WILD THYME, WINTER LIGHTNING

L. P. HARTLEY

ANNE MULKEEN

Wild Thyme, Winter Lightning

THE SYMBOLIC NOVELS
OF L. P. HARTLEY

Wayne State University Press, Detroit, 1974

Published in the United States of America
by Wayne State University Press
Detroit, Michigan 48202

Published simultaneously in Canada
by Copp Clark Publishing Company
517 Wellington Street, West
Toronto 2B, Canada

Printed in Great Britain

Library of Congress Cataloging in Publication Data
Mulkeen, Anne, 1927–
    Wild Thyme, Winter Lightning; the symbolic novels of L. P. Hartley.
    Includes Bibliographical references.
    1. Hartley, Leslie Poles.   I. Title.
PR6015. A6723Z78   823'.9'12   73-18047
ISBN 0-8143-1494-5

For most of us, there is only the unattended
Moment, the moment in and out of time,
The distraction fit, lost in a shaft of sunlight,
The wild thyme unseen, or the winter lightning
Or the waterfall, or music heard so deeply
That it is not heard at all, but you are the music
While the music lasts. These are only hints and guesses,
Hints followed by guesses. . . .

T. S. ELIOT

CONTENTS

PREFACE

WHEN Leslie Poles Hartley died in London in 1972, just before his seventy-seventh birthday, he was awaiting publication of his seventeenth novel. During the long career begun with *Simonetta Perkins* in 1925 he had been awarded some of Britain's highest literary honours, including the James Tait Black Memorial Prize in 1947 for *Eustace and Hilda* and the Heinemann Foundation Prize of the Royal Society of Literature in 1954 for *The Go-Between*; he had lived to see *The Go-Between* win further awards in 1971 as a Joseph Losey/Harold Pinter film, and was looking forward to the filming of *The Hireling*. Now headlines in *The Times* obituary mourned him as 'Distinguished English Novelist and Consummate Artist.' David Holloway's tribute in the *Daily Telegraph* was perhaps more precise in defining Hartley's contribution: 'By his death we have lost one of the most singular and most English voices among those writing today.'

L. P. Hartley's Englishness made him one of the twentieth century's best, most gently satiric documenters of a vanishing upper-middle-class milieu and its characteristic world view (or non-world-view). To many this seemed his essence. Apart from his experience as a gunner in World War I, Hartley had lived his part of the century as a typical Harrow- and Balliol-bred British gentleman, who for years reviewed books for *The Spectator*, *Saturday Review* and *The Observer*, and quietly wrote his own on the side. Even some of his most faithful readers saw his novels mainly as intricate reproductions of the British social existence he had known and comic commentaries on his own peaceful life.

But the singularity Holloway mentions stemmed from

Hartley's own vision, one which he perceived as long vanished from the British scene but needing to be stressed as enduringly valid. For Hartley—and this made his social comedies unique in twentieth century British writing—the real world was the unseen one beneath the decorous surfaces. There agonizing struggles ranged evil forces against the good, there growth, happiness and redemption came only through pain, supreme renunciation, even sacrificial death. 'The point of intersection of the timeless/With time . . .' was Hartley's real fictional world: to find a fictional form capable of embodying this constant suggestion of the cosmic beneath the commonplace became the subject of his lifelong literary experiments. Some were extremely successful, some much less so, but the quest itself has intrinsic interest in that it highlights central thematic and technical concerns of the twentieth-century novel.

For this reason I shall here, while stressing those works which seem most to deserve to endure (the *Eustace and Hilda* trilogy, *The Go-Between*, *The Boat*), examine all of Hartley's more serious work, trace the course of his experiments in combining realistic with symbolic genres, and attempt to show that, seen whole, Hartley's work suggests an overall 'myth' which casts additional light on the earlier and better novels.

*

At first glance L. P. Hartley's delicately wrought novels can seem out of place in a world where the young and angry have been confronting us constantly with the brutal truths of our civilization. Carefully observed, subtly shaped, such books as *The Go-Between* and the trilogy *Eustace and Hilda* seem to ask us to go back in time, to involve ourselves with the egos of sensitive post-Victorian youths struggling for self-discovery—a hard-to-justify pastime in time of revolution.

Only as we enter fully into L. P. Hartley's world do we realize that its aim is to reflect, illuminate, evaluate our own. Hartley's romances and mock-romances, a gallery of quests for selfhood by unusual individuals in special circumstances, are also—seen as symbolic forms—his anatomy of the twentieth century: its pre-history, its wars, its problems, its concerns, its philosophies. Most importantly, the best of them are complex metaphors of the universe in which twentieth-century man finds himself—searching, like all men before him, for meaning and salvation; searching, unlike them, with the perhaps unrecognized assumption that God is dead and humanism discredited. The sensitive Edwardian youth trying to fight his way out of the constrictions of the past is—was —man beginning a new era; the dilemmas he faces, seeking out a path between old absolutes and new relativisms, have shaped our century and continue at the heart of today's troubled consciousness.

'To imitate the surface of life, as Trollope did, without trying to interpret it, no longer satisfies serious modern novelists.' Here, in a 1946 article on 'The Future of Fiction',[1] Hartley locates for us the central concern in his own lifelong experiment in fictional form, and indicates his admiration for the Nathaniel Hawthorne who distinguished so carefully and frequently between the more mimetic Novel and the more fantastic Romance. Like Hawthorne, Hartley wished to aim at 'the truth of the human heart': to interpret, not merely to simulate, life in our century. It is a century whose people, places, events he could portray with warmth and realism—but we best penetrate L. P. Hartley's works when we begin to read them symbolically, and in terms not of individual symbols alone, but of comprehensive symbolic patterns.

In an article which has helped suggest the basic premise of this book,[2] Giorgio Melchiori shows how much Hartley owes to Hawthorne and the American Puritan and transcendentalist origins of symbolism—symbolism as a way of seeing, a kind of double vision in a universe of correspondences, where the world of physical appearances is only the near end, tiny and deceptive, of an infinitely more vast, more beautiful, more terrible whole. In demonstrating Hartley's affinity for Hawthorne, Melchiori (dealing primarily with *The Go-Between*) stresses 'the constant presence of this symbolic level', this 'plurality of levels of significance which has characterized the poetry of all ages'.[3]

In Hartley, Melchiori contends, a strain of contemporary

British fiction, while remaining thoroughly British, manages to incorporate within itself the American symbolic tradition—thereby finding a way of bridging the gap between traditional nineteenth-century novel structure and the extremes of twentieth-century experimentalism.[4] Essentially he would seem to see Hartley as pioneering among contemporary British novelists in producing a new genre: the contemporary novel of 'double vision', uniting the portrayal of 'an authentically English scene'[5] with the symbolic extension of that scene.

Two in particular among Hartley's other critics stress this symbolic richness in his fiction: Lord David Cecil, in the 'Introduction' to the 1958 edition of *Eustace and Hilda*,[6] and J.-P. Vernier, in a 1960 article in *Études Anglaises*.[7] For Vernier, who sees *Eustace and Hilda* as having three levels—the social, the psychological, and the metaphysical or spiritual vision which gives to the whole its profound unity—Hartley's aim seems less the description of individuals in their personal situations than the exposition, through them, of '*une vision personelle de la condition humaine*'.[8] That vision—of a universe in which each person is '*le jouet de forces maléfiques*', caught in a gigantic conflict between the forces of love (life) and death—would make our condition seem indeed pitiable, Vernier says, except that Hartley renders this tragic life as beautiful, as worthwhile, and except that all the characters, by their different paths and their different sufferings, seem to come at the end to a kind of salvation.[9]

This study, while owing much to all Hartley's critics, will lean more heavily upon the insights of those like Cecil, Vernier and Melchiori who stress mythical and metaphysical elements in his work than upon those of Peter Bien,[10] who tends to concentrate upon Freudian suggestions in the symbols, and their interpretation in individual psychological and moral terms. While this level is as surely present as it is in Hawthorne's own works, it is only one of many levels, and Hartley at his best is concerned with far more than individual neuroses.

Hartley, then, will be examined as a romancer and as a satirist or mock-romancer: a man who has incorporated romance patterns into the modern novel, has wedded representationalism and abstract design, to give us a unique kind of 'double vision' whereby characters and objects and events are seen as at once themselves—particulars, individuals—and as suggestions of, embodiments of universals, essences, archetypes. For insights into Hartley's use of symbolism here I am also indebted to E. K. Brown, whose *Rhythm in the Novel*[11] develops E. M. Forster's notes[12] on 'expanding symbols' (those accumulating complexity of suggestion through their repetition in a variety of associations, contexts, juxtapositions). Brown could be describing Hartley's method and its effect when he says that

> By the use of an expanding symbol, the novelist persuades and impels his readers towards two beliefs. First, that beyond the verge of what he can express, there is an area which can be glimpsed, never surveyed. Second, that this area has an order of its own which we should greatly care to know—it is neither a chaos, nor something irrelevant to the clearly expressed story, persons and setting that fill the foreground.[13]

'Repetition', he says again,

> is the strongest assurance an author can give of order; the extraordinary complexity of the variation is the reminder that the order is so involute that it must remain a mystery.[14]

The following chapters will deal first with the concept of romance—especially as analysed and placed in context by Northrop Frye[15]—and with Hawthorne's and, after him, Hartley's adaptations of its patterns; then with Hartley's works in an order designed to allow them to illuminate each other, and beginning with a glance at his sketches and short stories, many of which experiment with methods and themes to come into their own in the later works. In analysing the novels I shall try to take account of all previously published interpretations of Hartley's work, but shall stress in particular the elements of patterning, of the non-realistic, and the vision of reality which these seem to me to reveal. My emphasis throughout will be upon Hartley's earlier work, up to and including *Poor Clare* in 1968, because the more recent novels, on the whole less seriously intended and executed, might tend to cast false light upon what has gone before.

For making this book possible I am grateful first of all to Professor Paul L. Wiley of the University of Wisconsin, who introduced me to L. P. Hartley's work in the course of two seminars on the modern British novel, and generously and painstakingly advised me through every stage of my doctoral dissertation on Hartley's novels. Work on the manuscript and a visit to Mr. Hartley in England were made possible with the encouragement of my colleagues—especially Dr. James L. Sanderson—at Rutgers University in Camden, and through grants from the Penrose Fund of the American Philosophical Society and the Rutgers University Research Council. Most of all I am grateful to Leslie Poles Hartley—for his books, and for his warm reception, in 1970, of my visit and my work.

CHAPTER ONE

INTRODUCTION:
NOVEL, ROMANCE AND SATIRE

[a]

IN distinguishing four major tendencies in prose fiction—novel, romance, confession and anatomy or Menippean satire—Northrop Frye warns us that the great romancer should be examined in terms of the conventions he has chosen and not 'left on the side lines of prose fiction merely because the critic has not learned to take the romance form seriously'.[1] The distinction seems pertinent in broadening one's understanding of L. P. Hartley's work. Rich though his evocation of an age, a place may be, or intricate and painstaking his creation of a character, these are only means to an end. He creates seemingly realistic social and psychological portraits only so that they can play their parts in larger designs: symbolic patterns which carry a more universal significance than their surface verisimilitude suggests. There is more of the delicacy (and depth) of the fairy tale in a book like *Eustace and Hilda* than of the weightiness and social inquiry of the Victorian novel; the first step in understanding Hartley's complexity here ought to be a grasp of the nature and implications of romance in fiction, and of its structural opposite, satire or mock-romance, a form which Hartley also uses.

The essence of romance would seem to be its affinity with the world of the imagination, as contrasted with the world of ordinary experience. The romantic tendency in literature, according to Frye, is midway between myth and 'realism': it displaces myth in a human direction and yet, in contrast to realism, it conventionalizes and idealizes content.[2] The romance abstracts, designs

I

—suggests implicit mythical patterns in a world not mythical, but human.[3] Frye's *Anatomy of Criticism*, exploring romance as a mode and as a specific fictional genre related to that mode, gives us many clues to Hartley's method and meaning.

'The essential difference between novel and romance', according to Frye, 'lies in the conception of characterization':

> The romancer does not attempt to create 'real people' so much as stylized figures which expand into psychological archetypes. It is in the romance that we find Jung's libido, anima, and shadow reflected in the hero, heroine and villain respectively. That is why the romance so often radiates a glow of subjective intensity that the novel lacks, and why a suggestion of allegory is constantly creeping in around its fringes. Certain elements of character are released in the romance which make it naturally a more revolutionary form than the novel. The novelist deals with personality, with characters wearing their *personae* or social masks. He needs the framework of a stable society, and many of our best novelists have been conventional to the verge of fussiness. The romancer deals with individuality, with characters *in vacuo* idealized by revery, and, however conservative he may be, something nihilistic and untamable is likely to keep breaking out of his pages.[4]

The romance deals with heroes, Frye specifies—midway between the novel, which deals with men, and the myth, which deals with gods.[5] Romance approaches the wish-fulfilment dream—projects an ideal, usually in the form of the archetypal quest of a hero for a great good, his perilous journey, his overcoming of the enemy at great cost, and his final exaltation. 'The central form of romance is dialectical,' Frye says; 'everything is focussed on a conflict between the hero and his enemy, and all the reader's values are bound up with the hero.'[6] Hero and enemy partake of Messianic and demonic qualities according as the romance approaches myth proper; the usual three-fold structure of romance comes close to the three-day rhythm of death, disappearance and revival in the myths of the dying and rising gods. Usually linked to the conflict in a romance is the cyclical movement of nature in this our 'middle' world where the conflict takes place—the enemy being associated with winter, darkness, confusion and sterility, the hero with all that is springlike, fertile and young. Archetypal and symbolic figures such as witches, guardian spirits, helpful animals and sibylline mother-figures recur—emphasizing how much the quest-romance 'has analogies to both rituals and dreams'. And points of epiphany, of 'breakthrough' between the temporal and eternal world (the mountain-top, the island, the tower, the lighthouse, the ladder or staircase) are among the most important poetic symbols.[7] Translated into dream terms, the romance's sequence of marvellous adventures can be seen as 'the search of the libido or desiring self for a fulfillment that will deliver it from the anxieties of reality but will still contain that reality'; in ritual terms the quest-romance is 'the victory of fertility over the waste land'.[8]

The romance in its most basic form, then, suggests a world-view: Frye several times denotes romance as 'the form in which an ascendant class tends to express itself' and project its ideals.[9] Those who question the world-view, the ideals, have traditionally utilized the form of mock-romance, and Frye sees satire, structurally, as essentially a parody of romance: 'the application of romantic mythical forms to a more realistic content which fits them in unexpected ways.'[10]

The adapter of the romance form most helpful to our understanding of Hartley's work would seem to be Nathaniel Hawthorne: a writer whom Hartley admired and has frequently discussed,[11] and one whom Frye uses to exemplify the use in more modern fiction of romantic and ironically mythical design.[12] Hawthorne himself made notable use of the term Romance to define his own aims and methods. Introducing *The House of the Seven Gables*, he assumes the Novel, as epitomized in the work of Anthony Trollope, 'to aim at a very minute fidelity . . . to the probable and ordinary course of man's experience'. The Romance, while it must not swerve aside from 'the truth of the human heart', has a right 'to present that truth under circumstances . . . of the writer's own choosing or creation'.[13] Hawthorne goes on to suggest that such circumstances might include a touch of the Marvellous, or a setting in the past: whatever might remove the artist's 'fancy-pictures' from identification with the realities of the moment.[14]

Here and in his other discussions of the 'Romance', Hawthorne

3

is, as F. O. Matthiessen emphasizes, stating the aim of romance to be not the idealization or evasion of reality, but the more direct seeking of it—actuality disengaged from mere appearance, truth as distinguished from 'facts'. The role of art was to distinguish the universal beneath the particular, and Hawthorne's art, as Matthiessen saw it, was built on the conviction that man, living through the events of time, should simultaneously be penetrating their eternal meaning.[15]

Almost every Hawthorne story, short or long, is more design than description, more symbol than simulation of reality. Hawthornian romance follows the Frye description in dealing consistently in some kind of dialectic or confrontation of opposites—the interplay of characters who are clearly representative of larger qualities, ideas, tendencies, in a middle world into which the demonic or heavenly worlds just beyond the visible scene are always threatening to break. The design, the pattern created by the clash of characters is usually recognizable as the shadowy modern form of an ancient myth we glimpse beneath the surface —or an entirely new 'myth' which has the same kind of force, the same capacity to put us in touch with recurring and enduring elements in the human story.

Hawthorne himself seems to point to the archetypal quality of the denizens of his *Blithedale Romance* when he talks about them as

. . . the self-concentrated Philanthropist; the high-spirited Woman, bruising herself against the narrow limitations of her sex; the weakly Maiden, whose tremulous nerves endow her with sibylline attributes; the Minor Poet, beginning life with strenuous aspirations, which die out with his youthful fervor. . . .[16]

In the essay in which he demonstrates his own extreme interest in Hawthorne's ideas and methods, Hartley notes several times this 'type' quality of Hawthorne's characters. According to Hartley, Hawthorne 'created very few characters whom we recognize as persons, existing in their own right . . . try as he would, he was more interested in what they *represented*, above all in their moral aspect, and as they illustrate the operations of the Moral Law'

4

(*NR* p. 97). Hartley also notes how often Hawthorne's characters illustrate the workings of Evil as a thing in itself:

> Sometimes he calls it the Black Man, a forest-ranging personage who is, to all intents and purposes, the Devil. It is he who accosts Young Goodman Brown, he who haunts the woods where Hester Prynne and her daughter wander in *The Scarlet Letter*. Sometimes he is made more corporeal: he appears in the substantial frame and rubicund countenance of Judge Pyncheon; he gleams at us through Professor Westerfeldt's gold teeth; we meet him in the catacombs at Rome and watch him being hurled off the Tarpeian Rock. He is enough of a human being to be killed by a fall from a precipice but no more: otherwise he is just an embodiment of evil, like Ethan Brand, after his successful search for the Unforgivable Sin.
>
> This view of Evil is something both inside us and outside us, the human condition, in fact, is implicit in most of Hawthorne's stories. It is the theme of *The Fall of Man*, told with many variations, and leading (in *The Marble Faun*) to the unorthodox conclusion that sin is as inevitable as sorrow, and must be accepted as part of the training of the soul on its way to a higher development: it has a regenerative power (*NR* p. 122).

Thus Hartley notes the operation of types, archetypes and myths, and particularly the myth of the Fall of Man, in Hawthorne's romances, and goes on to give that particular aspect of the romance a name of his own. 'This preoccupation with sin,' he says, 'makes Hawthorne an apocalyptic novelist.' The Book of Revelation, Hartley continues, explaining his term, is the prototype 'of all stories [like *Moby Dick* . . . like *The Divine Comedy* . . . like *Paradise Lost*] in which the main, the only issue, is the struggle between the good and the bad' (*NR* pp. 122–3). Apocalyptic novelists like Hawthorne, according to Hartley, are those who feel that 'the very fabric of the earth is as unstable as it is presented in the Book of Revelation' (*NR* p. 129). The only British novelist Hartley can place in this category is Emily Brontë.

Hartley gives us a further valuable insight into Hawthorne when he stresses that his romances, however 'apocalyptic', aimed at establishing contact with 'the hum-drum life of the ordinary man'. 'Hawthorne's sense of romance', he asserts, 'was transforming rather than interpretative: the more commonplace the object, the better he could invest it with his own special imaginative quality'—the town pump 'was a more rewarding subject for him than the fountains of Versailles or Trafalgar Square, or even the fountains of Rome' (*NR* pp. 82–3).

A good though perhaps over-simple example of the way Hawthorne's mind and double vision work in making 'romance' from everyday reality is the story called 'The Threefold Destiny', and subtitled 'A Fairy Legend'.[17] Hawthorne begins by a direct statement of what he is doing:

> I have sometimes produced a singular and not unpleasing effect, so far as my own mind was concerned, by imagining a train of incidents, in which the spirit and mechanism of the fairy legend should be combined with the characters and manners of familiar life. In the little tale which follows, a subdued tinge of the wild and wonderful is thrown over a sketch of New England personages and scenery, yet, it is hoped, without entirely obliterating the sober hues of nature. Rather than a story of events claiming to be real, it may be considered as an allegory, such as the writers of the last century would have expressed in the shape of an Eastern tale, but to which I have endeavoured to give a more lifelike warmth than could be infused into those fanciful productions.[18]

The story is of Ralph Cranfield, who comes back from travels in foreign climes ranging from Hindostan to the Arctic—back to 'a village, not in "Fairy Londe", but within our own familiar boundaries'. Since his youth Ralph has had within him a conviction 'we say not whether it were revealed to him by witchcraft, or in a dream of prophecy, or that his brooding fancy had palmed its own dictates upon him as the oracles of a sibyl'—that he would receive three signs to reveal to him the marvellous dispensations of his high destiny. A heart-shaped jewel and a prescribed exchange of mysterious words would reveal the beautiful woman who was to love him; a mysterious pointing hand would reveal a buried treasure; three venerable men, one bearing a staff or wand, would confer upon him leadership and power. Ralph has ranged the earth, looking in vain for the signs and his destiny. It is, of course, in his own village, in very humble, ordinary and unexpected shapes, that the signs finally occur and his great destiny is fulfilled. The mysterious hand and inscription appear on a tree-trunk at his own door, cut there, at least in part, by his musing boyish self; 'Squire Hawkwood and the two other selectmen' come to offer him the exalted post of local schoolmaster; on the breast of his childhood sweetheart he finds the heart-shaped brooch he himself whittled for her long ago.

Hawthorne calls his story an allegory, and points a very direct moral at its end, about those who cherish wild wishes oftenest finding 'their sphere of duty, of prosperity, and happiness, within those precincts, and in that station, where Providence itself has cast their lot'.[19] But the story and its characters and events have resonances beyond mere allegory and the mere working-out of such a moral. We suspect from Hawthorne's point, and much of his language, that he is demolishing romance: he has Ralph, for example, sitting 'half unconsciously gazing at the three visitors, and enveloping their homely figures in the misty romance that pervaded his mental world',[20] and then in the last paragraph we learn that 'the wild dreamer was awake at last'.[21] But the actual effect of the story has been to stimulate our imaginations rather than to discourage them. We do not disbelieve in great destinies and mythical patterns and Providential or magic signs because of this story—rather, we tend to see them operating on every street corner. Hawthorne has managed to show us archetypal patterns at work in the life of Every Man, bringing to him the Woman, the Work, the Fortune meant for him. He has done it by using the symbol-making imagination of Ralph Cranfield within his story first to create a home-made myth reminiscent of all myth, then to see the particulars of his own everyday existence in the light of that myth. Because the myth does connect with all myth, does deal in archetypes, the story is fuller and wiser than mere allegory could be. It exorcizes purely visionary romanticism, but makes pure prosaic myopia also impossible; it calls for vision (double vision) by being its own best example; it reveals Ralph's destiny as a design which he both perceives and himself creates. The longer one looks into this little tale, the more it has to say.

On a more complex level, John C. Stubbs, in a recent *PMLA* article,[22] treats the nineteenth-century romance as a specific genre and explores Hawthorne's approach to that genre in *The Scarlet Letter*. Stubbs claims the primary goal of the romance to be 'artistic distance', aimed not at expressing *ambiguity* (the term

7

most often applied to Hawthorne's work), but rather at something approaching its opposite, *structured complexity*. The romance's goal was to be gained by an approach to human experience 'much more ordered, much more arranged than the reader's chaotic meeting with it in his daily life', and to achieve this, romancers struggled for a balance, in their work, between verisimilitude and ideality, between the natural and the marvellous, and, lastly, between history and fiction.[23]

Stubbs discusses at some length Hawthorne's own work at achieving these balances: trying to achieve verisimilitude while yet agreeing with the point of view that 'the work should be determined by the writer's conception of experience, not by his imitation of experience';[24] concerned to excite the reader's interest and to gain distance by use of the marvellous without entering into sheer fantasy; setting his fiction in a historical context within which he can, however, operate with considerable imaginative licence. Stubbs shows how the balances operate in *The Scarlet Letter*, set as it is in historic New England, remote and legendary while at the same time touching Hawthorne's readers' own era and experience. He shows how Hawthorne takes a traditional New England romance situation—the individual alienated from the Puritan community—and uses the (expanding) images of prison and rosebush to emphasize the two sides of the debate between two type characters, Hester and Chillingworth: heart, freedom and joy vs. reasoned law, severity and punishment. In the figure of the repentant Dimmesdale, according to Stubbs, Hawthorne internalizes and synthesizes the conflict, converting 'the simplistic confrontation of the opposites into a complex study of a human being'.[25] Stubbs's analysis also recalls F. O. Matthiessen's suggestion that Hawthorne's method in general consists in these confrontations of extreme and incomplete opposites—showing the tragedies of people who insist in seeking only the temporal or only the eternal, only the fact or only the ideal, whereas human existence must reconcile the two elements, must somehow manage to live on both levels at once (as a Hawthorne story usually does, but as none of its characters can).[26]

It is this double-visioned, two- (or three-) worlded genre which Hartley seems to be trying to adapt for his own exploration of twentieth-century man: a genre which expresses by its very essence some of what seem to be Hartley's main concerns about the postwar, post-Christian, post-humanist world. Romance or myth, as Jung himself showed us,[27] can and does consistently point to such questions as the split in man's nature today; the risk of ignoring the unconscious, the irrational, the dark sides of reality; the need for a religious or numinous element in man's life (seemingly not forthcoming from devitalized institutional religion); the integration of the individual as prerequisite for the healing of the times; the contribution of myth and symbol and dream to that integration.

Basically, Hartley's novels seem variations on the *Bildungsroman*, the traditional novel of quest for selfhood. In each a more or less sensitive, perhaps slightly neurotic protagonist (young man, middle-aged man, old man; young girl, career woman, suburban housewife) undergoes some part of the inward journey from innocence through experience to higher innocence, in a setting documenting one of the crucial moments in recent history: the beginnings of the century and life among the country houses of the Edwardian era; World War I; English society in between-the-wars Venice; World War II; the Welfare State and the crumbling of the class system; the post-World-War-III future.

Hartley analyses time, place and personal growth with care, subtlety, and verisimilitude. But ultimately each of his heroes is Everyman, and each of his designs is meant to ask, squarely and urgently, the great questions of the twentieth century. How then does man live after two world wars have shown him beyond all doubt how much it is in his nature to murder, to torture, to destroy? Where does the humanist turn whose optimism, whose easy answers have been mocked by the bitter experience of 'this hideous century we live in' (*GB* p. 279), the perversity of life and death and history and fate, his neighbour's vices and his own? How does one deal with great universal forces for which one no

9

longer has a name but which inflict suffering and death upon guilty and innocent alike? Where does one find foothold on the shifting ground between the dead abstractions and false gods of the past and the threatening anarchy, the potential ugliness of a future world without standards and values?

Hartley is an explorer of our own age, not a gentle fabler of the past. At his best he asks more questions than he answers; he tries to let us experience in microcosm and think about the dilemmas and contradictions and polarities of living when and where we live. With the protagonists we sway between imaginativeness and a sense of reality, between going along with the current of sense life and trying to go against it, between a regard for one's own selfhood and the call to place others before that self. From the dialectics emerge, from time to time, evidences of forces which insist upon being recognized, though we have sworn they are not there. Hartley's universe keeps suggesting at their work those mysterious realities which we used to call evil, grace and Providence—and to which, he seems to imply, we may have to give new names and new responses.

Hartley's world is recognizably that described by Camus and Sartre, in which man must at length face his absurdity, his pitiable fate, his burden of guilt, and act in full knowledge of his impotence. But it is also a world which would have been quite comprehensible to Emily Brontë, whose poems he quotes so often as epigraphs, in which 'A thousand thousand glancing fires' can break out in 'noonday Dream' to assure the ponderer upon the moor that death is the beginning of everlasting day.[28] Hartley's world would be recognizable, too, to the Sir Thomas Browne several times evoked in *The Betrayal* (1966)[29]—who believed so strongly in an 'invisible fabrick' of which 'this visible world is but a picture . . . wherein as in a pourtract, things are not truely, but in equivocall shapes, and as they counterfeit some more reall substance. . . .'[30] and whose philosophical approach, according to a contemporary critic, 'leans to that one (Platonic and Hermetic) which stresses the unity of the physical and spiritual universe and the immanence of God'.[31]

To this sternly-limited material, experiential, existential world

10

in which we live Hartley introduces a genre which questions the opacity of that materiality, which casts upon it light calculated to reveal monstrous shapes and shadows above and behind. His characters try to be, like Hawthorne's, representative and illustrative, his plots attempt the apocalyptic—but they are built upon a base so realistic in characterization and social examination that it is often mistaken for Hartley's essential contribution.

[c]

How then should one read Hartley? *Carefully*. With him, one has to heed William Blake's advice about symbolic painting:

> . . . that the Spectator will attend to the Hands & Feet, to the Lineaments of the Countenances; they are all descriptive of Character, & not a line is drawn without intention, & that most discriminate & particular. As Poetry admits not a Letter that is Insignificant, so Painting admits not a Grain of Sand or a Blade of Grass Insignificant—much less an Insignificant Blur or Mark.[32]

It is all there in the text: Hartley is not asking us to play guessing games, but merely to attend. He describes the 'Lineaments' of a face, an object, a landscape so that they begin to take on significance for us. Here, for example, is Emilio, the gondolier of *Simonetta Perkins* (1925), as seen by a heroine weary of Bostonian moral fervor:

> He smiled when you smiled, generally. He took you where you wanted to go. He forced nothing upon you. He demanded nothing of you. He had no questions, he had no replies. At every moment he was accessible to pleasure; at every moment, unconsciously, he could render pleasure back; it lived in his face, his movements, his whole air, where all the charms of childhood, youth and maturity mingled without losing their identity.[33]

Again and again through the book Hartley shows us Emilio linked with images of effortless movement, total expressiveness, complete harmony with nature. For Lavinia, struggling as she is with her Puritan past, he has a 'lustre'; he is attended always by something of a glow, or the colour of gold or rose. In one encounter, 'The gorgeous fruits framed his glittering smile, and their abundance went well with his loquacity' (*SP* p. 15).

Yet in a remarkable and very characteristic passage at the end of the book Hartley links Emilio—and through him all his accumulated associations with the beauty and force and abundance of nature—with the dark side to Venice's art and life which Lavinia has been absorbing, half-unconsciously, as she has been discovering her own sin and weakness.

Emilio is taking her to an illicit rendezvous, pulling powerfully at his oar, steering the gondola through the dark canals. The symbolism is strongly sexual. Then,

> The alternation of stroke and recovery became dreadful to her, suggesting no more what was useful or romantic, but proclaiming a crude physical sufficiency, at once relentless and unwilling. It came to her overwhelmingly that physical energy was dangerous and cruel, just insofar as it was free; there flashed across her mind the straining bodies in Tiepolo and Tintoretto, one wielding an axe, another tugging at a rope, a third heaving the Cross aloft, a fourth turning his sword upon the Innocents. And Emilio with his hands clasping the oar was such another; a minister at her martyrdom (*SP* p. 95).

Such 'key' passages abound in Hartley—tying together at a crucial moment several symbols which have been accreting a variety of associations; bringing to protagonist and reader, through this juxtaposition, a moment of illumination into the meaning of the story and Hartley's vision of reality—here his strong intuition of an evil, fallen side to Nature. Usually such a moment of insight (rather than an external event) is the climax of the story—and the reader who has not been following Hartley's language very closely is likely to miss the moment's significance and not realize that there is at least the possibility of a resolution quite contrary to outward appearances.

Significances in the earlier and better Hartley are rarely allegorical—rarely the simple one-to-one relationships which Forster attributes to so-called 'banner' symbols.[34] In *The Brickfield* (1964)[35] and *The Betrayal*, for example, two of the chief recurring symbols, the barren Brickfield and the successful Brickworks, begin as literal physical settings, then, as the story proceeds, take on meanings identifying them respectively with death and life, but by the end have completely reversed these meanings. In *The Hireling* (1957),[36] careful attention to the central cathedral symbol is essential because its implications change and interweave so subtly: now the cathedral's architecture expresses ideal human relationships (*H* p. 98), now its association with the Virgin carries over to Lady Franklin (*H* pp. 103, 152). With the help of this symbol one comes to feel by the end of the book that the relationship between this man and this woman is itself a symbol of universal spiritual laws. To understand *Facial Justice* (1960)[37] we must connect the glorious and godlike Michael with such things as the story of the child and the Pretty Gentleman which serves as pre-history for the strange world of the future, and then guess that perhaps this little fantasy is meant to be read on many levels, like a miniature *Divina Commedia*.

Sometimes meaning is suggested by out-and-out symbolizing on the part of the protagonist. In *Simonetta Perkins*, when Lavinia looks for and finds a vine in an old church, she tells us, by her reaction, her own state of soul: '. . . its greenness had gone grey, its leaves were falling, and the defeated tendrils, clawing the air, symbolized and reaffirmed her failure to recapture the emotion of her first visit' (*SP* p. 56).

Sometimes it is a play on words, a misunderstanding or a joke which reveals to us that there are at least two sides to everything. In the same book Lavinia says something to her mother about the 'whoredoms' of Jezebel, and her mother, shocked, asks how she dares to use to her 'the language of the marketplace'—only to be reminded by Lavinia that it is the language of the Bible (*SP* p. 50). A seemingly casual juxtaposition—but in context it suggests that the Bible is often, for the religious, not really part of the marketplace of everyday life, and that their appreciation of it is likely to ignore its more grim aspects. It also suggests that Lavinia, perhaps for the first time, is discovering that the Bible can have relevance to daily problems and that some of its stronger revelations about human nature are truer to her own life than she had supposed.

Sometimes one must note, as in *Eustace and Hilda*, the three-fold pattern in everything (as also in Frye's archetypal romances) —the three Shelters on the way to the lighthouse at Anchorstone (*EH* p. 59), the three movements of the Bach Concerto Stephen

13

plays at Oxford (*EH* pp. 254ff.), the three stages of Eustace's climb from Lowcross to Hilda's home for crippled children at Highcross (*EH* pp. 318–21)—and then connect with them the threefold movement in the book as a whole, and in Eustace's steps towards manhood. Sometimes one finds oneself matching up colours or habits—wondering why Lady Nelly always wears pearly, shimmering colours (*EH* pp. 367, 473) and always travels by water, and why Jasper hates to set foot in a gondola (*EH* p. 440). One could grow impatient and accuse Hartley of being much too intricate and involute in his symbolism—perhaps one should not have to read and re-read a novel, searching for recurrence of colours, in order to understand what is happening to the hero. But the correspondences are not esoteric—Hilda's red dress, which does not suit her, helps to convey something of the uneasy passion and pain of her offstage affair with Dick (*EH* pp. 481, 533–5, 519); Anne's grey suit, 'like her expression . . . had the air of reducing all occasions to one' (*EH* p. 339). And in forcing us to *look* at the things of his world, think about them, relate them, question them, be frustrated by them, Hartley gives us a sense of experiencing the mysteries and frustrations of life itself and conveys its complexity in a form (and world-view) which might otherwise seem too simply achieved. One can make no easy abstractions from these shifting symbolic patterns—there is always something that doesn't fit. The real achievement here is not the contriving of an ingenious puzzle which can be solved by mathematics, clever analysis and *The Golden Bough*. It is, rather, the creation (in his best works) of a truly baffling universe, a mirror of the one in which we live.

The form of Hartley's novels is, like the typical romance Frye describes, dialectical. Characters are linked to attitudes, world-views, dreams, ideas: usually inadequate by their very over-abstraction, over-simplification. Interaction with others and with life hardens or alters or reverses these attitudes. At the end we are usually confronted with a death, real or symbolic, and the problem of deciding whether that death represents utter tragedy and failure, or signals a successful resolution—the only possible resolution—of the dilemmas of life. Man, living, must always be torn between the opposing forces of matter and spirit, fact and ideal, Hartley seems to say—the best he can do, living, is to accept polarities and conflicts as the stuff of existence. Peace and reconciliation are somehow bound up with death—or with managing to give over one's material existence to a spiritual one. Whether this is a horror or the beginning of new life Hartley does not quite tell us.

If he suggests answers at all in his old-yet-new universe (and I am not sure that he does), they would seem to be along the lines of a somewhat existentialist approach to Christianity: a Christianity willingly relinquishing its pretensions to superior knowledge and power and affirming its oneness with human misery and helplessness; a Christianity cleansed of the abstract, the legalistic, the overly rational, and stressing above all the personal, the concrete, the leap of faith, the centrality of love and self-giving; a Christianity facing the universe with all the agony and unknowingness of modern mankind, yet willing to die for others—the Christianity of Pascal and Blake and Kierkegaard. . . . The following pages will look at L. P. Hartley as a writer of romance who at times manages to achieve, in forms of beauty and vision, a realism at once courageous and terrible: a confrontation with man's contemporary agony that admits of no easy affirmations, yet points, within that agony, to beauty, love and self-giving.

CHAPTER TWO

CRYSTALLIZATIONS:
HARTLEY'S SHORTER FICTION

... What should we be without
The dolphin's arc, the dove's return,
These things in which we have seen ourselves and spoken?
—Richard Wilbur[1]

In his analysis of the romance form, as distinguished from the novel proper, Northrop Frye points out that a comparable distinction exists in short forms of fiction, and that 'the tale form used by Poe . . . bears the same relation to the full romance that the stories of Chekhov or Katherine Mansfield do to the novel'.[2] Hartley's short fiction (with the exception of some which can only be classified as 'sketches') seems in general to fit into this category of the tale.

If one comes to these tales after acquaintance with Hartley's more sophisticated and complex longer works, there is bound to be disappointment. Of Hartley's first volume, *Night Fears* (1924),[3] a *Times Literary Supplement* reviewer says that Hartley 'writes with such elegance and conscious care that one regrets that lack of body which is the dominant characteristic of his volume'. Furthermore, 'aiming at subtlety', Hartley 'achieves too often an effect of deliberate, almost conscientious futility, as though to create characters in the round, and show them in action, were a gaucherie he was determined to avoid'.[4]

Reviews of later collections have much the same ring up to and including those on *Two for the River* (1961),[5] which *TLS* characterizes as containing 'artful little tales' in which we are rather too aware of the creator's 'discreet manipulations', and upon which the reviewer pronounces, 'Mr. Hartley is one of our most professional writers, but in *Two for the River* there is not a great deal that shows him at anything near his best'.[6] Most reviews seem to agree with the one on *The Travelling Grave* (1948),[7] which judges that Hartley is 'more at ease with a larger canvas'.[8]

Almost all of Hartley's short stories, many of which are brought together in the recently published *The Collected Short Stories of L. P. Hartley*,[9] are best seen, perhaps, as studies, sketches, experiments for those larger canvasses. Here, over the years, he creates characters to embody themes, attitudes and points of view, finds objects to symbolize inner life and change, broods over and highlights events which seem to reflect mysterious universal laws. If Hartley's earlier novels can so finely suggest the density and complexity of experience, it is surely because in exercises like the stories he has painstakingly tried to capture, to explore and elaborate, one by one, the individual elements and perspectives which go to make up his vision of complexity. Here again he seems to follow his master Hawthorne, of whom Q. D. Leavis says, 'What he had worked on and crystallized out in *The Minister's Black Veil, Endicott and the Red Cross, Young Goodman Brown, Main Street, Rapacini's* [sic] *Daughter*, and *The Maypole of Merry Mount* he swept into a finely organized whole [in *The Scarlet Letter*], so that every portion is concentrated with meanings and associations and cross-references.'[10]

It is possible to see the short stories as coming, roughly, in three waves; one might even say three layers, and identify these layers both with the three 'levels' in a novel like *Eustace and Hilda*[11] and with a progression in the setting of Hartley's novels from the more romantic and timeless to the more contemporary and socially relevant. The same themes and concerns weave in and out of all Hartley's stories, but in the first group he seemed to experiment mainly with expressing mental or psychological states; in the second, his more farfetched Gothic tales, with metaphysical statements about the whole of human existence; in the later volumes, with the locating of his enduring dilemmas in very contemporary problems like the relation between the artist and society, the pitfalls of modern sexual mores and modern marriage. Yet in all three types of stories, Hartley is talking about the same

17

things. From *Night Fears* onward, he is concerned with the life of the mind in its relation to the 'real' world, and looking for ways of catching, in a symbolic event or tableau, the discrepancy between ideal and actual, between the imagined, the abstracted, the mentally organized, and the complexity of experience. His overall theme seems to come close to that which he ascribes to Hawthorne in the previously-mentioned 'Nathaniel Hawthorne' essay:

> . . . the contrast between life as it is lived by hopeful and healthy human beings . . . and those who . . . would try to find an explanation of life apart from, and almost unconnected with, the mere, gross act of living. It is the essential Hawthornian problem, and it is perhaps a blessing for mankind that so few of us are troubled with it. The only interpretation of life is one that comes out of the act of living—that is, I suppose, Hawthorne's existentialist conclusion, though he could not adapt it to his own life (*NR* pp. 115–16).

Hartley's own chosen method of symbolism seems appropriate to his own 'existentialist conclusion'—the symbol or symbolic situation in which he embodies each new version of the dilemma is, itself, in its concreteness, a contradiction of abstraction and idealization (while at the same time attesting to the need for the imprint of mind and imagination).

A number of the stories in *Night Fears*, including the title story itself, stress the *power* of the mind, its ability to create its own reality. In 'Night Fears' the protagonist is a newly-hired night-watchman, alone for the third night in a rectangle of darkness and light, forced into a strange new acquaintance with his own thoughts. Suddenly there is a figure, back turned, sitting on the barrier of the compound. In the conversation that ensues, this mysterious stranger touches, encourages, builds to tremendous intensity all the watchman's incipient fears and worries—that people do not like him . . . that the money will not be enough . . . that inability to sleep in the daytime could drive a man ill, mad, to suicide . . . that his children will not know him, since he is never at home . . . that his wife might be unfaithful. His mind in chaos, the normal daylight world completely lost, the watchman takes out his knife. . . . Later in the night, the stranger steps over his dead body and leaves. Crossing the street he enters 'a blind alley opposite, leaving a track of dark, irregular footprints; and since he did not return it is probable that he lived there' (*NF* p. 47).

A projection of the night watchman's own fears—the blackness within any human mind, welling up in the strange world of darkness and solitude. This would certainly seem to be Hartley's meaning. But those footprints! It is the kind of 'multiple choice' device Matthiessen attributed to Hawthorne,[12] which Yvor Winters later named his 'formula of alternative possibilities'[13] and Richard Harter Fogle his 'pervasive ambiguity':[14] that vagueness surrounding a given strange event (such as the appearance of the gigantic *A* in the sky of *The Scarlet Letter*) whereby we might equally well believe it to be caused by supernatural, usually evil agencies or, on the other hand, to be imagined by its overcredulous beholders.

But Hartley, exploiting this Hawthornian device, can be fairly sure that his audience will not be tempted to believe in a literal Black Visitor from the Other World: the tangibility of the Visitor, the warming of his hands at the brazier, his irregular progress over and into the blind alley, are meant to leave us with a strong sense of the reality and power of the creatures of the imagination. Night fears are not shadows to be laughed away. They can be stronger and more powerful than daylight assurances —they can kill. And people who discount the invisible world live with only a fraction of reality.

Along the same lines, 'A Sentimental Journey' pictures a man whose whole rejuvenation and success has depended upon believing that someone (the verger of a church he had toured, once, in a crowd) had rightly recognized him as a man of distinction. 'Talent', on the other hand, is the glimpse of a failure whose only possibility of coping with life is through convincing himself he never had the poetic gift which, in fact, he probably had. 'The Tonic' is about a lonely man trying to assert that he does not have the serious heart condition which is about to condemn him to a bedridden existence and a lingering death. 'A Visit to the Dentist' is about another lonely man who eagerly embraces pain to convince himself that his meaningless life *has* some point, some interest, some challenge. 'Witheling End' is more strongly comic: the protagonist's hyperactive imagination transforms his host's over-eagerness to please into a malevolent desire to be rid of his guest. 'A Summons' is a highly imaginative man's rationalization of his own morbidity and fear. His little sister is having a nightmare, due no doubt to his recounting of his own dreams in her presence. He does not get up and go to her aid—for a million ostensible reasons. In fact, he must really speak to her some time about her morbid streak. . . .

The stories in *Night Fears* are among the earliest, the simplest, the thinnest of Hartley's sketches where, in particular, we see him developing his approach to character and characterization. Another group of stories in this volume finds ways of demonstrating man's constant tendency towards abstraction, towards finding an informing principle to life other than his own selfhood. 'A Beautiful Character' sets two portraits side by side—portraits expressing two clashing views of life which will appear over and over again in the novels. The narrator of the tale within the tale, appropriately called Speedwell, seems to believe in taking life by the horns and managing it. He imposes his will, but perhaps, according to the narrator proper, by not 'giving the future its fair chance . . . being rather cruel to its boasted attribute of uncertainty' (*NF* p. 110). Speedwell has somewhat the same effect upon us as upon the narrator: 'Almost the first words I exchanged with Speedwell chilled me' (*NF* p. 109).

Druitt, on the other hand—the man whom Speedwell's story describes—believes

> . . . one should live from day to day and from minute to minute; receptivity should be strained to the utmost; attention should never flag. . . . Personality must be poured out like water from a bucket. . . . In the end this expense of spirit would lead . . . to the creation of a beautiful harmony . . . enriching life without the meretricious expedient of contrast and division' (*NF* p. 117).

Druitt, as Speedwell describes him to us, is left by his philosophy completely deflated and disillusioned, 'sagging and crumpled and inert' (*NF* p. 121). We are left to wonder about and perhaps identify with the narrator's more ordinary and pragmatic way of life—he who likes 'simple souls who believed in institutions, had plenty of corns to tread upon, who availed themselves of traditional prejudices and of the organized and canalized endeavour of mankind' (*NF* p. 116).

'The Telephone Call' gives us a version of the one type again: a 'drifter' who refuses to move, to make decisions—but whose very indecision makes decisions and creates more and more dilemmas. 'A Condition of Release' gives us, on the other hand, a little man trying to be decisive, to control the situation, to pride himself on his ability to stride off and take a cold swim—and his comeuppance by the vagabond who steals and dons his trousers, and then tricks him into helping him take them off. These stories assure us over and over again of the basic irony of Life—it is never to be organized, conquered, captured; yet man's whole bent is to keep trying to do just that.

A few stories give us the men who seem to have succeeded, to have grasped the life they figured out for themselves. 'The New Prime Minister' had risen, caught up in his ideal, like a pure flame; now he is finding that the achieved heights, lived with day by day, amount in fact to being bogged down in petty details and the inevitable dislike of the thousands he cannot satisfy. The Rupert of 'Apples', growing up to accomplish the satisfaction of all his sensual desires, finds that they cloy.

'St. George and the Dragon' gives us a frustrated schoolteacher who tries to organize two men in her life into a neat triangle, with herself at the apex—but they refuse to be placed. 'The Last Time' finds a man with a limited time to live trying to finish everything off neatly. The rough, frayed edges, however, refuse to be trimmed. His always tentative, unsatisfactory romance with Helen d'Estrées will not, even at his near-deathbed, consent to take a graspable shape. After bright conversation, Helen leaves him with a few polite phrases.

'The Island', the longest and most complete story in this collection, has also perhaps the most resemblance to a parable, or complete symbolic tale, with a number of possible interpretations. Here we have an island, set apart, and on it a house barricaded off from the surrounding ferocious sea, and having a peculiar white-ness, dustlessness, soundlessness. The house and the life within are the essence of luxury and comfort—the very angles of the walls have been rounded to eliminate the possibility of stumbling against *edges*. In this hermetic world Mrs. Santander entertains her lovers; her husband has left for South America.

But there is much that has what G. K. Chesterton would call 'the wrong shape'—the glasses with 'twisty stems' (*NF* p. 6), the Wolf music, 'full of strange chords and accidentals' (*NF* p. 5), the Chinese figures with their expressions of 'ferocious pleasure' (*NF* p. 7)—finally the torn fingernail of the mysteriously-returned Mr. Santander: 'a jagged rent revealing the quick, moist and gelatinous' (*NF* p. 25). When in the final scene, the sea and rain pour in through the shattered casement window, we are not surprised to find Mrs. Santander, strangled, in the dark library, while her husband crashes to the rocks and surf below. We cannot live, Hartley shows us, as if evil and suffering, the 'edges' of life, the cruelty of the sea are abstractions that can be shut out from a perfectly planned and organized life. Inherent in *any* life, in human nature as well as the threatening nature without, are inescapable contradictions, evils, uglinesses—a blackness, a chaos at the heart, perhaps. And we are foolish and self-condemned if we do not recognize them, allow them their due in our scheme of things.

In 'A Portrait' and 'Friends of the Bridegroom' Hartley seems to comment on his own method. 'Friends of the Bridegroom' gives us a little tableau in which we experience perspective, point of view as revelatory. Here stands the bridegroom, here the bride. It is through the presence of the sardonic, yet pitying friend and his interaction with the bride—not through anything explicit that anyone says—that we come to see the groom as a well-to-do nonentity for whose money the bride has sold herself. This is an exercise in indirection which finds its point in the methods of characterization and the unusual comic effects of many of the novels. And with 'A Portrait' we have an artist catching an 'ideal' Mrs. Marchmont, expressing on his canvas the quintessence of 'all that was most charming in her many expressions'. Again the ideal is contrasted with the 'real', but perhaps this time with the weight on the ideal side. The artist captures, in a sense *creates*, the essence of her personality in a way it can never exist in life. Yet *which* is true; which is 'real'?

What do we take from these first of Hartley's sketches? Concerns and a method that were to last him all his life long. The complexity of reality, the oftentimes sinister chaos at its heart, the seeming impossibility of capturing the truth about any aspect of life or reality in abstractions or categories. On the other hand, the restlessness of the human mind, free to override mere reality and experience and to be creative of its own versions of existence; the constant, constantly frustrated striving after meaning, form, a principle. Overall, the duality in us and in our universe. . . .

Usually these sketches make tangible (as tangible as they really are) the little neuroticisms, fears, guilts, illusions by which we all live—like Hawthorne's tales, as described by Hartley himself, they exploit the possibilities of the subconscious mind, 'but always with the intention of throwing light on the human predicament in its entirety. . . .' (*NR* p. 72). In *Night Fears* Hartley first begins to *embody* states of mind: to give arms and legs and actions to the hidden halves of men's personalities; to let guilt and fear and Puritanism and hedonism become actors in little dramas.

Hartley's symbolism is of several kinds. First of all, the basic situation of each sketch is an embodiment of a moral question, perhaps of varying points of view—usually highly visual, perhaps static. These are tableaux, comparable to scenes in a well-made film by someone like Antonioni in which the visible relationships between the characters' positions in a room suggest all that is going on beneath the surface. Here we have a night-watchman's conversation with a faceless stranger—in a rectangle of blackness, lit only by a brazier; here a wet, naked gentleman, pleading for his trousers before a rowdy member of the lower classes; here a burly military man and a weak and bookish schoolmaster brought unwillingly to blows over a conniving spinster; here an unsuccessful poet in a sleazy restaurant, unable to retrieve his hat from the dusty floor until his pitying friend reassures him that his poems were never any good.

In general, Hartley reinforces his central situational symbolism and meaning by finding other symbols to echo and extend it. Sometimes this is in the use of a single, central, emblematic symbol, like that of 'Apples'. Rupert as a child wants those apples when he wants them. He will inconvenience his Uncle Tim, break his little sister's doll, to try to get them, all unripe as they are. Rupert as a sensual, self-indulgent man of thirty finds overripe apples falling all about him—and they make him sick. The apples are a kind of objective correlative for Rupert, his goals, and what happens to him and them; his attitude towards the apples, at both stages, is an index to his character and his happiness. (Here and elsewhere Hartley seems to suggest that man continually sets petty goals for himself, hankers after worthless absolutes because he must be constantly striving. But those who find their petty goals fulfilled, their striving cut off, achieve only unhappiness. Man's mind, capable of infinite striving, must have an infinite goal.)

More generally, Hartley adds emphasis and extra dimensions to his meaning with a variety of incidental symbolism. He experiments, often over-obviously, with furniture and clothing and natural surroundings—as, for example, in 'The Island' (see above). At the beginning of that story, also, we are given a horrifying image of nature's destructiveness when the narrator tells us that Mrs. Santander's island looks like 'some crustacean, swallowed by an ill-turned starfish, but unassimilated' (NF p. 2). (Incidentally this type of image returns often in the short stories and, most notably, in the shrimp and anemone image of *Eustace and Hilda*.)

When Helen d'Estrées comes to see the dying Hector Stanforth in 'The Last Time', 'A bedroom chair would have prefigured too plainly the brevity of the interview; the almost sofa on which Helen sat down had been sidled awkwardly into the room to suggest permanence and talk indefinitely prolonged' (NF pp. 218–19). For the victory feast shared by 'The New Prime Minister' and the 'second place' narrator Grampus, there is a scheme of changing the flowers on the table with every course— and the meal proceeds from lilies of the valley to poinsettias, which last the disillusioned Prime Minister dismembers with

24

'irritable fingers', 'piling the crumpled rays, bruised and dark with their own juice, in a little heap by his plate' (*NF* p. 147). The artist in 'A Portrait' props his easel up with a twig taken from the garden—a seeming reference to the dependence of art (but only in part) upon life. And the morbid-minded brother of 'A Summons' meditates about a blue-bottle fly as perhaps drawn to his bedside by its ' *air* for putrefaction' (*NF* p. 123), mentally sees the virginia creeper cut from his window as lying below, withering, with the 'pathetic, strained curve of a creature that curls up to die' (*NF* p. 124).

The Killing Bottle (1932)[15] and *The Travelling Grave* (1948) are, in the main, collections of Gothic horror tales and ghost stories. Studying them gives us further insight into how Hartley developed some of his favourite themes in and through some of his most frequently recurring symbols. In general, the Gothic, the grotesque or horrible or exotic or other-worldly, tends to serve him as a medium for dealing with invisible forces in man's existence, and with questions of the meaning, the hidden laws of that existence.

Often-recurring types here and later in Hartley's novels are the unsophisticated observers (often Italians, sometimes women or children) who are superstitious, credulous—believe in curses, revenants. Mario, the gondolier in 'Podolo', evidently believes with the rest of his fellow-Venetians that it is unlucky to kill cats, whatever your motives. His scruples do not arise from the cat's suffering: 'He did not mind the animal dying of slow starvation; that was in the course of nature. But deliberately to kill it!' (*TG* p. 24). Interference with nature's laws is unwise—perhaps his superstition is an older, deeper human wisdom which knows that nature *has* mysterious and terrible laws.

The other side of this coin is the often-recurring type (usually a bluff Englishman—like Lord Morecambe in *Eustace and Hilda*) who has only contempt for the superstitious foreigners or easily-influenced women. There is the hard-drinking pair in 'Three, or Four, for Dinner', for example, who insist on sending an un-suspecting Italian boy to invite to dinner the man (actually the corpse) in their gondola. It is they, not the boy, who suffer when

25

the invitation is accepted. The servants at Low Threshold Hall in 'Feet Foremost' are inclined to take its hereditary curse seriously; the more sophisticated ladies and gentlemen refuse to admit that the curse is being fulfilled under their very eyes.

Hartley's ghost stories give us intimations of the apocalyptic universe which moves in the background of each of his novels. The visible world we live in is surrounded by, in touch with a greater and more frightening invisible one of spirits, forces, connections and consequences. It is one organic world, and the settings of Hartley's stories—remote country houses during weekends or extended visits (e.g. in 'Feet Foremost',' The Killing Bottle', 'The Travelling Grave', 'A Change of Ownership'), exotic places like islands near Venice, or fairy-tale countries ('Podolo', 'Three, or Four, for Dinner', 'Conrad and the Dragon'), the ritual of a masked ball ('The Cotillon')—are microcosms carefully designed to give us an experience of that world in little. In several cases Hartley calls our attention to the fact that he has created a *theatre*—that in quite ordinary settings and moments a portentous drama is being enacted. Thus Podolo Island forms a kind of natural amphitheatre. 'As we sat in the gondola we were like theatre-goers in the stalls, staring at an empty stage' (*TG* p. 22). And in the church of 'The Thought', where Henry Greenstream meets his devil, 'The sunlight coming through the window below them fell on the chairs, picking them out in gold and making a bright patch like the stage of a theatre' (*TG* p. 141). This theatre-creating emphasizes a conscious or unconscious bent towards Hawthorne's method as he explains it in the Preface to *The Blithedale Romance*; his concern with the socialist community of Brook Farm, he insists, is

. . . merely to establish a theatre, a little removed from the highway of ordinary travel, where the creatures of his brain may play their phantas-magorical antics, without exposing them to too close a comparison with the actual events of real lives.[16]

(Similarly, in the later *Eustace and Hilda*, as the entire houseparty company waits at Anchorstone Hall for the return of Dick and Hilda from their aeroplane, the lights are dimmed and the curtains opened:

It was like being in a theatre when the lights went down. The window was the proscenium arch and the night the stage. . . . But . . . the thought crossed Eustace's mind, 'Perhaps it is we who are on the stage, and the night is looking in at us with its thousand eyes, waiting for us to do something' [*EH* p. 420].)

One of the first discoveries we might expect to make—and do make—is that there is mysterious evil in this universe, in man and seemingly in untamed nature within and without him. Hartley deals extensively in curses ('Feet Foremost'), haunted houses ('A Change of Ownership')—sometimes involving commerce with the devil ('The Thought'), but usually revolving around the return of someone or other from the dead to avenge his attempted destruction ('A Visitor from Down Under', 'A Change of Ownership', 'The Travelling Grave', 'The Cotillon'). Vengeance, retribution, return from the dead is the favourite theme—and we begin to see that, in general, evil has laws. It begins in someone's mind or heart, often with jealousy or the desire for another's possessions ('The Thought') and breaks out in murder, as in 'A Visitor from Down Under', 'A Change of Ownership', 'The Travelling Grave'—or in the kind of cruelty and lack of love which is equivalent to murder, as in 'The Cotillon'. 'I know it sounds melodramatic to say it, but you have spoilt my life, you have killed something inside me', Harry Chichester writes to Marion Lane (*TG* p. 104) before shooting himself. When his ghost returns and hands Marion a revolver, it is simply the embodiment of the inexorable law that evil, lack of love, lives on, perpetuates itself, encompasses the destruction of its perpetrator. 'The Killing Bottle' personifies this principle in a madman who destroys all who are unnecessarily cruel to living things; 'The Travelling Grave' symbolizes it in a trick coffin that chases after and snaps up its victims (most appropriately snapping up its owner and proprietor as he tries to use it on a guest); 'Podolo' shows it to us in a nameless unknown monster on a ghastly island, who devours the too-innocent 'Angela' when she flouts the dreadful economy in nature and tries (out of misguided humanitarianism) to kill a stray cat. Here more than retribution is involved—there is a hint of the terrible demand for *food* which is

27

the most basic of urges and commitments and which makes animals and possibly men, if pushed to it, eat each other. 'The Killing Bottle's' terrible images hint at the same underlying need of life to prey on life—the snails' shells on a stone which mark, according to Rollo Verdew, 'the thrushes' Tower Hill' (*TG* p. 206); the butterfly dying in the killing bottle (*TG* p. 221), 'its straining, delicate tongue coiling and uncoiling in the effort to suck in a breath of living air'—suddenly, 'with a violent spasm', giving birth to 'a thick cluster of yellowish eggs'. 'Blood calls for blood', Randolph Verdew says (*TG* p. 213). More terribly, Oscar Wilde's epigram on each one killing the thing he loves seems to be the meaning of 'Podolo' (see *TG* p. 26). There is evil at the heart of life; there is an evil side even to love.

But if un-lovingness and misdirected love kill, as Hartley suggests, he seems to suggest also that authentic love, the real placing of another's good before one's own—gives life. The image he uses for this kind of love, at least in the story where his meaning is most clear, is sacrificial death (or the *willingness* to undergo death for another). In 'Feet Foremost', the ghostly Lady Elinor's love for Antony, born of her own hatred and mistreatment during life, is a curse. She will possess him and kill him; her caress is a stranglehold (*TG* p. 96). Killing the cat-woman, as Maggie tries to do, is no solution. The only thing that will save Antony from death and possession is a substitute victim, and Maggie is willing to accept this death and ultimate violation for his sake. Chance substitutes another victim, but we understand that it is her love that has changed the balance in the universe and bought his freedom.

Hartley's incidental symbolism is carefully worked-at to fill out this sense of a huge economy of good and evil, love and non-love. The country houses are all replete with Gothic wings, disused churches, slimy moats—touches that set them apart in the realm of the past, or that perhaps set the scoffed-at beliefs of the past against the flatness of the sceptical present, to ask which is greater truth. Hartley delights in using children's games and songs ('Hide and Seek' in 'The Travelling Grave'; 'Oranges and Lemons' and 'Who will you have for your Nuts and May . . .'? in

'A Visitor from Down Under') to epitomize the meaning of the whole and make Mr. Rumbold's murder, for example, a working-out of the black philosophy of the 'Oranges and Lemons' song he has just heard: 'Here is a candle to light you to bed, / And here comes a chopper to chop off your head!' Like the superstitious yet worldly-wise Italians, children have an instinct for the blacker realities.

Hartley also focuses upon rituals like the Cotillon with its masks and its succeeding figures in which, for example, one chooses a partner in a mirror or through a sheet (the sheet falls in folds about Marion, like a shroud [*TG* p. 111]), because he, like Marion, is conscious of the force of the dance's 'mimic drama' (*TG* p. 109) to symbolize inner happenings. He experiments also with dreams and fantasies which serve as integral parts of the stories' progress, their disclosures of meaning. In 'Podolo' the gondolier appears to the narrator in a dream and explains that Angela has disappeared because 'We loved her and so we had to kill her' (*TG* p. 26). In 'Feet Foremost' Antony dreams about 'Possession' and its nine points, and cats and their nine lives—before the nearly-fatal, possessive love of the cat-woman Lady Elinor takes him over (*TG* p. 77).

And all the time, in Hartley's dialogue, life is also taking place on two levels. The most ordinary words and relationships and events, we begin to feel through this technique, have enormous, powerful reverberations in the economy of the universe. 'He is not *de notre monde*, perhaps?' the Count equivocally asks the two Englishmen at the Lido in 'Three, or Four, for Dinner'. His question refers, though with seeming innocence, to the corpse they have irreverently invited for dinner. 'It's the chance of a life', Mrs. Verdew writes to Jimmy in 'The Killing Bottle' to urge him to leave her husband's estate for a mythical appointment in London. He does not know she is offering him an escape from a mad murderer.

There is 'multiple choice' throughout these stories. If you like you can read them as pure and simple tales of the activities of ghosts and devils who carry out these laws by which we, all unknowing, must live. In 'The Visitor from Down Under', the mysterious killer leaves 'an icicle on the window sill, a thin claw of ice curved like a Chinaman's nail, with a bit of flesh sticking to it' (*TG* p. 20). In 'The Cotillon' the ghost of Harry Chichester leaves an open window in the ballroom and an oval smear on the floor nearby. Jack Manning asks if people think it's a footmark, and 'No one could say' (*TG* p. 119). But Hartley also gives us, of course, ample evidence for taking the strange happenings as workings-out of guilt and hatred and remorse—the toll taken by an evil conscience. Just as in 'Night Fears', the personalities of these guilty and fearful men and women split into their incompatible halves, and their guilt and terror (seem to?) take on flesh and blood and character of their own to destroy their originators. This is most clear in 'The Thought', where a man tortured by guilt returns again and again to the empty country church where he has wished evil to his enemy. He is so convinced that he belongs to the devil and that only death will atone for his crime, that the devil takes on shape and comes to get him. And in 'A Change of Ownership', the face, the hateful murderer's face which looks back at the terrified Ernest from outside the window, is his own (*TG* p. 132).

All these stories, despite their macabre premises and images, have a sort of playfulness which fits well with the ambiguity of this genre. Two in particular are much more light in manner than the rest, though differing not too much in their picture of the universe. There is 'Mr. Blandfoot's Picture', which uses names (Mrs. Pepperthwaite, Mrs. Stornway, Settlemarsh, the Pergola, Antony Mellish), architecture, landscaping, furnishings (the cocktails at tea-time of the newcomers; the 'sombre trophies from India and the Boxer Rebellion, scraps of armour without faces, scraps of faces without armour, pallid wooden hands projecting from hollow sleeves supporting flower pots . . .' of the old guard) to symbolize lifestyles, social standing and old and new forms of social snobbery. Mr. Blandfoot defeats Mrs. Marling and her pet lion, the author Hesketh, by accepting her invitation to exhibit his famous picture at her salon—and then revealing it to be tattooed on his chest. The point he is making to Mrs. Marling might be that a man's worth is himself and not his possessions.

'Conrad and the Dragon', on the other hand, is a charming, wittily-told fairy tale/satire which could even be political in nature if attached to any particular time and events. It tells of a princess whose every prospective husband is killed by a ravening dragon—until the one man shows up who doesn't particularly want to die for her (he assumes she has enough intelligence not to want him to). This quite unusual man—Conrad—manages to wound the dragon, which then turns out to be the princess herself. Basically, Hartley seems again to be talking about love—sexual love—and the fact that men themselves make women into monsters by the way they treat them, and by their assumption that love must be predatory and possessive.

Two more recent volumes of short stories, *The White Wand* (1954)[17] and *Two for the River* (1961), show Hartley still exploring. —one might say playing with—many of the same basic themes, posing the ideal/actual, One vs. Many dilemma in ever more sophisticated, though usually more ordinary and contemporary forms.

The artist or writer character (that favourite of Hawthorne's) comes forward prominently in *The White Wand* to stand alternately for good and bad sides to the human faculty of aspiring, idealizing, 'looking behind appearances', as writers are supposed to do ('The Two Vaynes', *WW* p. 168). 'A Rewarding Experience' shows us a writer, Henry Tarrant, who has become too isolated, lost his contact with experience, Nature—and hence his gift for writing. An encounter with a lady and her dog at his front gate bring blood and dirt within his too-immaculate house—to his great relief and the probable re-grounding of his art in life. 'W. S.' is a comic horror story exploring the relationship of an author with his creation. Hartley probably had much fun putting this story together around the somewhat remote middle-aged author Walter Streeter, who keeps getting postcards from a 'W. S.' who accuses him of fence-straddling, not getting to grips with people, being over-ambiguous in what he writes. 'W. S.' finally arrives—or seems to—and turns out to be the one thoroughly evil, Iago-like character Streeter had created in his youth when things were apt to look more black and white to

31

him. Because Streeter can not, for the cause of goodness every-where, allow W. S. a redeeming spark, he has to submit to a very logical strangulation by this totally evil creature. This is an explicit example of Hartley's use of the *doppelganger*. Streeter knows that most of his characters are projections of himself, or his antithesis, and that all his self-hate probably went into W. S. It is his self-hate, then, which begs for leniency and, not getting it, throttles him. For all his middle-aged feeling for the ambiguous, the good-and-evil mixtures in life, Streeter cannot deny his knowledge of the real evil in himself.

'Up the Garden Path' poses an ineffectual, artistic type who loves flowers (Christopher) against Ernest, the brute realist who has achieved success and, seemingly, won Constantia's love from his too-ethereal rival. Christopher commits suicide when his garden, his last hope for meaning and success, seems to fail. But, dead, he is strong, and his memory comes between Ernest and Constantia.

Here we have several ways of looking at the same persons and events. Seen one way (Ernest's way), Christopher is ineffectual, impotent, and, finally, a failure. He was unable to come to terms with life and so had to die. Seen from another angle (as his fare-well letter and the actual beauty of his garden, recognized even by Ernest, help us to see) he is competent as an artist, a lover of beauty—but desperately needing love, recognition, commerce with the 'realists' to succeed. His friends, those who should have loved and sustained him, have failed in their responsibility. 'Was it too much . . . or too little' (*WW* p. 212) that he asked of life? Hartley here gives us another parable of the relationship between ideal and actual, body and soul, imagination and reality—specifically the artist and society, the ordinary world. When art, the soul, is split off from the body of life, it fades and fails—and leaves the average citizen to his own inadequate resources and unsatisfactory love.

'The Price of the Absolute' shows us Timothy Carswell willing to pay a fantastic price for a vase which speaks to him of perfection, especially when he realizes how few among all the world's millions could create such a thing. 'Had his life been a quest, it would have ended here' (*WW* p. 144). Again Hartley is portraying the strength and centrality of the human desire for an absolute—and, as he is so often to do in the future, he lets an art object be that in which the individual human being tries (usually unsatisfactorily) to satisfy his search, his aspiration towards perfection.

'The White Wand' is a culminating point in the study this book makes of the aspiring and creating aspects of the human mind. 'The White Wand' is a long short story, almost a novella, and therefore more complex than the rest: playing off against each other some of the elements and themes caught and crystallized in the shorter sketches.

There is a story within the story; hence, two points of view on the events, with the overall narrator's impressions only suggested as a counterbalance to the wildly-exaggerated inner story being told by 'C. F.', the obviously hyper-sensitive, neurotic writer. The overall narrator is a happily married, settled, seemingly quite balanced person, a kind friend, unwilling to let his rational mind and instinct for fair play be ruled by prejudices and personal animosities; C. F. says in exasperation that he 'would defend the Devil' (*WW* p. 22). C. F., on the other hand, is a bachelor writer who has lived a pampered, protected life in the society and 'civilization' of pre-war Venice—who has seen the war as almost a personal affront to his comfort, who has cut himself off from people for years because of his inability to tolerate imperfections in his friends or servants. As he tells his striving-to-be-sympathetic friend about the idyllic love affair he had in Venice after the war, we realize with horror—through what he lets drop and through his friend's reactions—that, in fact, his neuroticism, his self-imposed isolation from imperfect human society, have betrayed him into constructing this idyll for himself. If there is any reality at all, it is in a completely false relationship with a crippled and dying girl, who humoured him because she did not want to be unkind.

The 'white wand' of the title is one of our clues: it is the sick girl's wasted arm, as seen by C. F. from his window, across from hers. Hartley also brings forward many of the symbols and

33

corresponding themes with which he deals more extensively else-where—'face-saving' and dishonesty as basic human faults which C. F. recognizes in the small faults of others, especially the Italians, but not in himself; the *'doppelganger'* who reveals to C. F. and to us that he is really old, and not the youthful delight he fancies himself to be; the choice of views from two windows: one revealing a decaying palace of old Venice, with the 'white wand' in its window; the other exhibiting more ordinary, func-tional architecture: a campanile like a water-tower, a chimney stack, and 'a lot of other things that I didn't like, but they didn't vanish just because I didn't like them. They weren't so accom-modating as she was' (*WW* p. 29). And here, all day long, the swifts are 'dive-bombing and screaming'.

C. F. chooses the view of the past, of romantic, decaying Italy, but he abstracts it, turns it into geometry and imagined view. In the sick girl's room, when he finds it, he seeks to escape the contradictions of actual contemporary existence, as revealed in the just-ended war, with its dive-bombers, and to go back to the 'flux', where 'forms had no time to harden into matter' (*WW* pp. 52–3), to 'the raw material of facts, the inchoate substance of experience before it becomes one's own', symbolized by 'the indeterminate springing greenness' of her plants (*WW* p. 55). The nameless narrator tells us here how C. F., telling him the story, rubs, closes and uncloses his eyes, 'Whether to keep his mind's eye clear for its inner vision or to brush the vision aside I could not tell' (*WW* p. 53). In any case, we are clearly dealing with the making real of an inner vision and its clash with actual physical facts. And Hartley relates this individual self-deception to the larger problems of human relationships, including the war; to pre-war aestheticism and individualism and the separation of art from life; to the post-war tendency of British art, perhaps, or the British upper classes, to long for the serenity and irresponsi-bility of the past and a no longer viable beauty and culture; to all current temptations to ignore reality, the hard lessons of the war, the challenges of the present. In such dissections of his own class and profession, Hartley seems to be grappling with the problems and contradictions he feels within his own being—that is why he

34

can present them with such complexity and balance and leave us with very real questions instead of simplistic answers. This story does seem to coincide, also, with his own post-war effort to find utterly contemporary settings for his questionings and to make his bachelor writer heroes more or less his own age at the time of writing.

The volume *Two for the River* seems to hit hard on the other side of the dilemma—the power of nature and brute reality, especially the unrecognized potential evil in a force like sex. 'The Pylon' and 'Someone in the Lift' stress the father-son jealousies and antagonisms related to awakening masculinity, the way in which adult masculinity can threaten and negate a child's imaginative and sensitive sides. The central symbol of 'The Pylon', while obviously phallic, is also linked, more broadly, to pride and strength and even the atom bomb (*TR* p. 219). It is an ambivalent, good-evil symbol, and fits in with a frequent tendency on Hartley's part to use masculine and feminine to symbolize self-assertion and self-sacrifice, and to relate these principles to war, life and death, and the balance of good and evil in the universe.

'*Per Far l'Amore*' is extremely explicit. Mr. Henry Elkington is disturbed, sick, oppressed by the heat and mosquitoes which characterize Venice in August—and also, subconsciously (we see by his reflections and dreams), by the too-great-freedom of his daughter Annette, about whom young men 'as like each other as mosquitoes' (*TR* p. 157) are continually buzzing. Annette and her perhaps repressed, too romantic (*TR* p. 156) mother do not see danger in Annette's spending hours at a time, unchaperoned, with one or another of the young men. Mr. Elkington worries that 'She seems to think that love today is different from love at any other time' (*TR* p. 167).

As usual embodying attitudes and points of view in tangible form, Hartley sets up a party at which guests take refuge from heat and mosquitoes in tents marked and furnished according to their tastes: for misanthropy, conversation, cards, or '*per far l'amore*'—making love. It is in one of the latter tents that Mr. Elkington discovers his daughter at the end of the party— strangled, with the tent's pennon tied around her throat to proclaim that *'per far l'amore'* is always playing with fire, with death, with passions that should not be too naïvely risked.

'A Very Present Help' discriminates between two kinds of *'l'amore'*. Mrs. Buswell, the warm and solicitous daily housekeeper, gives George Lambert a 'vision ... of reciprocal affection dominating, softening, yes, and even sweetening physical love' (*TR* p. 131) after he has been left alone in his sickness by his capricious mistress Deirdre O'Farrell. Playing with his usual symbols of 'love in terms of money' vs. 'money in terms of love', and of ordinary people as agents of Fate or Providence, Hartley has Mrs. Buswell teaching George that he should take as well as give and—by her loud clattering of dishes in the kitchen all through his final interview with Deirdre—getting him to dismiss Deirdre, who stands for mere sex, and to look for real friendship/love in a woman.

'The Crossways' is, quite unashamedly, a fairy tale—though modern in its analysis of personalities and the marital relationship. Lucinda is a dreamer, beautiful, from a far country. Her husband Michael, is a stern, poor woodman, scarred by his earlier encounter with a bear in the dangerous woodland. A pedlar from Lucinda's own country passes by, inducing her to buy beautiful things, wooing her with his tales of the road to the Land of Heart's Desire that can be found at the Crossways in the heart of the forest.

When Michael, in response, grows morose, quarrels, drinks, Lucinda flees 'to where her heart calls her' (*TR* p. 148). The children follow, and, at length, Michael, his eyes wild, comes too to find them at the Crossways—where all the signposts, leading in so many directions, have turned out to be blank.

Michael admits how unkind he has been, that he is not worthy of Lucinda, that she must go where she wants to go. She, on the other hand, has hurt her foot and cannot go on unless he carries her. With their rediscovered love and agreement to return home, the signpost becomes clear. The Land of Heart's Desire, for them, is on the homeward path they have begun to follow.

Only the agreement of body and soul—the working together and mutual respect of aspiration and reality, art and life, the spiritual and physical—can achieve the Land of Heart's Desire, in marriage or in any human endeavour. With love and imagination, one's own place and life can become rich and beautiful. It is Hartley's usual problem, but here seemingly resolved in balance, in marriage. Finding a crossways and trying to make a clear choice—setting up dichotomies—is no solution; imagination and reality cannot live apart, nor art and society, nor the physical and spiritual aspects of the sexual relationship. This little fairy tale, this symbolic construct, embodying archetypal relationships in modern form, and carrying with it so many possible meanings, might serve as one of the clearest clues to what Hartley is all about and to his method of presentation.

A brief summary has already been given[18] of *Simonetta Perkins*, Hartley's first, very short, novel, published in 1925. The rather lurid book jacket on the second (1952) edition tries to catch something of the opening tableau in which Hartley sets up his central problem. Lavinia Johnstone, a carefully brought-up model of behaviour from Boston, is sitting in front of her hotel, in Venice, reading a treatise on Love and being bothered by its highly-coloured assertions just as she is bothered by the exuber-ance of Italian Baroque—especially that of Santa Maria della Salute, opposite her, 'rising like a blister out of the inflamed and suppurating stonework below' (*SP* p. 7). The book she is reading says something about 'the eye of desire' and Miss Johnstone takes exception:

> 'What execrable taste!' she exclaimed. 'The eye of desire, pooh!' She raised her own eyes, as though to record a protest to the heavens, but her outraged glance never climbed to the zenith. An intermediate object arrested it. Posted in front of her, . . . a gondola lay rocking . . . and the gondolier was sitting on the poop and staring at the hotel. No, not at the hotel, decided Miss Johnstone, at me (*SP* p. 11).

The story of Miss Johnstone—torn between her accepted idea of her own virtue and its worth, and the 'desire' she soon begins to experience for Emilio and all that he represents of complete expression of one's passions—is Hartley's means of asking, in the free-for-all world of the twenties: What, then, are the standards to be in the new age? Are there standards at all—and if so, where does

37

one find them? Or how does one arrive at them? The particular issue in the story is sexual freedom, and Hartley manages to deal quite directly with this thorny question, setting before us in an unusual way the spectacle of a young and virtuous girl discovering her own strong erotic impulses and facing the problem of what to do about them.

Lavinia has very clear options before her. There is her proper Bostonian suitor Stephen Seleucis, who embodies the Puritan code by which she has lived thus far, to the admiration of her less spotless friends. Stephen sees Venice as a task to be done, a map to be checked off, piece by piece, as part of one's education. He is relieved to find that Lavinia objects only because she doesn't *want* to do it this way. 'Why, of course you don't,' he replied. . . . 'No one does. But we've got to. That's what we Americans come here for. Now, try again' (*SP* p. 44).

On the other side stands Emilio the gondolier, the complete hedonist, pictured for us on the same page unselfconsciously exhibiting the effortlessness and economy of 'a thousand years of watermanship' in managing himself and his gondola; at every moment 'accessible to pleasure' and ready to 'render pleasure back' (*SP* p. 44). Lavinia begins to understand the repressiveness of her background, the falseness of her response. 'What was the effect, psychologically, of saying you wanted something that you passionately did not want? Did it do you any good? How did the will, thwarted, revenge itself?' (*SP* p. 51).

Little by little freeing the opposite response in herself—lying about the tickets in order to stay in Venice, joining up with the despised Kolynopulos in order to be near Emilio—Lavinia finds herself, in a letter, creating another personality, Simonetta Perkins, to bear the brunt of the fact she hates to admit: that she has actually developed a passion ('a shorter word describes it better' [*SP* p. 84]) for a gondolier. She has now become a split personality—half Puritan, half hedonist, with neither half able to face the other. The only way of resolving the problem, after some struggling, seems to be to become all hedonist. 'The rivers of her being, long forced uphill, turned back upon themselves, joined and flowed away unhindered in one dark current' (*SP* p. 92).

Lavinia/Simonetta goes off in the gondola with Emilio to follow up Mrs. Kolynopulo's coarse suggestion that gondoliers function as something like male prostitutes (*SP* p. 57).

Hartley's presentation of Lavinia's awakening to, and trying to cope with, a more realistic picture of herself, is sensitively developed within the scope of 96 pages. Now, pressing on in the gondola through ever-narrowing canals on the way to her assignation, Lavinia suddenly comprehends what is happening to her as part of a whole new grasp of the drama of existence. In the four sentences (quoted in part in Ch. One) in which Hartley details her recognition we have a 1925 adumbration of the mysterious symbolic world which was to figure in the background of all his subsequent novels:

> She was afraid to look back, but in her mind's eye she could see, repeated again and again, the arrested rocking movement of the gondolier. The alternation of stroke and recovery became dreadful to her, suggesting no more what was useful or romantic, but proclaiming a crude physical sufficiency, at once relentless and unwilling. It came to her overwhelmingly that physical energy was dangerous and cruel, just in so far as it was free; there flashed across her mind the straining bodies in Tiepolo and Tintoretto, one wielding an axe, another tugging at a rope, a third heaving the Cross aloft, a fourth turning his sword upon the Innocents. And Emilio with his hands clasping the oar was such another; a minister at her martyrdom (*SP* p. 95).

This passage gives us all of Hartley, in miniature. In a few sentences we have an equation of the gondola's movement with the purely physical side of sexual intercourse, having no spiritual component; with all brute physical power uninformed by the human spirit; with the epitome of human cruelty and victimization, the Crucifixion. Hartley could be saying, as a believing Christian, that the one drama of Christ's Crucifixion goes on constantly, is the universal meaning of history: that in every human act one either joins with the brutes, the haters, the killers, or with the lovers, the givers (inevitably the victims)—who, dying, are really overcoming in the only way it is possible to overcome in a terrible world. Or, again, Hartley can be using the Christian apocalyptic view as a simile, as Lavinia seems to be doing. In either case, Hartley seems to be giving Lavinia—and the new world of the twenties—some kind of basis for the moral decisions of each moment. All human life and action are inseparably intertwined; our deeds, whatever they are, reverberate throughout the human universe and kill or give life. We can never simply follow our brute inclinations without being aware of this; cannot honestly seize upon the hedonistic answer any more than upon the Puritan. Earlier Simonetta has mused, '... but then cruelty is a thing apart; no one can want to be cruel' (*SP* pp. 53–4); now she is seeing cruelty as part and parcel of any purely 'natural' act unredeemed by human care and love. Notable, too, in this passage, is the use of art as revelatory—also a continuing element in Hartley's vision. It is those Venetian fixtures Titian and Tintoretto who show Lavinia the meaning of Venice and Emilio and the gondola in the great scheme of things. This, Hartley would say, is the role of the artist, whatever his specific subject.

Lavinia seems, despite her sudden revelation, to be completely hemmed in at this moment by fate, events, the misery of life. She feels herself to be going down a tunnel that is growing smaller and smaller with something after her and escape less and less possible. 'She ran, she crawled; she flung herself on her face, she wriggled. . . .' (*SP* p. 96). But at this last moment, something in her makes it possible to say the magic word '*Torniamo*' to Emilio (a word symbolic of moral change which Eustace also speaks at a crucial moment [*EH* p. 634]). Lavinia has perhaps begun to find her Self, an 'I', the pinpoint of inviolable freedom at the heart of all her entanglements which makes it possible for her to reject the Emilio-solution on her own terms and decision, and not merely because she has been brought up that way. '*Torniamo*'. The finding and assertion of the 'I', the solving of life's problems in the act of living them, is the only way out of abstract (and therefore false) moral dilemmas.

Hartley's ending of *Simonetta Perkins* comes quickly and says little that is explicit. On the Paris-bound Orient Express, Lavinia thinks of Emilio and knows, 'I shall never forget him' (*SP* p. 96). Harvey Curtis Webster says 'At the end of the book it is left open to the reader to decide whether she has come to terms with both her wishes and God's [this is how Webster sees her dilemma], which she understands only partially'.[19] And the *TLS* reviewer, after talking about Hartley's delicate vivisection of the 'butterfly' of the Bostonian soul, says, 'He exposes it to our curiosity, not to our derision, and then lets it flutter away free. Whether quite the same butterfly or not he will not definitely say.'[20]

Hartley does not definitely say, but as our study of his sketches and experiments has revealed, his object is to show, not to say. We have followed Simonetta/Lavinia from her initial self-assurance through her temptation, her agonized examination of her Puritan code, her reckless yielding to its opposite, her seeming touching upon the living point of Self, deep within, which makes nonsense of all abstractions. This seems to be the nearest Hartley feels a child of the twentieth century can come to moral standards, given the dilemma he has pictured so clearly, and the inadequacy he seems to see in both the code of the past and the licence of the present.

Simonetta Perkins in its relative simplicity helps to show us, too, whither Hartley's shorter experiments have been going. Fully rounded characters in action as usually given to us *are* perhaps a gaucherie Hartley is determined to avoid,[21] because he means all his characters, the fabric of his whole book, together, to give us the inner and outer portrait of a personality in a manner quite different from that of the ordinary novel. In telling us that Hawthorne clothed thought in circumstances (*NR* p. 115), that he was interested in his characters for what they *represented*, above all in their moral aspect, and as they illustrated the opera-tions of the Moral Law (*NR* p. 97), Hartley describes what sounds very much like Ralph Freedman's concept of the 'lyrical' novel (another concept related to romance, and to Hartley's own work). The lyric, says Freedman, 'objectifies not men and times but an experience and a theme for which men and their lives, or places and events, have been used'.[22] Most of Hartley's shorter sketches are satisfactory only when understood in this light, as his first efforts to find, to create a language which could explore in the twentieth century the kinds of themes Hawthorne had pursued in the nineteenth. In *Simonetta Perkins* he begins to show us that his search could be worthwhile.

CHAPTER THREE

EUSTACE AND HILDA:
AFTER THE FINAL NO

After the final no there comes a yes
And on that yes the future world depends. . . .
—Wallace Stevens[1]

[a]

THE trilogy *Eustace and Hilda* (1944–47) is thought by many to be L. P. Hartley's masterpiece. A subtle and sensitive detailing of a life and of the relationship which dominates, characterizes and seemingly destroys that life, the trilogy is first of all the tragedy of Eustace, who dies because he and Hilda can no longer exist in the same world, because one can only live at the expense of the other. But *Eustace and Hilda* seems also the story of the achievement, the strange salvation of Eustace, who dies after learning what few manage to learn—to love.

The story of Eustace and Hilda is also the story of an age—our age—at its inception. The years of Eustace's growth and struggle and defeat (or victory) are the years of the death of the Past: the death not only of Victorianism, but of absolutes, of assumptions, of God. Eustace's is the world which pronounces all the gods dead, all the wars fought, all the faiths in man shaken; it can offer him nothing but death. But in the baby Eustace, born to Barbara and Jimmy at the trilogy's end, we see the birth of the new twentieth-century man. 'What a one, think you, shall this man be?' Hartley seems to be asking in this trilogy which looks back at the century's beginnings from the perspective of the post-World War II years.

And the story of Eustace and Hilda is also, at its most basic, a parable of the perennial and seemingly insoluble problem of man, raised again by this particular life and death at this particular turning-point in history. Bastard blend of 'squalor and splendour' (*EH* p. 613), inevitably at odds with his own nature, is man doomed forever to oscillate between time and eternity, goodness and pleasure, the desire for perfection and the disappointment of the actual? Can the one only be gained by the loss of the other? Hartley's story has at least three dimensions—but the deepest impression we receive from our growing comprehension of and sympathy with the Eustace-and-Hilda relationship is that of the duality, the complexity, the seeming dichotomy of everything in man's tragic existence.

Seen as one large novel, *Eustace and Hilda* has a well-defined circular—or perhaps spiral—shape. A frame of prologue and *dénouement* set in the coastal town of Anchorstone, in Norfolk, surrounds the central portion, which takes the Eustace-and-Hilda relationship through adventures in Oxford, Anchorstone Castle and Venice.

The prologue, *The Shrimp and the Anemone*, sets the central tension or problem of the novel—the relationship between nine-year-old Eustace and his sister Hilda, four years his senior and in almost every way his opposite. The children are being raised by a strict, puritanical Aunt Sarah and their rather weak father. Hilda —strong-willed, beautiful, rigid and literal-minded, always ready to act, to impose her will, to wrestle with the universe—has charged herself with the moral education of Eustace. He—by nature pliant, receptive, imaginative, able to escape mentally from the harder facts of life—struggles, but usually bends to her will, whether it be in building a walled pond on the sand or speaking to a crippled and unprepossessing old lady on the cliff path above. When we see the children confronting the cruel spectacle of a beautiful plumose anemone devouring a shrimp, we can hardly help assuming this to be a direct symbolic revelation of their destructive relationship.

We are soon aware that there is symbolic significance to everything at Anchorstone: the carefully-described beach with its seaweed-covered rocks far below the red cliffs, the green land-scape above and the path with its First, Second and Third Shelters leading to the white-domed lighthouse. But we can as yet only guess at these significances; they will grow and be revealed only with the development of the story. All we begin to realize is that the stuff of the story itself—the characters, gestures, clothing, colours—the everyday reality of Anchorstone 'shimmers' with meaning.[2]

The Shrimp and the Anemone covers Eustace's childhood years; *The Sixth Heaven* takes him on to Oxford and initiates him, with Hilda, into what is to be a catastrophic friendship with Dick Stavely of Anchorstone Hall. The third book, called *Eustace and Hilda*, sees the sister and brother through the developing (and parallel) stages of that relationship: Eustace playing at authorship and the romantic life in Venice with Dick's aunt, Lady Nelly; Hilda back in England having a love affair with Dick. The climax of Eustace's Venetian experience (which comes at about the same time that Hilda visits Anchorstone Hall for Dick's birthday party) is the great festival of the *Redentore*, or Redeemer, high-lighted for Eustace by a projection, in fireworks, of the thorn-crowned head of Christ on the façade of the *Redentore* Church, and a ritual bath in the Adriatic. Called back to England when Dick's abandonment of Hilda causes her paralysis, Eustace is somewhat purged of the dreaminess and unreality and over-innocence that had made him an instrument in promoting the Dick-Hilda affair. But he over-exerts his weak heart in an effort to shock her into recovery; she does manage to walk again, but at great cost. Eustace, in bed after his ordeal, dreams first of passing a difficult examination, then of being on the sands with Hilda. They are children again, but now with a sense of complete union, a knowing of each other's thoughts and wishes. She disappears, he goes to seek her—and finds the anemone. The book ends with what Walter Allen calls 'the quietest, most subtle and therefore most shocking death in contemporary English fiction'.[3]

The white plumose anemone was stroking the water with its feelers.
The same anemone as before, without a doubt, but there was no shrimp in its mouth. 'It will die of hunger', thought Eustace. 'I must find it

something to eat', and he bent down and scanned the pool. Shrimps were disporting themselves in the shallows; but they slipped out of his cupped hands, and fled away into the dark recesses under the eaves of the rock, where the crabs lurked. Then he knew what he must do. Taking off his shoes and socks, he waded into the water. The water was bitterly cold; but colder still were the lips of the anemone as they closed around his finger. 'I shall wake up now', thought Eustace, who had wakened from many dreams.

But the cold crept onwards and he did not wake (*EH* pp. 735–6).

It is very possible—especially if one reads Hartley's ever-present symbols and the dreams and fantasies he gives to Eustace in a conventionally Freudian sense—to see this novel only as the sadly comic tragedy of a boy destroyed by his environment: specifically his sister's domination, his own guilt and death wish. Peter Bien, for example, sees *Eustace and Hilda* as 'a study in neuroses'. He points to Eustace's fantasies as revealing an unconscious incestuous attraction for Hilda, ending in Eustace 'dead, impotent, decapitated', in 'one of the most horrifying images of frustration in modern literature'.[4] (Here he refers to the above-quoted section on Eustace's death.)

It is certainly true that *Eustace and Hilda* is tragic, that it points to terrible forces at work in man's life, that much of its basic plot can be interpreted in a coherently Freudian way. But it is important to see that Hartley's symbolism (like all true symbolism) is multivalent. We may read *Eustace and Hilda* as a Freudian psychological study, as we may read much of Hawthorne. But we may also, and I think here more importantly and inclusively, read the trilogy as the kind of 'apocalyptic' work Hartley attributed to Hawthorne.[5] In Hartley as in Hawthorne, good and evil are the main, the only issue—though, as in Hawthorne, we may see the good and evil as relating primarily to one's own complexes, guilts, fears and their effects, *or* to a supernatural order in which God's (or Someone's) Providence directs, rewards, punishes. Or perhaps both Hartley and Hawthorne are saying that the two are one.

Seen from one point of view, Hartley's story is indeed, as Walter Allen says, about a 'morbid relationship, but . . . sterilized of morbidity by the treatment. Hartley's detachment, which is that of the affectionate comic writer, not only sets Eustace in perspective but also universalizes him.'[6] This not-so-farfetched situation of neurosis and domination is a jumping-off point—but from the beginning of *The Shrimp and the Anemone* Hartley's careful, significant delineation of Anchorstone, his barely-perceptible emphasis upon and repetition of colours and shapes and objects points to hidden, greater realities. The events, the entire physical world of objects and people take on more and more possible meanings as the story proceeds and these events, objects and people are linked with, paralleled to others. Set down by the third book, *Eustace and Hilda*, in Venice, in the midst of St. Mark's Plaza, in the summer, we know immediately that we are within a huge structural metaphor. The city is flooded with sunlight—but some people prefer shadow. It is a city of water—in which, however, some people deliberately choose to travel on land. Throughout the book light is opposed to darkness, heat to cold, Venice to England, Baroque to Gothic. One senses that silence, speech, language all have their shimmering significance, as well as L-shapes, arches, squares, circles and all the colours of the rainbow. All the motifs touched upon so lightly in the first two books sound out strongly in this one, collecting to themselves all the earlier resonances. Symbolic meanings touch and shift and interrelate; one thinks one sees a coherent pattern in the world of value and significance which radiates from and surrounds the visible, material one. One grasps at it and tries to fix it, and it shimmers again and shows another face. The following reading, attacking the complex of symbols in the crucial third book and then returning to trace the emerging pattern through from the beginning, can only be partial and suggestive.

[b]

The third book of the trilogy opens with an epigraph from Walt Whitman: 'Of the terrible doubt of appearances, / Of the un-certainty, after all, that we may be deluded' (*EH* p. 433). The rest of the poem, which Hartley does not quote, suggests a possible interpretation of reality quite opposed to the usual and obvious;

46

it suggests also the pre-eminence of love as the one unquestionably real thing, the key to all the unanswerable questions. 'May-be the things I perceive, the animals, plants, men, hills, shining and flowing water,' says Whitman, 'The skies of day and night, colors, densities, forms, may-be these are (as doubtless they are) only apparitions, and the real something has yet to be known. . . .'[7] But, he concludes, 'I cannot answer the question of appearances or that of identity beyond the grave, / But I walk or sit indifferent, I am satisfied, / He ahold of my hand has completely satisfied me.'[8]

One of the most important clues to our interpretation is the moment of enlightenment which comes to Eustace during the Festival of the *Redentore*. Hartley's description is memorable, reminiscent of the great Indian feast scenes in *A Passage to India*. In the evening, boats go side by side along the canal, some in the moonlight, some in darkness, towards the point where a newly built bridge spans the water to touch the open door of the great *Redentore* church. The scene is beautiful, mysterious, suggestive; it is also quite effectively desentimentalized by the ironic comments of Hartley's sceptical moderns and the *naïvetés* of his enthusiastic but not over-spiritual gondoliers.

At the end of the evening, Eustace, Lady Nelly, the gondoliers and Lord and Lady Morecambe watch the fireworks from the gondola:

'Good show,' said Lord Morecambe. 'A bit old-fashioned, of course, but good considering.'

'Considering what, my dear?' asked Lady Nelly.

'I don't want to hurt your feelings, but I saw some Italian shooting on the Isonzo, and I'm surprised they're so handy with fireworks. Of course, the sky's a big target, and doesn't hit back.'

'I wish you would try not to see things always in terms of bloodshed,' said Lady Nelly. 'Couldn't you stop him, Heloise?'

'I do try to make him think of something else,' said Lady Morecambe.

'Darling Heloise, I think of you all the time,' her husband said, and put his hand on hers.

Eustace was touched by this gesture, which he attributed to the liberating influence of the fireworks, and wondered how Lady Nelly would respond to a caress from him. Perhaps the same impulse was felt in all the hundreds of little boats that gently rocked beneath their lanterns on the windless, unfretted water; perhaps every heart sent up a rocket to its objective in the empyrean of love. The thought pleased Eustace, and he tried to make the symbol more exact. Viewless, perceptible only by the energy, the winged whizz of its flight, desire started up through the formless darkness of being; its goal reached, it burst into flower—a flower of light that transfigured everything around it; having declared and made itself manifest, it dropped back released and fulfilled, and then at a moment that one could never foresee, it died, easily, gently, as unregretted as a match that a man blows out when it has shown him something more precious than itself (*EH* pp. 512–13).

It is possible to see this vision of the consuming of oneself in love as the heart of the book, and to trace it through quite consistently. In the book as in life, death, suffering, is a 'given', a constant; it is certainly a constant for Eustace, whose every attempt at accomplishment, independence, escape from Hilda seems doomed to failure. As he sits there, Eustace is marked out for death, but so is everyone sitting and watching with him; death is, after all, the one certainty in all human life and success. The shrimp and anemone principle is at the heart of life: a terrible law, fact, which must be faced. But perhaps suffering and death have two sides, can be met in two ways. Perhaps there can be meaning in life and death if they become a willing giving of self in love for others—and only if they do.

Perhaps this is the main thing Eustace has to learn during his life—to be this kind of hero rather than one in the style of the dashing Dick, who is associated throughout the novel with guns, hunting, war: killing rather than loving. (Note the opposition of war to love in the above quotation, but also the just *possible* equation of bloodshed and love; 'seeing things always in terms of bloodshed' and thinking of Heloise 'all the time'.) One can be the kind of hero (or shrimp) that dies giving life to something as beautiful as the anemone, or, as in the book's last terrible image, one can flee from the anemone, under the rocks, only to be eaten by the crabs—a much more terrible death.

Directly after Eustace's musing about the rocket, and love, comes the brilliant spectacle of the Church of the Redeemer flooded with golden light, and the firework of Christ crowned with thorns—another emblem of love consuming itself for

48

others. And then comes a passage which suggests a totally different, a *transformed* perception of reality:

> Silence had fallen on the spectators; in the light that was now as bright as day and with a much more startling power of visibility, he saw the backs of countless heads all motionless and all turned the same way, and in the stillness it seemed to Eustace that the sound of crackling was borne across the water. For one timeless instant the appearance on the church glowed with an increasing brightness that transformed not only the scene but the very sense of life; reversing the lighting system of the mind.
>
> Dazzled, Eustace closed his eyes, but a shadow pressed against his eyelids and they opened on darkness (*EH* p. 516).

Eustace alone, of Lady Nelly's party, takes part in the dawn ritual bath which follows and which concludes the feast; he finds himself, at first unwilling, drawn along by the huge crowd to plunge into the Adriatic as the sun rises. The entire description of the bath is filled with baptismal and death imagery, and we sense that a kind of education about death and rebirth is taking place in Eustace. It is one of the many images of death by water (and otherwise) that recur throughout the book—recalling particularly an earlier scene when Eustace, in the bathtub, hears of Miss Fothergill's funeral and begins to think that death, which he fears, might also mean peace and harmony and release. Here, immersed in the Adriatic with the anonymous masses, he experiences a certain sense of unity with humanity and a certain acceptance, again, of the universal fact of death. He goes back to Lady Nelly's *palazzo* seeing Venice (literally) in quite another light: everything in Venice looks darker to him, even off-colour (*EH* p. 526); the glow and sunlight have gone. He seems, too, to have found a more mixed and tolerant attitude towards people; he can be philosophical about the changeable moods of the family who bring him back across the Styx-like canal, can think that 'people are like that: Happy and pleasant one moment, cross and disagreeable the next' (*EH* p. 528). His 'death', in fact, seems to have brought about a definite change in him, which everyone notices.

Eustace does not yet understand what has happened to him (nor has it fully happened), but what we can guess here is the possibility, at least, of a transformed 'sense of life', a reversed

49

'lighting system of the mind', in which the entire given world of glorious Venice could be something of a mirror image of itself—in which the blackness and the water and all that has begun to stand for *death* in our minds might very well be on the side of life. Certainly what *has* happened here is that Eustace at least glimpsed a more sober, balanced, realistic side of Venice and of the charms of a life devoted to pleasure.

The encounter with 'death', as a matter of fact, seems to be the signal for things to start moving in a downward direction in what has been, up until now, a rather idyllic dream-world experience. This is where the beautiful and ageless Lady Nelly begins to lose interest (seemingly) in Eustace, where he has a humiliating experience with old friend and siren Nancy Steptoe, and where he hears from home that something is wrong with Hilda: the end of his independent life in Italy is in sight. This is also, however, the point at which Eustace hears that his younger sister Barbara is expecting a baby. Eustace's dying has begun, but so, Hartley suggests, has a new life.

Eustace and Hilda could be seen as a *Bildungsroman* in which the lesson Eustace has to learn just may be that 'he who loses his life shall find it'. Throughout his life Eustace is being prepared, step by step, for the most important moment of his life: that moment when he meets the unknown someone who, in his most frequently-recurring dream, waits for him in the rain somewhere under a sort of railway arch. He must not be late; this will be his 'moment of freedom', the moment which he later tells the paralysed Hilda she also may expect:

. . . at any moment, just when you're least thinking about it, you'll get better, just as the woman did in the Bible, just as the Sleeping Beauty did, when the prince waked her. And then all the past will seem as though it was just leading up to that, your moment of freedom (*EH* p. 712).

The mysterious, ambiguous Lady Nelly, Eustace's chief educator, who sometimes cherishes, sometime neglects him, seems to be an everyday embodiment of the goddess Fortune—often described as a 'queen' (*EH* p. 556), living in the *Palazzo Sfortunata*, buying clothes at Fortuny's, appearing to Eustace in one overpowering vision as 'Inside by the column under the arch, on a tall crimson chair with finials carved like a crown . . . her soft white hands folded in her lap, her figure all curves and comfort' her amethyst eyes shining mistily, her voice warm with welcome, (*EH* p. 633). All the women in Eustace's life, including Nancy and Miss Fothergill, are aspects of his education. Hilda—who sits characteristically, so that her legs form a V and her back a question mark (*EH* p. 26)—is also its goal. In one terrible vision, Eustace sees 'Venus with the face of Hilda clinging to her prey; and look, where she relaxed her grip, the victim's skin was wrinkled and old from the long pressure of her ageless flesh' (*EH* pp. 642–3). Hilda is Venus—Love—which he must come to accept and value; but Venus is a terrible force indeed. In the *Redentore* scene the love, death and unity or ecstasy symbols are linked. Hartley describes the setting minutely. The façade of the church, opposite them, is at the apex of the triangle, 'a slender black-and-white V', made by the bridge across the canal and a ribbon of moonlight. Crowds of people, 'slow-moving and tiny', are crowding across the bridge and disappearing into the shadow of the high door-way (*EH* p. 511).

An equation, though something of an impertinence to Hartley's subtle novel, may be of help here. It seems that in the concatenation of symbols in *Eustace and Hilda* as a whole:

Events and people of everyday life		Fortune (teaching, leading)		Love/ Death (Reality's two faces)		Unity, peace, immortality (God?)
	=		=		=	

Note that these elements can be seen in a time sequence, as an educative process, or as a kind of eternal present and identity. The way to the goal, in other words, is already the goal. One reading of the story of Eustace, I would suggest, is that it is the ever-repeated saga of man trying to flee from the acceptance of reality in which lies his only salvation—but being brought back to reality, almost inevitably, by its very inescapability (and, possibly, by the action of a kind of Providence—also equal to Reality). It can be seen that Hartley's picture of the workings of the universe strains towards what Northrop Frye identifies as the apocalyptic—'the imaginative conception of the whole of nature as the content of an infinite and eternal living body which, if not human, is closer to being human than to being inanimate'.[9] Strange and terrible though Hartley makes this universe, it is recognizable as our own absurd one—but also, essentially, as that of Judaeo-Christian tradition.

Perhaps it may be helpful at this stage to go back to the beginning and try to see the growing pattern of the novel in the light of this suggested core-meaning.

Just as *The Shrimp and the Anemone* functions as prologue for the psychological implications of Eustace's story, it functions also as part of the symbolic frame which gives that story its universality. There is something primordial in the setting in which the children play, on the beach at Anchorstone. There, on the sand, among the rocks, one has reality at its most basic: and Eustace-and-Hilda, struggling to tame the destructive sea with their walls of sand, tied together in their awkward three-legged unity (Eustace carrying his wooden spade, 'symbol of Adam's destiny' [*EH* p. 197], wearing his stained 'Indomitable' cap [*EH* p. 27]), are certainly man himself, admirable and pitiable, divided within himself and set against an enigmatic universe.

To return again to the mysterious Hilda, it is possible to see her under all the terms of the above equation. She is a person, a concrete reality in Eustace's life which must be met and dealt with; she is therefore a kind of personification of Reality (at least for him, the Love/Death principle at the heart of life with which he must come to terms). We note that she often sits on a rock— Gibraltar on p. 26—or is, during her paralysis, identified with Andromeda *chained* to a rock [*EH* p. 703]. It is also possible to see her as an aspect of Eustace: his sense of reality (his body, even, with its mortality, its finitude), or, at times, his conscience, his will, insisting that he conform to what *is*, or that he act, strive, make. This last meaning of Hilda is linked to the first in that it is Hilda the *person* who has been most responsible for creating Eustace's sense of reality and his moral sense.

Hilda, then, is all these things (and more) at once. Eustace, similarly, can represent the imaginatively inclined person that he is, who must learn to face his personal weaknesses and his dominating sister; he can be Imagination or Romance (or the Soul), exerting a strong pull against Hilda's earthy Reality; he can be Man, torn between his Eustace and Hilda sides and the need to integrate them.

Without the other each, seen as a person or a quality, is a monstrosity, just as either one, pulled too far to the other's side, is a monstrosity. The visions of perfect unity, balance and harmony which keep recurring in Eustace's life are the dreams of every man, torn and divided; here they are connected variously, through symbols, with union with Hilda (or Reality); with human effort and art (incarnating spirit, marrying body and soul); with self-giving; with death; with eternity. There is, for example, the childhood experience of building the pond with Hilda: 'They had imposed an order, they had left a mark; they had added a meaning to life. . . . The experience was ecstatic and timeless, it opened a window upon eternity, and while it lasted . . . they felt themselves to be immortal' (*EH* p. 165). (In the end-dream of the trilogy, at Eustace's death, the pond is built, and 'his sense of union with Hilda was absolute. . . . Inexhaustible, the confluent streams descended from the pools above; unbreakable, the thick retaining walls received their offering; unruffled, the rock-girt pond gave back the cloudless sky' [*EH* p. 735]). There is the West Window (under the arch) of St. Eustace's Church at Frontisham: 'he seemed to be experiencing the ecstasy—or was it the agony?—of petrifaction' (*EH* p. 152). There is even his painful but blissful hot mustard foot-bath shared with Hilda (*EH* p. 236).

The Shrimp and the Anemone contains prophecies or epitomes of what is to come in the main part of the book. Eustace tests his strength against the Try-your-grip machine (which is flanked, incidentally, by two others: 'on one side by a bold-faced gipsy offering to tell your fortune, and on the other by an apparatus for giving you an electric shock' [*EH* p. 163]), and can only push the indicator to point 10 on a dial which reaches to 130. Since we have just been told that it is ten o'clock, and since the machine states that the ringing of the bell indicates moderate strength, we may perhaps see the dial as the whole range of Eustace's life and education to come, being measured throughout by the watches and clocks he keeps looking at and the bells he keeps ringing (mostly to summon waiters or maids). The object is to educate his 'strength' to point 130, where he will be able to exercise his 'moment of freedom'. This may seem extraordinarily exaggerated analysis—but it seems to me that Hartley's book is just this playfully complex.

Another frame-image (completed in the last part of *Eustace and Hilda*) is that of the walk along the cliff-edge with its three Shelters and its watertower and the white-domed lighthouse at the end. The description of this landscape is given by degrees and must be pieced together, but it seems to point to and accompany stages in Eustace's life. It is after passing the First Shelter, and coming next to a 'storm-bent hedge' clinging to the cliff's edge (which later disappears), that he first speaks to Miss Fothergill, the frightening invalid who initiates him into a love for ease and leaves him the means to pursue it. After his return from Venice, it is at the Second Shelter, with its blue roof (*EH* p. 663), that he has an important moment of meditation on the beauty of ordinary reality, showing us that something of an integration has begun to take place in him. The Third Shelter, we are told on the next page, is red-capped and close to the edge of the dangerous sixty-foot drop of the red cliffs. After this there is a slight rise, and then the lighthouse, the pharos of Anchorstone. The lighthouse is not the same as it had been in their childhood: 'Gone was the white summit with the golden weather-cock, gone the circular glass chamber, shrouded with dense white curtains, within which gleamed the rainbow-coloured lantern' (*EH* p. 664). The lighthouse had become a Tea Room: 'The god had deserted his shrine and commerce had taken it over' (*EH* p. 665). The place which used to be a 'place of awe, fearsome to approach' (*EH* p. 664) now was surmounted by a sign of hands open in invitation. All this seems an indication of Eustace's growth (as well as a summation of contemporary social history). A false 'religion' with an unapproachable god has given way to something more concerned with reality and human beings. 'If the lighthouse had outgrown its usefulness,' Eustace thinks, not regretting the transformation, 'far better that it should be turned into a tea-shop, where many people might refresh themselves' (*EH* p. 665). But it is important to note that the red cliffs and the fall to the abyss come before the lighthouse.

Colour imagery is extremely important in the trilogy, as the above description would indicate. In *The Shrimp and the Anemone* Hilda is always associated with dark blue, and Eustace, when we first see him, has on a blue jersey which, under stress, is 'hanging about him in ungainly folds' (*EH* p. 22). One gets a direct clue to the meaning of some of the colours later, in *The Sixth Heaven*, when Anne arranges flowers and tries to make 'the men's blue and upstanding, the women's pink and fussy and drooping' (*EH* p. 340). Blue seems always to have some relation to one's closeness to a 'realistic' or active or *assertive* quality; Hilda's blues are quite dark (perhaps approaching black?); her father has light blue eyes. Red seems to stand variously for love, passion, sacrifice and pink (see above) for romance, perhaps sentimentality. (Anne says that 'They have different ways of doing flowers now, all in a heap with reds and pinks together, which clash to my eye.' She says her views are probably old-fashioned [*EH* p. 340]. Her expression is grey like her suit—that of 'a grey day . . . resigned to the unlikelihood of change' [*EH* p. 339]. The elder Staveleys have quite a bit of grey about them, though Sir John's eyes are bright blue, especially when he is making a penetrating remark.)

Miss Fothergill, who mitigates Hilda's influence, is associated with lion imagery and her living room looks like 'the skyline of some fabulous city' (*EH* p. 116); she sets Eustace on his way to Venice. And Dick first raises doubts in Eustace about 'those beastly rocks' (*EH* p. 103). When Eustace goes off to school, his cap will no longer be inscribed 'Indomitable', but will have on it a white horse reminiscent of the romantic Dick. In short, though the book begins with a picture of the human condition—man struggling against his barren, rock-strewn world—Eustace the child is not ready to face the meaning of the shrimp and the anemone, or the fact that the butcher's name (*EH* p. 58) is Love.

He has begun to be caught up in a more romantic, unreal vision of the world; his own version of love at this stage is sharing his new money with Hilda. It is, perhaps, 'blood-money' (*EH* p. 193), buying her off, purchasing his freedom. It is also his entrance into a world more and more removed from the excessively 'real' one where she has tried to confine him.

One of the main themes in *The Sixth Heaven* is that of perfect union and harmony—in an extended section on Bach's Concerto for Two Violins (compared to the Eustace/Hilda relationship), in a number of references to machinery (in which the pliant Eustace is compared to the oil that makes it go), and, above all, in the picture of Barbara's very happy marriage. There is continual suggestion, also, of oppositions and resolutions of forces, of a pendulum (*EH* p. 316) and poles (*EH* p. 317), even of the Parliamentary system of checks and balances (*EH* p. 332). Eustace's friend Stephen is notable for combining utility and decoration in his room (*EH* p. 245), and for urging Hilda to a natural, organic pace in her usually impetuous undertakings (*EH* p. 326). (Stephen is perhaps the closest thing to a norm in the trilogy: he has integrated his Eustace and Hilda sides and learned to live with them.)

The basic movement of the book, however, is to bring Eustace —and Hilda along with him—to Anchorstone Hall, that realm of grey, pink and green-gold (suggesting tradition, romance, and something of an ideal and hope—perhaps a false one). The brother and sister are separated, significantly, almost from the moment they arrive.

Hilda's flight in Dick's aeroplane is a 'sixth heaven' (notably not a real or ultimate one) of unity and fulfilment for Eustace, who hopes for a romance between the two. (As Cecil says, Eustace's spiritual problem would be solved: 'their union would be the union of the two conflicting strains of his nature, and Hilda would be off his hands' [*EH* pp. 7–8].) Bien uses this flight scene to indicate Eustace's vicarious sexual relationship, through Dick, with Hilda.[10] But it seems to me that Hartley is stressing the relationship between Hilda and Dick—and the fact that Eustace, while causing it, is unaware of its destructive possibilities. This interpretation would be borne out by Hartley's comments, as quoted by Bien, on Hilda's hands, bruised in her violent Billiard-Fives game with Dick: 'I think they meant to show Eustace's concern for Hilda, especially for her *physical* state; he half guessed, but tried to conceal his knowledge from himself, that she had been having an affair with Dick Staveley, and the hands are a kind of symbol of her physical violation.'[11] Eustace (or man in general) does not want to face the darker implications of life, love and 'romance'.

In the Venice section of *Eustace and Hilda* this closed-eyed over-innocence is the situation which prevails. It is important to see that *both* Hilda and Eustace are in the world of romance—she in the grey, green-gold and pink of Anchorstone Hall (and in the novel Eustace is writing); he (always carrying a small stone paperweight) among the grey, green-gold and pink room decorations and buildings of Venice. The settings and events are linked by numerous repetitions—the Serpentine in Venice and the Serpentine in Hyde Park (in Eustace's novel); the L-shaped salon in the Palazzo Sfortunata and the L-shape of Anchorstone Hall; the similar symbol for pounds and *lire*. If one notices carefully, one finds almost a parallel in what is happening to Eustace and what is happening to Hilda: their initial happiness and success, their 'death' and illness. The entire double-experience of Eustace and Hilda here can be seen both as the tension between reality and romance (body and soul?) in the one man, or as the painful education of two badly-balanced individuals.

The news of Hilda's serious illness finally brings Eustace to the edge of 'the abyss' into which he dares not look. The strange deserted garden into which his feet and the conniving streets of Venice lead him (*EH* pp. 612–13) is strewn with artefacts symbolic of his life-experience. It is a maze, overshadowed by a great arch and leading to a life-like statue—a combination of squalor and splendour which reminds Eustace of himself. (An interesting parallel: Ralph Freedman, in discussing the 'lyrical novel' as the progressive symbolic portrait of a 'self', gives as example a novel by Novalis in which 'The center . . . is a scene in which Heinrich views an image of himself.' The scene 'not only clarifies the work

57

in which it takes a prominent place but also elucidates the very concept of the lyrical novel').[12]

Back in his room, Eustace reads Stephen's letter laying bare Hilda's affair, and looks up, at last, 'from the bottom of the abyss' (*EH* p. 620). The shock has brought him back to words and thoughts and shapes 'like rocks, dark and slippery with seaweed, but with jagged edges, strewn on the floor of the abyss. His mind ventured near them and found they were not so strange as he thought. Indeed, to one part of his mind they were curiously familiar. Could he have seen them, one day, when he looked over the edge? Had he always known they were there, and ignored them' (*EH* p. 620)?

When Eustace goes back to Anchorstone, he is, then, going back to a newly-glimpsed reality. Surely in this return of the sobered Eustace to the house and sand and rocks of childhood there is a suggestion of the struggle to move from Innocence through Blake's world of Experience to that of Higher Innocence —where we can rediscover beauty and perfection in reality once we have faced and surmounted its ugly side. Hartley does not make the change in Eustace sudden and complete, nor unwavering —one of the greatnesses of this book is the gradualness, the subtlety of the character change. For a while Eustace tries to do away with his imagination entirely and to live a life of unadorned 'facts'. He and Hilda are again at Cambo, with Barbara and her husband, but now it is Hilda who is helpless and dependent and Eustace who is forced to be more assertive. He wavers between a masculine, independent self who wears a moustache and can speak sharply to Aunt Sarah, and the more romantic, visionary Eustace conjured back by letters from Venice. He also wavers between acceptance of Hilda's paralysis, entailing giving up Oxford and devoting his life to her, and a determination, on the other hand, to shock her into recovery. 'A shock, according to the doctor, might do it.'

Gradually, in Eustace, there seems to come a certain maturing balance between reality and imagination, between aspiration and the bitter present. This is perhaps most clear in the passage in which he examines a blade of grass on the cliff-path:

It was short and sapless and brown at the tip, and Eustace's imagination could take no pleasure in it. But remember, he admonished himself, its beauty is in its essential quality; it is not the totter-grass, or the sword-grass, least of all the Grass of Parnassus; it is ordinary common *grass*, but a Chinese painter might have given a lifetime to portraying it, and that without any idealisation, each patient stroke taking him nearer to the heart of grassness in the grass. And this demi-lune of bird's-foot trefoil . . . is not the strelitzia, the Queen Flower of Central Africa; it is not the Morning Glory convolvulus. . . . But Titian or Botticelli would not have disdained to give it a place of honour in their pictures. . . .

So Eustace mused, and meanwhile his steps were bringing him nearer to the red-capped Third Shelter and the cliff's edge (*EH* pp. 663–4).

Here also Eustace sees the transformed lighthouse, now a 'maroon' Tea House. In fact, Cambo itself, and Barbara's marriage, seem rather to be images of Eustace's new attitude and integration than (as Bien suggests) Hartley's indication that family life is the best compromise man can make with unhappiness.[13] At the end of *The Shrimp and the Anemone* there had been a suggestion that 'the white gate of Cambo' was the gate of Paradise (*EH* p. 198), the goal of man's struggle; but at the end of *The Sixth Heaven* Eustace had seen instead a vision of Lady Nelly's mansion, Whaplode, as Paradise, with 'portly rococo angels blowing trumpets' around its doorway (*EH* p. 432). This is the false Paradise in which he has been living; now he is back to one closer to ordinary earth.

The very pregnant Barbara, whose happiness is obviously the fruit of self-giving, is also a Venus-figure as she goes off to face suffering in order to bring forth new life, her pale face the apex of her huge body (*EH* p. 689). In short, Anchorstone, and all that Eustace does there upon his return, must be seen in terms of his coming closer to wholeness as a person—the only condition in which one can experience a 'moment of freedom' and sacrifice.

The important day arrives on which Eustace has determined to try to shock Hilda into recovery by pretending to let her wheel chair roll over the cliff's edge. First he takes a bicycle ride, meets Dick's sister Anne and visits Anchorstone—where he is told that Dick really loved Hilda but had always feared any attachment that threatened his independence. Eustace learns also that Dick, at the end, had offered Hilda money. He meets Dick's parents and is able to achieve with them a kind of sympathetic understanding and mutual compassion for human shortsightedness and unhappiness. Returning home, Eustace bicycles straight up a hill he had always been too weak or too afraid to attempt, and sees once more the beautiful West Window of Frontisham Church that is one of his symbols of eternity, unity and happiness.

Hilda is wearing the blue and silver Fortuny dress he has brought her, and during their evening walk Eustace forces himself to speak to her about Dick, to tell her that the experience has not been a totally bad one. He tells her what Anne has told him—that Dick actually loved her; that he had said she had made him a better man. Eustace himself has been changed, and Stephen also, he tells her. And he assures her that her illness is only temporary and that her 'moment of freedom' may come at any moment.

Eustace comes to the point at the edge of the steep red cliffs where he has planned to administer the life-giving shock. He turns the wheels of the chair towards the abyss and the chair begins to move—but he faints and falls. He only just manages, falling, to thrust his hand through the spokes of the wheel and stop the chair. Hilda, caught, hanging in space, sees Eustace lying 'as if his body had been tied to the wheel and shaken off' (*EH* p. 714). She comes to life, puts him in the chair, and brings him home.

The final chapter of the trilogy, also called 'Eustace and Hilda', shows us that the recovered Hilda is still very much the dominating sister. She starts to organize Eustace's time, insists on his planning to shave off the new moustache. Yet she has changed enough to laugh at a slightly ribald joke, something inconceivable in the Hilda of a few months before. When she goes upstairs, Eustace hears water running in the tub and decides she's having a ritual bath, a purification from the past, a preparation for a new future. He plans to tell her in the morning that he will keep his moustache.

While Eustace is sitting in front of the dying fire, the phone rings. Barbara has had her baby, which looks just like him and will be called Eustace.

In bed, Eustace dreams. He is taking an examination, along with everyone else who has appeared in the book; he is asked what he knows about the souls of the righteous. The scene is a funny one, with Nancy, Dick, even Nancy's divorced husband, all writing away, and Eustace unable to think of the answer. Finally he remembers and begins to write the text from Scripture which had so moved him at his first encounter with death—Miss Fothergill's funeral:

> 'But the souls of the righteous are in the hands of God, and there shall no torment touch them. In the sight of the unwise they seemed to die: and their departure is taken for misery, and their going from us to be utter destruction: but they are in peace. For though they be punished in the sight of men, yet is their hope full of immortality. And having been a little chastised, they shall be greatly rewarded: for God proved them, and found them worthy for Himself.' (*EH* p. 734).

Though everyone tells Eustace he has failed, he suddenly discovers he has passed. He has passed; he has brought new life to Hilda, symbolized by the fresh young Eustace to whom Barbara has just given birth. Or perhaps fresh young Eustace is the sign that for Eustace himself death has meant the beginning of a new life.

[c]

It seems to me that *Eustace and Hilda* best makes its mark, is most fully understood and of most lasting interest when seen as a romance in the Hawthornian vein, taking description and characterization that is often more realistic than Hawthorne's but transforming it into symbolic suggestion of the mysterious spiritual universe surrounding and enfolding its materiality. 'The skies of day and night, colors, densities, forms, may-be these are (as doubtless they are) only apparitions, and the real some-thing has yet to be known. . . .' Hartley has used Hawthorne's licence to the romancer to 'so manage his atmospherical medium as to bring out or mellow the lights and deepen and enrich the shadows of the picture',[14] and so we have characters like Hilda and Lady Nelly who are both real and obviously archetypal; we have constantly reappearing *leitmotifs*; we have a plot in which coincidence and repetition are basic elements.

At the same time we have incorporated into this romance genre all that both traditional and modern experimentation with the novel form has gleaned in terms of dramatization, naturalistic detail, point of view, psychological analysis, dream imagery, fantasy and stream of consciousness. A typical Hartley chapter in the third book of the trilogy, where his technique comes most fully into its own, might include, side by side, Eustace's bumbling adventures in Venice, 'the drawing room of Europe' (*EH* p. 435), his dialogues with Lady Nelly, with cynical aesthete Jasper Bentwich or the gondoliers Silvester and Erminio (who mangle the English language in a manner calculated to render it startlingly significant), his dramatized fantasies and daydreams, the letters he writes or thinks of writing, and scenes from the novel he is writing—which reflects at its highest peak his romanticizing of the Dick–Hilda relationship. We also have dramatizations of the parallel events going on in England through letters of varying point of view from Barbara, Stephen and Aunt Sarah (or from Dick's mother to Lady Nelly), and through the descriptions of Lord Morecambe, an English visitor.

These methods, mainly dramatic in form and consisting in great part of Hartley's witty and beautiful dialogue, keep the story moving along quickly, almost lightly, while at the same time conveying great complexity and density of both inner and outer experience, and the convergence of many points of view. Eustace is rendered lovable, pathetic, comic—as in the imaginary dialogue where he sees himself, as usual, missing a golden opportunity:

'Good morning, Shakespeare. Glad to see you. Kind of you to remember your promise to introduce me to the Mermaid. Let me see if there's anyone I know. Oh yes, there's Beaumont and Fletcher playing darts. I met them once. I adore "The Maid's Tragedy," don't you?'

'A lovely and moving piece of work.'

'And "Philaster" too! So sylvan and sunshiny—or did someone say that about "The Beggar's Bush"?'

'I'm not sure. The dear fellows excel themselves whenever they write.'

'I *wonder* what they are writing now?'

'They tell me it's called "A King and No King." Such a good title, I think. Wouldn't wonder if it turns out to be their masterpiece.'

'Didn't *you* once have a hand in one of Fletcher's plays?'

'Well, I did put a few lines into "Henry VIII" one morning when Fletcher had a hangover.'

'How wonderful for you. Beaumont is a gentleman, isn't he? I mean, he doesn't have to write for money?'

'Yes, lucky fellow, he writes for the pure love of the thing.'

'I wonder where he lives?'

'At Anchorstone Hall, in Norfolk.'

'What a divine house. Where do you live, I wonder?'

'At a place called Whaplode.'

'I'm afraid I haven't heard of that. But what a lot those two have done for poetry, haven't they? I adore their weak endings.'

'More than their strong ones?'

'Um—well, yes. Oh, look, isn't that John Webster? I met him once, too, but he didn't speak to me.'

'He's not very talkative. But what a good playwright. When I saw his "White Devil" I just threw down my pen.'

'I don't wonder. I'd give anything to have a word with him.'

'You shall. I'll introduce you—now, if you like.'

'*Thank* you—but first, isn't that Peele? We used to play together as children. What a joy his "Arraignment of Paris" is. Didn't he once write something rather rude about you?'

'No, that was Greene. Don't tell anyone, but they've both been dead for some years. You have missed an experience and so have they, if you see what I mean.'

'I'm not sure I do see. But what luck to have you with me! You're such a wonderful guide to the dramatic world.'

'Always glad to be of use [bowing]. Now that Webster's fortified himself with another tankard, shall I take you over to him?'

'Oh, do. It will be the most marvellous moment of my life' (*EH* pp. 475–6).

Hartley's version of romance, incorporating the most modern of novelistic techniques, builds on a foundation of realistic social and historical detail: asks its ultimate questions not in the abstract but in the context of our own age, its history, its bitter 'Experience'. Depicting 'the surface of life' as well as 'trying to interpret' it, Hartley gives a rich and faithful and perceptive picture of the early twentieth century and its changes in class structure and dominance, in religion, in styles of life and thought. His picture of the international set in Venice is an example of this kind of richness of detail, and Lord David Cecil says (with some exaggeration, one would think, remembering Evelyn Waugh) that *The Sixth Heaven* contains 'the only authentic likeness of fashionable undergraduate society in Oxford of the early nineteentwenties that has been written' (*EH* p. 11).

And there is, for example, the 'destroyer' theme that runs through the book. Dick, the romantic hero, is a destroyer—not only because of Hilda, but because of his penchant for hunting and for war. Anchorstone Castle grounds have been a drilling ground; the very streets of the town where Eustace grows up carry echoes of the Boer War.

Eustace also has his destroyer side, a tiny grain of explosive within, as one of his own fantasies recognizes: its going off means 'The rumble, the roar, the explosion, the tearing sound, the cities piled in ruins . . .' (*EH* p. 629). Like his mentor Hawthorne, Hartley is concerned with the dark mystery of the human heart. Unlike him, he is able to bring us to link that darkness specifically with the wars of our own century.

Eustace and Hilda, then, is a romance which gives us the story of a life, the story of an age, and the picture of a Plan—the vast, mysterious world-order within which man lives and dies. One can understand Eustace's 'salvation' on many levels, basically because this romance is a modern version of the universal 'monomyth'. The trilogy is unquestionably tragic—seemingly an acknowledgement that man, poor hybrid of clay and dreams, can only find unity and peace in death. But the final word, as in the monomyth, is not pointlessness, failure and destruction; rather, Hartley seems to be exploring the possibilities of heroism and selfrealization for neurotic, guilt-ridden modern man in a universe so terrible he can hardly bear to face it—a universe barren of God and devoid of clear landmarks or a coherent vision of life. One can read *Eustace and Hilda* as an expression of contemporary Christianity (Eustace associates himself several times with Christ carrying his cross, or crucified, before he really understands what it means; the legend of St. Eustace, moreover, is a popular one in England—that of a hunter converted to Christianity and martyrdom by his vision of a stag with a crucifix between its antlers). But Hartley also seeds the book with references to other versions of the myth of rebirth through death or sacrifice: in everyone from the Sleeping Beauty to Lady Godiva. The epigraph to Part II of *Eustace and Hilda* recalls Antony's love-death for Cleopatra: 'Come, then, for with a wound I must be cur'd' (*EH* p. 644).

In using the references to Christ and Scripture Hartley seems, too, to be stressing the sacred nature of *reality*—reality ranging from the most ordinary everyday experience to death itself. Hilda's quite ordinary bath, after her recovery, can be a ritual purifying from the past and a step into the future. Barbara's care of her invalid sister, her happy facing of childbirth, are her version of heroic death.

Eustace and Hilda is rich in implications. We concentrate mainly on Eustace's education and salvation; we see Lady Nelly, as Fortune, teaching him, for example, not to give money but love, himself. But the same process is going on for everyone in the book. Hilda's love and suffering bring Dick a little further along the road, so that he can for the first time be affectionate to his family (*EH* p. 698). Hilda, too, grows to be able to see her own suffering as life-giving for others. Her blue and silver dress seems to indicate a new blend of reality and imagination in her future, probably a marriage to Stephen.

In short, in this novel everyone is, to some extent, Venus or Reality for everyone else—an occasion of love, of sacrifice, of personal integration, and of new life. And it is important to see that Nelly, or Fortune, explicitly identifies herself with Hilda (*EH* p. 607); the terrible and beautiful forces which rule life are ultimately one. It is the beautiful, warm and loving Lady Nelly whom Eustace sees under the arch; the beautiful Hilda, the beautiful anemone to whom he surrenders.

Themes as well as form recall Hawthorne in *Eustace and Hilda*: the dialectical romance form, whenever it is used, tends to take up the same questions, the same eternal dichotomies which have always tormented man. In his essay on Hawthorne Hartley speaks of 'the characteristic duality of attitude in Hawthorne, which would neither accept nor reject' (*NR* p. 66); of 'the fundamental dichotomy in his nature—of if not in his nature, in the nature of his thought' (*NR* p. 95); of 'his characteristic gift of saying two opposite things at the same time' (*NR* p. 101). 'Truth to him,' Hartley says, 'was always two-faced, if not double-faced'; he had a 'double—or treble—vision.' He 'could not commit himself' (*NR* p. 101). 'So many constructions can be put on his stories that every reader will probably find a different one' (*NR* p. 105).

The very title and central symbols of *Eustace and Hilda*, once we begin to penetrate them, seem to indicate that Hartley himself saw this sense of duality in man, in the universe, as a problem needing to be probed for our time. In its own way, that is what the novel is about: polarity, division, dichotomy—and harmony.

Man himself is divided, between body and soul, imagination and reality, aspiration and acceptance. David Cecil speaks of one of the themes of *Eustace and Hilda* as 'the contrast between man's immortal longings and his mortal weakness' (*EH* p. 13). And everything in man's world has a twofold quality—love, death, suffering, sin, individualism, community. Each of these can be seen as evil, or as good—and are so seen at various moments and in various contexts, by various people and by us.

Hartley sees Hawthorne's basic dualism as a conflict between his Rousseauism (of the intellect) and his Calvinism (of the emotions). Hawthorne believed (alternately? at the same time?) both that man was good and capable of perfection and that the human heart was innately depraved and flawed. Human endeavour was important, and could lead to Utopia, the good society, an earthly paradise—or human endeavour was doomed to failure, and man to suffering and sin. (Only God, grace, another world could remedy this one.)

These are, after all, two of the most basic attitudes men have held about the meaning of human life—constant in all ages, and struggling with each other for dominance again in our own time. Hartley brings them before us again in *Eustace and Hilda*. Should we co-operate with nature, especially human nature: go along with it, count on its goodness, allow it to flower, and expect the Golden Age (e.g., as portrayed in Eustace's Venetian-

66

made romantic novel and brought about therein by the desired union between Hilda and the fictional Lord Anchorstone)? Or does nature inevitably go back on us, break down, cause chaos and suffering (like the *actual* relationship between Hilda and Dick)? Does it need to be controlled, feared, tamed, worked against, in the Puritan tradition, in which one is 'good' in so far as he is overcoming his inclinations? Hedonism/Puritanism; Pelagianism/Manichaeanism; activism/passivity; humanism/asceticism—most of Hartley's principal characters go through life encountering variant specimens of these classic positions, and trying them out as solutions for life's problems (solutions which, one after another, seem to fail). Here Hartley seems to suggest that because of the dualism, the true dualism in reality, one must not polarize, abstract, absolutize—must not create false dualities, nor see clear-cut dilemmas and choose clear-cut sides.

Hilda is too rigid, too Puritanical, too passionate, too insistent on imposing her will on reality. Eustace is too hedonistic, too passive, too *laissez-faire*. Only in some kind of combination or balance could they portray an adequate response to life—and such balance seems to be impossible for them. There is something in Hartley's *schema* which suggests he might have in mind Kierkegaard's classic divisions between the aesthetic, the ethical and the religious views of life,[15] in which the whole man, reborn in faith, who sees life from a central religious position, is the one who can also contain within himself the aesthetic and ethical elements which make up the complete personality.

No such whole Christian personality appears in *Eustace and Hilda*—at least, not in any explicit sense. But there are people who love, like Lady Nelly; and she, it will be noted, is exempt from the final judgement all the others have to undergo (*EH* p. 733). Love, for Hartley, seems to be the key, the thing that matters, that resolves the sharp polarities; love, in an inexplicable universe, is all that is left to us. In *The Sixth Heaven* Jimmy proposes a puzzle. The solution, spelled out with matches, is L, O, V, E. These same letters recur throughout the trilogy, in the L-shaped rooms, the great O of a street sign and of Fortune's ball (*EH* pp. 490, 527), the V of Hilda and the *Redentore*, the E of

Eustace's own initial. Each individual must find and put them together in his own way to understand the great puzzle of life. As Barbara leaves for the hospital on the final day of death and birth, her last words to Eustace are 'Love to Hilda! Love—' (*EH* p. 689).

This is, in the last analysis, a dark universe, and Hartley, like Hawthorne, probably leans away from 'the cheerful humanistic view of Emerson and his fellow-Transcendentalists' (*NR* p. 128) and ends finally with those who see suffering—death—Evil?—somehow related to sin and guilt—as the most constant presences in the world-picture. Hartley's basic story is invariably that of Innocence faced with bitter Experience, and he seems to suggest that this is the basic story of man's life, as well as the story of man himself in history: man who has had to face, in the wars and horrors of this century, the evidence of the inexplicable evil that can come out of his own nature.

Eustace, for all his sunniness and charm, must be brought to face 'the bottom of the abyss'. And frustration and death seem, in the end, the only solution for his personal agony. Hartley, like Hawthorne, like the modern existentialist, seems to be saying NO in thunder. He sees Hawthorne's theme as '*The Fall of Man*, told with many variations . . .' (*NR* p. 122), and this too is Hartley's own theme, embodied in personal life-stories, revealed at the heart of social history.

But, Hartley continues, Hawthorne's theme of the Fall is also dual; he is led, in *The Marble Faun*, 'to the unorthodox conclusion that sin is as inevitable as sorrow, and must be accepted as part of the training of the soul on its way to a higher development: it has a regenerative power' (*NR* p. 122). This *felix culpa* note sounds and resounds also throughout Hartley's work. As Lady Nelly says to Eustace about Hilda's unhappy love affair, '. . . such an experience has its value . . . it breaks the crust . . . and lets the song pour out' (*EH* p. 605). And Eustace himself needs to face the abyss in order to grow up, to attain the balance of reality and imagination, the capacity for sensitive love that he demonstrates in the final pages of the trilogy. In Hartley's universe all things, even sin, seem to work together unto good. It could be—indeed seems to be—a basically Christian universe ruled by an all-powerful, all-loving Providence. But it is also an absurd, a tragic, an inexplicable universe: one which would not be unrecognizable to today's most pessimistic existentialists. Naïve Christians who count on Providence to straighten things out at no great cost will be brought up very short.

Hartley says NO, then—perhaps even the 'final no' of Wallace Stevens. But after the final no there does seem to come a yes. Vernier speaks of the beauty of life as seen in *Eustace and Hilda*, despite the genuine tragedy. Hartley does seem able to suggest a kind of Higher Innocence, a radiance coming from life and tragedy accepted and love undertaken, a transformation of suffering and sin and death into life on a higher plane—perhaps even an actual new life to be begun after suffering and death have done their work of preparation. One cannot say certainly that this is what Hartley is proposing, any more than he can say it of Hawthorne. He quotes a letter of Hawthorne's to his wife: 'I first look at matters in their darkest aspect, and having satisfied myself with that, I begin gradually to be consoled, to take into account the advantages of the case, and thus trudge on, with the light brightening around me.' But, Hartley adds, 'as one critic has remarked, the light never grows very bright' (*NR* p. 113). In *Eustace and Hilda* the light, the beauty, the radiance *is* bright, and one cannot help but feel that, in the last analysis, Hartley loves the human tragicomedy. Perhaps the happiness he accords Eustace is the happiness of Sisyphus, to whom he compares him (*EH* p. 721). 'The struggle itself toward the heights is enough to fill a man's heart', Camus wrote. 'One must imagine Sisyphus happy.'[16]

Searching for criteria to judge the true artist of the present moment, Wright Morris writes that 'If the modern temper, as distinct from the romantic, lies in the admission that men are mortal, this admission determines the nature of the raw material with which the artist must work.' He continues, 'An element of despair, a destructive element, is one of the signs by which we shall know him—the other is the constructive use to which this element is put.'[17] It would be difficult to find a better summary of the uniqueness of *Eustace and Hilda*. Hartley, through his use of the great integrating and healing form of the romance, grown to twentieth-century stature and sophistication, has been enabled to go far beyond the surface of things and to touch the special 'squalor and splendour' of being a man in our time. His story is truly terrible and beautiful: to the same pathetic non-hero whom we now recognize as the image of twentieth-century man he has brought a comprehension, a compassion, a respect for the weakest man's uniqueness and heroism that is genuinely illuminating and worthy of our gratitude. One of the things which Hartley seems to illuminate (perhaps even to resurrect) is the religious question, and *Eustace and Hilda* can certainly be seen as presenting a kind of sketch for a new understanding of a non-abstract, non-institutional, existential Christianity. (There is an implicit critique of the traditional variety in Jasper Bentwich's testy complaint (*EH* p. 627) that Christianity 'makes people so intolerant of their friends'.)

'A violent order is disorder', says Stevens. We 'cannot go back' to the 'law of inherent opposites, / Of essential unity . . . as pleasant as port,' for 'The squirming facts exceed the squamous mind.'[18] But Hartley's assertion of unity and meaning in complexity does not come as a violent order—he is too honest, too willing to face, and adhere to, and insist on, the 'great disorder.' His opening towards a reconciliation seems, rather, like the 'small relation' that appears after honesty and purification: 'A small relation expanding like the shade / Of a cloud on sand, a shape on the side of a hill.'[19] The yes after the final no, 'the yes of the realist spoken because he must / Say yes, spoken because under every no / Lay a passion for yes that had never been broken.'[20]

This kind of yes, which really counts the costs, which defines love—but an utterly unsentimental love—as the only possible heroism for modern man, seems supremely valuable. If one could quarrel with Hartley here, it might be over what at times seems his almost total discounting of the value of human action. There are ways in which *Eustace and Hilda* would seem to be saying that no humanism—even Christian humanism—is possible, and that man's only hope is in a completely transcendental order. But the universe itself seems to say that to us sometimes, after all. And even *Eustace and Hilda* cannot say everything at once.

70

CHAPTER FOUR

THE TRUTH ABOUT UTOPIA:
THE BOAT

Through Jonathan Swift's dark grove he passed, and there
Plucked bitter wisdom that enriched his blood.
—William Butler Yeats[1]

[a]

M o s t of L. P. Hartley's work can be classified under the general
category of 'romance' if one accepts Hawthorne's broad definition
of that genre as concentrating on the interpretation of scenes and
events through symbolic extension rather than on their realistic
reproduction. But Northrop Frye's more finely-pointed division
of fictional genres may allow us an even more intimate appreciation of some of Hartley's darker stories, in that Frye puts before
us a form called 'Menippean satire' or 'anatomy' which combines
fantasy and morality into what is in many ways a mirror image
of romance, dissecting intellectual attitudes, dealing in caricatures
rather than in heroes. Frye sees satire both as an attitude, an
approach, and as a form of plot structure; what he says about
each[2] illuminates our comprehension of that unusual book *The
Boat* (1949)[3] as well as of many other Hartley postwar productions.

It is important to note that all Hartley's novels (with the
exception of *Simonetta Perkins*) are postwar productions, written
by a man already in his forties when World War II began. All
those novels are haunted by that war, as Hartley's consciousness
and world-view seem to be; yet *The Boat* marks his most direct
attempt to grapple with the war in itself. Even here he deals not

in battlefields and victories but in the crises of a diffident middle-aged writer who tries to live out the war years in the comparative peace of the little village of Upton. But in the tragicomic story of Timothy Casson Hartley is exploring as schematically (and as pessimistically) as he can the present state of Western civilization.

Peter Bien is surely right in linking this novel directly with Hartley's own life and war experience.[4] One can, in fact, see most of Hartley's novels as a very personal continuing dialogue with himself, at various ages and in various circumstances, about the meaning of life. He gives us some right to do this by contending in 'The Novelist's Responsibility' (*NR* p. 2) that the author's created world 'must, in some degree, be an extension of his own life . . . ,' and, in 'Nathaniel Hawthorne' (*NR* p. 62) that 'It is, of course, unsafe to assume that a novelist's work is autobiographical in any direct sense; but it is plausible to assume that his work is a transcription, an anagram of his own experience, reflecting its shape and tone and tempo, and its main preoccupations.' Yet in Timothy Casson Hartley is giving us not just L. P. Hartley, or the Artist in Wartime, but another Everyman—the type of English middle-class, middle-aged liberal humanist whose day, this war and its side-effects seem to proclaim, is now over. Hartley takes over five hundred pages to tell the pathetic story of Timothy's obsession with his boat, an obsession which cuts him off from the local gentry and eventually from all human communication, which involves him in a Communist plot and divides the village into hostile factions; which, in the end, costs two lives. But the five hundred pages serve also to anatomize the world of the 1940s and its backgrounds, to set forth almost all the possible human attitudes towards experience as revealed in the glaring light of war, and to leave us with what seem to be Hartley's gloomy questions about the future of England and humanity. If, as Mrs. Purbright believes, 'we've sold our capital of happiness, our reserves are gone', can we 'build them afresh' (*B* p. 134) as she feels we must? No one seems to be doing so at the end of the book, and Mrs. Purbright is dead. Perhaps Timothy has at least learned that liberal humanism is not enough—but Hartley leaves us still in the midst of war, with the outcome, and future, precarious.

Hartley's method, in *The Boat* as elsewhere, is to deal with the tension between the 'real' and ideal worlds by having myth-making, fantasizing minds within his story expand the meaning of objects and events through investing them with symbolic significance. The mind which, above all, works at this in *The Boat* is Timothy Casson's. His friend Tyro accuses him of this tendency at the end of the book, and sees it as the fault which has caused all his troubles:

> ... He likes things to be raised to a higher power—some instinct of worship, I imagine—just as he likes people to be types of themselves. Miss Cross and Mrs. Purbright were; and no doubt we are, too, in his eyes (*B* p. 507).

We see Timothy practising his fatal flaw, rather ludicrously, in his purple prose writings about British ruins—turning each into a glowing symbol of what the war is all about, turning the down-to-earth servants Beatrice and Effie into those 'intelligent and decorative nymphs' Damaris and Chloe who accompany him on searches for 'Pictures of Britain'. We see him constantly at his mythologizing in his musings about people and life in Upton, in his continual attempts to mould all his increasingly unpleasant experiences into a pattern, in the dreams in which he idealizes the Italian past, or sees the present as torture in a concentration camp (*B* p. 377). Above all we see it in his attitude to the boat (which he obligingly transposes, for author Hartley, into the emblematic, expanding symbol at the heart of the book). From the beginning the boat represents a kind of liberation for Timothy, 'the sum of psycho-physical sensations that ... [he] would capture with the first free stroke of his free sculls on the free water: the release, the renewal' (*B* p. 30). The boat has definite religious associations for Timothy from the first, and gradually he tends to worship it as a god or goddess (*B* pp. 23, 30, 103), though an increasingly tainted one (*B* pp. 104, 373, 375). But tainted or not, the boat becomes Timothy's outlet for 'the pure spirit of striving' that expresses the 'needs of the soul' as such minor, over-specified goals as 'the quest of the Holy Grail, the search for the Philosopher's Stone or the North West Passage' do not (*B* pp. 287–8).

Here we are dealing with the modern non-hero who wants very much to be a hero—who wants something to worship, to die for, to strive for; who, not finding it in Upton or in modern England, creates it. The humanist, the man for whom beauty is the highest good, for whom the world of the spirit supposedly does not exist, seems to be Hartley's target (though compassionately aimed at) in Timothy; such a man must romanticize, must create a false spiritual world, must let his 'instinct for worship' betray him into nonsensical rites, unreal visions, the defence of false causes. Such romantic liberalism causes war and death in Upton just as it has caused the war and death in the world surrounding Upton. Timothy is a kind of timid Raskolnikov longing for a cause, for martyrdom, for self-fulfilment, self-spending, in a great cause. Like Raskolnikov, he does a great deal of mischief, and for the same reason—because his humanist world is flat, anti-heroic, empty of God, of evil and of greatness.

To show all this Hartley combined his favourite modern romance genre with something like Frye's satire (and perhaps points to his intentions by his several references to Swift, early in the book [*B* pp. 24, 41]). Frye sees the structure of satire, or ironic myth, as a parody of romance;[5] he believes that in terms of attitude or approach,

> The Menippean satire deals less with people as such than with mental attitudes. Pedants, bigots, cranks, parvenus, virtuosi, enthusiasts, rapacious and incompetent professional men of all kinds, are handled in terms of their occupational approach to life as distinct from their social behavior. The Menippean satire thus resembles the confession in its ability to handle abstract ideas and theories, and differs from the novel in its characterization, which is stylized rather than naturalistic, and presents people as mouthpieces of the ideas they represent.
> . . . Petronius, Apuleius, Rabelais, Swift, and Voltaire all use a loose-jointed narrative form often confused with the romance. It differs from the romance, however (though there is a strong admixture of romance in Rabelais), as it is not primarily concerned with the exploits of heroes, but relies on the free play of intellectual fancy and the kind of humorous observation that produces caricature.[6]

Satire, then, tends like romance to have somewhat stylized characters—here representing ideas rather than psychological archetypes. The 'anatomy', as Frye also terms this genre, likes to dissect a society intellectually.[7] Often recurring in the *mythos* of satire are such themes as the disappearance of the heroic, the killing of the monster (representing society, convention), the destruction of simplifications, superstitions and false philosophies in the face of the more complex experience of life itself. Often the norm figure, the reverse-hero who is used to show up the grand-scale follies of society, is what Frye calls 'the Omphale archetype, the man bullied or dominated by women, which has been prominent in satire all through its history. . . .'[8] *The Boat* is both romance and mock-romance, in these terms. Somewhat like Hawthorne's 'The Threefold Destiny', dealt with above, in Chapter One, *The Boat* is about a man's symbolic vision of the world. It criticizes and demolishes whatever is over-romantic, obsessive and destructive in that vision—but at the same time it suggests that the world, objects and events are (or at least might be) alive with spiritual meaning. Timothy is perhaps not so totally wrong as he seems to be; his problem, like ours, like the modern world's, is looking for the right thing in the wrong place.

The plot of *The Boat* establishes a 'theatre', as Hawthorne would put it, in the little village of Upton (a mock-Utopia?) where forty-nine-year-old writer Timothy Casson has come, in 1940, with a five-year lease on the 'Old Rectory' (whose name would seem to signify the vestiges of Christianity which are his). Timothy is the sort of 'go-between' character in which Hawthorne and James specialized—an observer-writer type around whose comparatively innocent head huge controversies can rage and enormous polarizations can take place through the agency of characters more strongly committed than himself.

Forced by the war to leave his beloved Italy's culture and beauty, Timothy is trying to find a way of carrying on, despite the war, with the 'life of aesthetic appreciation' to which his guardian had introduced him (*B* pp. 128–9). In Upton-on-Swirrel he will write journal articles about monuments of British culture and

75

keep 'the banner of friendship flying' in a time when, unfortunately, 'The clear call of one personality to another was muffled by a drum-beat' (*B* p. 58). His one small request of life is that he be allowed peacefully to row his boat (called the *Argo*, as testimony to his heroic longings) on the Swirrel River. Unfortunately, however, this seemingly unquestionable right does seem to be in question—mainly because it might disturb the long-established fishing rights of the local gentry. The boat therefore becomes for Timothy a symbol of his own personal freedom and fulfilment which must be upheld and asserted at all cost. After all, 'the right and duty of each human being to treat another as an end in himself, not as a flag or a coloured shirt or a sinner, these were what we were fighting for' (*B* p. 58). Little by little the boat—and his own rights, his sense of being in the right—become the focus of all Timothy's thoughts and actions: estranging him from the old guard of the village and from all his friends; making him an easy prey to the blonde *femme fatale* Vera Cross and her Communist conspiracy to set Upton's upper and lower classes at each other's throats; turning Timothy gradually into a 'pocket Führer' (*B* p. 400) engaged in his own private war.

Hartley uses the boat as the central symbol, in close connection with the go-between character Timothy, of an intricate plot that could and does suggest many meanings. The boat, as Bien points out,[9] shifts constantly in its associations and reverberations, according to the way Timothy himself changes and according to his current version of the way the world works. But always the boat is intimately connected with Timothy himself and the selfhood and liberation he desires and sees as ultimate good.

Centre of the plot, then, is the slightly pathetic humanist clinging to his boat as he clings to his implicit worship of selfhood, of the human person. Around this centre Hartley ranges his type characters, his 'Pedants, bigots, cranks, parvenus . . .'. There is Esther, who stands for convention and tradition and country life and England as 'every country's other self', the 'sanity and spiritual health of the world' (*B* p. 56). Timothy helps us place her by the thermos flask he sends her for Christmas (*B* p. 16), just as he characterizes Magda's 'aesthetic . . . view of life' (*B*

p. 18) by a gift of perfume, and Tyro's strong moral sense by a copy of Swift's 'Conduct of the Allies' (*B* p. 24). Magda, incidentally, works at the Ministry of Appearances, and Tyro at the Censor's Office in Liverpool: details which show us that their type-hood is not only in Timothy's mind. A stream of letters back and forth between Timothy and these three widely-different correspondents helps to give us their three representative views on life as well as boats and self-assertion, and particularly on the war, its causes, and the issues at stake.

Upton itself is a microcosm wherein Hartley embodies almost every question of modern history in architecture, social events, gossip, family relationships, even the books left out on the hillside to be picked up in a salvage drive (All those Victorian favourites, 'elderly, unfashionable children of the humane century . . .' [*B* p. 269]). Hartley is able to sum up in a fleeting thought, a single word of Timothy's (relating to his missing evacuee guests) the decade which was the prelude to world war: 'Kidnapped! The word had horrible associations. It had gone screaming through the nineteen-thirties, warning mankind that the age of clemency was over' (*B* p. 164). With much the same talent for finding precisely the right symbol, he populates Upton and its environs with a number of very alive people who nevertheless serve as types and representatives of a culture in process of change: Beatrice and Effie, the servants who cow their bachelor employer; Wimbush, the very Hawthornian man of the soil, of Nature, with his perpetually earthy hands and his equally earthy personality; the local gentry in their clipped grey moustaches, their Roman-nosed, steady-eyed ladies in grey, rust-brown and purple (*B* p. 81), in contrast to the newly-come villagers in their 'flashy, not to say fast' clothes, their '. . . well, irregular' relationships (*B* p. 37); even lovely young Désirée Lampard, saying thoughtfully for the next generation that 'Sometimes I think one ought to be' a Socialist (*B* p. 158).

The boat, however, and the question of whether Timothy will be allowed to use it, holds the centre of the stage as it does of Timothy's mind. And soon there appear, one on either side of Timothy and his boat, a bad and a good angel—one urging him to self- (and boat-) assertion, one to self- (and boat-) giving: Vera Cross and Volumnia Purbright.

Volumnia Purbright, the wife of Upton's rather choleric Rector, is a Christian—a real, a modern, one might say an existential Christian. Loving, sympathetic, understanding, she seems to live up to her first name by seeing good and God in all. Hartley paints her carefully, though very comically—she stands in this novel for the clear call to a renewal of Christianity: of the Christian faith and love and self-giving which, Hartley seems to say (not too hopefully) are the only things that might save us.

Mrs. Purbright functions in *The Boat* as a kind of comic Cassandra (*B* p. 219), a 'prophetess' (*B* p. 224) who, like Timothy, has visions, sees more than the bare surface of things ('An inner glow, he knew, absorbed her vision; of the outer world she saw only what she chose to see' [*B* p. 215]). She lives, appropriately, at the New Rectory, but her religion contrasts completely with that of her husband, the Rector, who first appears to Timothy as a 'policeman' (*B* p. 33), quibbling about the legality of transferring petrol from one car to another; who is a 'tall ascetic-looking man' with what seems a 'permanent shadow' on his face (*B* p. 33); whose mind, in contrast to his wife's fluidity, is 'as plain sailing as a channel marked out by buoys' ([*B* p. 144]: note the boat and water imagery which appear at every level of this book). The conventional Rector sees the fact that his parishioners laugh uproariously at a rather profane joke as evidence 'that my twenty-five years' ministry in this parish has borne so little, and such bitter fruit' (*B* p. 193); in a crisis, he makes the 'practical' rather than the 'emotional' decision: to do nothing—since acting 'might even earn me a rebuke from my Bishop' (*B* p. 412). His wife's Christianity is not conventional; it is also not the aesthetic and sentimental remnant to which Timothy clings, and she is not at all elated when he tells her:

'I like the feeling of being in church . . . the bowed heads, the subdued movements, the ritual, that varies so little and so much. And the sense of worship round me is comforting to me, even if I don't share it. . . .' (*B* p. 131).

Mrs. Purbright is a rather zany version of Eustace's Lady Nelly. When we and Timothy first meet her,

> Very tall, she had draped herself across a chair and a footstool so casually that she almost seemed to be putting her feet up; she was smoking a cigarette through a long black cigarette-holder tipped with silver, with which from time to time she made a wide gesticulation (*B* p. 73).

Her outstanding characteristic seems to be an 'air of vague and comprehensive benevolence' (*B* p. 73); her eccentric appearance and sudden appearances, the apparent randomness and rambling-ness and inconclusiveness of her remarks add to the sense of vagueness. Where Lady Nelly is all curves and softness and pale diaphanous garments, she is all drape and fluidity: she approaches 'Plunging and dipping . . . like a pinnace' (*B* p. 215). Yet as with Lady Nelly, we realize by the end of the book that there is a single impulse behind everything Mrs. Purbright does.

Mrs. Purbright's sense of the universe and the interrelation-ships of people and things is as of something completely organic —one, yet made up of the harmony of many different things, and always fluid and changing. To such a universe one must respond with the kind of fluidity she herself exhibits. She meets Timothy, after a month's separation, quite aware of the fact that he is by now a changed person (to stress this, she points out, with one of her frequent organic images, how much the garden has changed in a month. It 'was full of roses when I went away. Where are they now? And these nettles. . . . The year has grown much older since I went away' (*B* p. 216]). She urges him not to be too fixed on his boat by picturing for him the effect his obsession will have on the relationships within the whole community, as well as within his own being (*B* pp. 219–20). She is convinced of the effect of one person upon another, upon the fabric of life—worries that she is Timothy's 'evil genius' (*B* p. 142), shows him what power, for good or evil, is his (*B* p. 221), tells him, even, that part of his guardian's happiness in heaven may depend on his con-tinuing sense of relationship with him after death (*B* p. 130). She stresses unity and co-operation above all, always—but it is a unity as great and complex as the world in which people are 'much less

79

interesting if the corners are rubbed off' (*B* p. 87); in which 'There are many kinds of beauty' (*B* p. 88); in which she urges Timothy to 'Be yourself . . . people will appreciate you far more for what you are than for what you want them to think you' (*B* p. 218).

The world and everything in it is dual, complex, for Mrs. Purbright. 'Life is so complex,' she says to her husband. 'Think of all the strands of beauty in it. Does one want to tear them out, even if one could?' And 'I wish you could feel, as I do, that beauty and goodness can no more be separated from other qualities than the flame can be separated from the coal it springs from' (*B* p. 405). It is the same lesson that her life and death just may finally teach Timothy, if one is to judge from the dream in which she calls him on the telephone and says that the 'evil' Vera, who died with her, won't go away—because 'we're both together in your mind'. Vera's voice affirms it: 'we look so nice twined together, you couldn't tell where I end or she begins.' Timothy wants to know 'But shan't I ever see her alone again?' and Vera answers, 'No darling. . . . Your girl-friends are inseparable. I know you'll hate it, darling, but you can't have her without me' (*B* p. 502).

It is the lesson Mrs. Purbright has always very indirectly, very delicately, tried to teach him: not to abstract, to polarize, to seize on any conviction or any object or desire as an absolute. Early, she fears his growing obsession with the boat and wishes he could use it 'before you come to want it too much' (*B* p. 136). Later, she warns of 'the over-development of the will at the expense of the other faculties', and the way that 'dwelling too much on one thought' can stop up 'the avenues of experience' (*B* p. 220). After his series of fixations upon first Vera, then Felix, then the beautiful vase which is broken, she gives him another beautiful vase, but urges that it be 'a handmaid, not a magnet to your thoughts'. Here, as so often, Hartley uses a work of art to sum up a world-view; the vase seems to be an image of the universe as Mrs. Purbright wants Timothy to see it:

> Timothy rested his eyes on the lustreless, grey-green enamel of the vase, upon which, each enclosed in a margin of dull gold, floated flower-forms of every shade between pink and mauve and brown, with butter-

flies to match; and as he looked it did seem as though the whole mass was in motion, turning slowly round, like a revolving globe; and the petals, so firmly embedded, did seem to have a certain liberty of movement in relation to each other, and to widen or decrease the gap between them. So indeterminate and recessive were its lines that, for all its bulk, the vase seemed to have been conjured out of air—a materialisation of garden tints at twilight (*B* p. 339).

Mrs. Purbright warns Timothy of 'the dangers of purpose-fulness' (*B* p. 138) and is emphatically sure that 'one would not wish to feel altogether in the right' (*B* p. 219); even her husband is quite aware that 'My wife's Christianity is of a more elastic type than (I am afraid) mine is, she sees evidences of spiritual-mindedness where I cannot' (*B* p. 193).

The firm core to Mrs. Purbright's fluidity is her love: a genuinely 'comprehensive benevolence' indeed seems to be the sole constant in her life and value-system. No matter how Timothy flouts or hurts her, 'the elusive current of her sympathy, a sort of Gulf Stream lapping against the shores of his mind' (*B* p. 75) is always there, reaching out to understand and excuse the motives for his outrageous conduct. Startlingly, for the wife of a village Rector, she is 'hospitable to all ideas', arranging each new one 'in a position where it harmonized with the rest' (*B* p. 87)—her 'catholicity of taste', her ability to value each person, each thing in and for itself, is symbolized by her art collection (and linked with world problems and world peace):

> ... Timothy ... saw all round him, clustered on tables, piled on cabi-nets, balanced precariously on brackets, glimmering from behind glass, the most heterogeneous agglomeration of objects that he had ever beheld in any human habitation. Hanging from the ceiling, clinging to the walls, springing up in thickets from the floor, were spoils from the four corners of the world. Of all styles, shapes, sizes, colours and substances; of ebony, ivory, mother-of-pearl, silver, lacquer, china, tortoiseshell and lapis-lazuli, they solicited but did not clamour for attention. A League of Nations! But how much more decorative, how much more effectively creating unity out of diversity, than parallel assembles at Geneva and the Hague! ... Here, they each contributed their own quota of beauty to a collective beauty that was not their own (*B* pp. 71–2).

Mrs. Purbright is not even slightly shocked at Timothy's

improper laughter at the improper joke (*B* p. 217). To him, suffering over the ridiculousness of his affair with Vera and feeling like 'the elderly hero of a French farce' (*B* p. 259), she is able (indirectly, of course, by talking about someone else—she always talks in analogies and parables, like Hartley himself) to say that 'It may sound unconventional in a clergyman's wife, but I should not want to criticize. . . . Autumn hath violets as well as spring, and age its sweetness hath, as well as youth.' Afterwards, for him, 'the fires that blazed upon the crests or smouldered in the deep hollows of the autumn woods' carry a message: 'If there was such beauty in corruption and decay, then perhaps he might claim for his love that it was not just a warning beacon, a brothel gas-fire set upon a hill' (*B* p. 261). Nothing is outside her sympathy, nothing eludes her response. 'She wasn't just un-selfish, she was self-*giving*', says Timothy at the end, summing up Mrs. Purbright's whole message for him and for the book:

> 'She didn't merely put *herself* in your place, she had the imagination to feel as you would; she really understood you. And at the same time she never lost sight of her own values. She kept them . . . not priggishly of course . . . as some people keep their choicest things . . . well, cakes and so on, for a visitor. . . . Whatever one did, they were always there . . . to tempt any appetite for good that one might have' (*B* p. 491).

Aware as she is of the need for affirming each self, each nature, person, thing in its own distinctive being, Mrs. Purbright is aware that the kind of freedom and fulfilment Timothy is looking for is not found in self-assertion or in the possession of any object, and that being convinced one is absolutely in the right narrows and constricts one's being, one's openness to life and growth, to the All which should be one's centre. She sees Timothy seeking to fix his affections, his striving, on the dog Felix, then on the first bowl, in that order—an order of diminishing demands upon his adaptability. At the moment of his greatest obsession with his boat, his Communism, he feels that 'He only wanted to meet his own kind'—people who would agree with him at all points (*B* p. 440). Perhaps one should live by 'absolute suppression of the personal', he thinks—'make oneself independent of human contacts. . . . Left to themselves, unheeded and unheeding, the emotions would atrophy and petrify, leaving the consciousness as hard and gemlike as the bowl was. . . .' (*B* p. 294). After all, Kant's maxim that every human being be treated as an end in himself was 'a counsel of perfection, for any human being, so treated, would see to it that his requirements were unending' (*B* p. 332). So, little by little, Timothy's obsession, his tendency to absolutize, makes him shrink. Hartley surely chose with great care the name Timothy gives himself when he is trying to conceal his identity from Mrs. Lampard: ' "Peabody," she repeated, dreamily. "What a curious name. It suits you, I think" ' (*B* p. 299).

Mrs. Purbright knows that love, on the other hand, would release and expand and fulfil Timothy's personality; having to adapt to the 'infinite requirements' of others, and of reality in all its multifariousness, would bring him the growth and freedom he desires. For her, 'in self-surrender lay the finest fulfilment of self' (*B* p. 494). Even Timothy's love for Vera, insofar as it *is* love, helps to free him from 'the chains of self' (*B* p. 365). All this Mrs. Purbright knows, and with it she tries to tempt Timothy's appetite for good. She practices always the tactics of ju-jitsu in which 'the victory goes to the one who best knows how to yield' (*B* p. 409), and her advice to Timothy about his boat is to sacrifice it, to burn it. If he persists in his self-assertion, the river may run with blood. But 'all this could be averted if he would make one sacrifice'.

> I reminded him of the value of the spectacular in turning people from a fixed idea; I said that his act, like a column of fire shooting up to heaven, would change the character of everybody's thoughts. They would be lost in amazement; their minds would go up, with the leaping flames; they would join hands and dance round the great pyre singing hymns of thanksgiving and praise (*B* pp. 221–2).

Timothy is for the moment tempted by this good angel; he understands for a moment that keeping the boat and holding to his rights contracts his very being, and that in the projected sacrifice he would realize all the liberation for which his soul was really longing:

> . . . an enlargement of himself, a holocaust on to which he could gloriously fling every impulse, great or small, that he had ever entertained, every

accretion of experience, every variation of personality, that had visited him since the dawn of self-consciousness (*B* p. 222).

But alas, Mrs. Purbright is not to prevail. For reasons of prudence Timothy decides to sell the boat, not to burn it, and the effort at sale is unsuccessful. And as he returns from that effort, who should suddenly loom up on the other side of the boat and the question but Vera Cross—angelic-looking, innocent-faced blonde, with her 'halo-like' bright hair (*B* p. 344), her look as of a young nun (*B* p. 94), her constant pleading with Timothy to assert himself and take the boat out on the Swirrel, to win her love and favours by becoming the hero of the River Revolution.

Mrs. Purbright, who loves Vera's beauty, cannot think of her as other than 'Miss Angell', but Hartley helps us, through a look at Edgell Purbright's somewhat lurid spy stories, to recognize Vera in the blonde adventuresses 'too beautiful to ignore, too ambiguous to trust' (*B* p. 352) about whose habits Edgell seems to know so much. In a parody of the usual situation, Hartley has the innocent Timothy laugh off Edgell's insights; Edgell, Timothy thinks, 'saw life not as it was, but in terms of shocker values' (*B* p. 353). Timothy has to learn that life *is* a shocker, that evil exists and usually looks very pretty.

Vera is a type of the blonde *femme fatale*, she is an evil angel; she is also a Communist. She urges Timothy on to self- or boat-assertion, but she has no concern whatever for personhood. What matters to her is the cause, and she hesitates not at all to exploit Timothy's love for her, to deceive and lie to him, to trick him into serving her purpose, and then to desert him. Essentially he is right when he sees the boat as a 'direful deity' and Vera (in a very Hawthorne-like vision) as 'the priestess of the cult, all silvery white down one side and black through the rest of her body' (*B* p. 375). To sacrifice *to* the boat, or to sacrifice the boat (with Mrs. Purbright as prophetess, darting forward with an inarticulate cry to 'fling upon the conflagration sweet-smelling oils, filling the air with the scent of jessamine and honeysuckle' [*B* p. 224]): this is the choice Timothy has to make; he makes it wrongly. Urged on by Vera, he makes the boat the symbol of a proletarian uprising and takes it out on the river during a flood.

The boat crashes on the Devil's Staircase, nearly drowning Timothy and his passengers; Vera and Mrs. Purbright (at last aware that 'Miss Angell' is a 'wicked woman' [*B* p. 427]) struggle in Lover's Lane and fall together into the water and their deaths. A chastened Timothy leaves town with the conventional Esther and the moralistic Tyro—he will probably join Tyro in working at the Censor's Office.

Hartley's story of Timothy and his boat seems at times only a very small part of the huge world-picture Hartley creates in this book. Closely paralleling each stage of the main story are at least three systems of imagery which, taken all together, create some-things like the effect of the Great Chain of Being operating in the background. Much of the symbolism, as previously mentioned, comes from Timothy's often over-working imagination, but much also comes from Mrs. Purbright, and some seems quite objectively rooted in the nature of things. One must, in each case, take note from whence and how it comes, but in general the parallels between Timothy's story, the passage of the seasons and the progress of the War are mutually illuminating and suggest how much Hartley is saying when he is saying any one small thing.

All through the eighteen months Timothy is at Upton we are constantly aware of the seasons changing in the background, linking always with (though often in contrast to) his own emotional state, as well as with the objective situation of the war. There is snow on the ground when Timothy first comes to the Old Rectory; Timothy is the same old Timothy he has been for quite a while; Britain is as yet only involved in the 'phony war'. The 'wonderful summer of 1940' starts early and with promise, but comes over-soon to a ripening, a turning-point, as Mrs. Purbright helps Timothy to see his own life has done (*B* pp. 118, 216). A little later we find that all his life Timothy has expected nature—his own human nature—to come to automatic fulfilment, but that something has happened:

> All his life he had beguiled himself with the mirage of a coming fulfil-
> ment; he had no idea what it would be, any more than a plant can foretell
> its flower, but he believed implicitly in the movement towards fruition.

> And now it had stopped; the sap no longer rose; the flowers had withered and on the branches hung fruit that was not good to eat. . . . (*B* p. 328).

He has, perhaps, gone the wrong way at the turning-point, and the summer of 1941 echoes his mood; it is 'but a faded transcript of its predecessor'.

> The sunshine was paler, the vegetation less luxuriant; it was as though Nature had exhausted herself, like an artist whose best work is over. One could not lose oneself in the rapture of the season's mood, for like one's own, and like the world's it was discouraged (*B* p. 346).

There is more here than the pathetic fallacy, though the passage does serve to elaborate Timothy's mood. But there is a suggestion on Hartley's part that the whole order of things has gone wrong: that man, frustrating himself, fighting himself, is rejecting and perverting and exhausting the bounty of nature. Mrs. Purbright's continual organic images accord well with her sense of the oneness of all living things and their participation in the divine goodness and Plan. Hartley's own constant paralleling of natural, supernatural and manmade events is calculated to suggest just such a mysteriously unified universe—in this constant suggestion of the 'organic metaphor' he recalls Goethe and the American romantics as well as more traditionally Christian conceptions of the Mystical Body of Christ.

Water imagery, as a particular manifestation of Nature, is constant throughout *The Boat*. We have already noticed it in descriptions of the Rector and Mrs. Purbright, and mentioned how often the river and the boat seem for Timothy a symbol of the freedom and infinite outlet for which his soul longs. Seeing a branch swept away by the current, he longs to be like it; 'shedding all resistance, with no pace of its own, only the impulses of the water round it, it glided swiftly past him to vanish round the bend. Timothy felt glad for it, as if it had achieved a liberation' (*B* p. 104). There is much talk about 'the current' of one's being or one's emotions (*B* pp. 115, 135) and Timothy is relieved to feel his being 'running one way' when his mind gives in completely to his emotions and he follows Vera's lead in defying his neighbours. Timothy wants this kind of freedom and liberation for everyone; he sees Upton, converted to rowing, as a kind of watery Utopia in which children's innocence is never lost:

> If they could only stay like that—if the bright water could continue to be a condition of the spirit in which they could always play—they would never want wars or commit the horrors we are always reading about' (*B* p. 395).

But the current of Nature is stronger, more hazardous than Timothy realizes; in the happy moments of his affair with Vera 'dimly' he descries himself 'struggling in gigantic, rainbow-tinted seas' (*B* p. 246); when she leaves him, petulantly, 'in the huge, encircling seas not a raft, not a spar appeared; not a gleam from the shore he had started from, not an intimation of land ahead' (*B* p. 376). In actual fact, Vera is able to lead him on to a literal shipwreck because he does not take account of the fact that the river is in flood and does not believe in or prepare for the Devil's Staircase.

Hartley's war imagery, paralleling the Matter of the Boat throughout, is of two kinds. In the first place, we are always aware of stages of the actual War going on in the background of this pastoral—from the war clouds of summer 1939 (*B* pp. 19ff.) through the early days of 1940 when Timothy thinks 'It looks as if the war might fizzle out, doesn't it?' (*B* p. 16), through the invasion and fall of France, the 'discouraged' summer of 1941, Germany's declaration of war on Russia, even Lord Haw Haw. . . . With each of these allusions we are made aware of Timothy's own attitude. Apolitical in 1939, he still thinks, during 'The tremendous, bewildering international events' of May 1940, and with 'the far-off rumble of guns' making his windows rattle, that the war is 'something that was taking place outside his experience'; 'something that was happening in a history book which it would one day be his duty to learn' (*B* p. 144).

But meanwhile, Timothy's own efforts on behalf of the boat carry with them their own consistent imagery of battle, and Timothy: self-assertion succeeds in bringing the War to birth within Upton itself. Mrs. Purbright hints that he is becoming 'a general at the head of his army', splitting the village into two camps because of his being 'so certain of being in the right' (*B* p. 219). He blows hot or cold in his belligerency according to whether her influence or that of Vera Cross is uppermost: for a time he becomes 'neutral', after 'the revolutions, the street fights, the changes of government that had taken place in his heart and mind . . .' (*B* p. 231), but soon he is looking at Upton again 'as it must appear to the pilot of a German bomber, carrying his lethal load. Should he drop it, or shouldn't he?' (*B* p. 270). He does: he writes a letter that brings suffering and madness on the Lampard household which has been an agent of his own troubles.

In the suffering visited upon him by his isolation and the failure of all that he tries to seize upon and make a centre for his life (Vera, Felix the dog, the beautiful vase) Timothy experiences his own Belsen and Buchenwald (*B* p. 379). But with Vera urging him on, he fails to see that *he* is the totalitarian, the persecutor, ready to 'liquidate' his enemies in behalf of his cause of 'freedom', and its 'benefit of the poor and the oppressed' (*B* p. 433). By the point of climax of the book *he* is the one writing a fanatical letter to Tyro, saying, 'it seems to me that what happened when I came here was a kind of Munich. I ought to have "declared war" *at once*, on the fishermen, put my boat on the river and taken the consequences' (*B* pp. 435–6) in full conviction of the absolute rightness of his cause—quite openly contrasting the clarity of the conflict in 'his war' with the muddiness of 'their war', the big one, 'in which the issues were so confused that none of the parties, except Russia, was certainly in the right' (*B* p. 436).

So, seemingly, does Hartley tell us that wars start in the heart of the individual man, in his pride and self-assertion. For this is one of the main lessons Timothy (and in him the romantic, progressivist humanists whom Hartley seems to be blaming for the war) has to learn from the war and death he causes: man's insufficiency as mere man, his propensity to evil, his inability to create a Utopia or even an Upton without giving it over to hatred and factions. Mrs. Purbright, idealist though she is, does know there is evil in the universe, in human nature, in herself—something Timothy does not know or does not wish to know when he comes back from sunny Italy, deplores the war as somebody else's doing, and settles down to uphold English culture and dream of a watery Utopia where all children can play happily with their boats. He is a real romantic, in fact. Writing to Tyro about his boat paradise, he sees the local young people

> . . . in the open air, communing with Nature, benefiting their health, and enjoying each other's society in any way they like (I'm not a puritan) in romantic and poetical surroundings, the influence of which will remain with them through life, quickening their response to the beautiful—which is also (I'm sure you will agree with me about this, so I won't stop to argue it) to some extent, the good (*B* p. 394).

Mrs. Purbright, despite her love of beauty, is not at all as sanguine about the goodness of Nature or human nature. In the face of the continued recalcitrance of Beatrice and Effie, Timothy's servants, she gives him surprisingly strong advice: 'You must get rid of them . . . misery-makers, enemies of happiness.' Her vision is apocalyptic: she says that he 'must be the angel with the flaming sword' to make them go (*B* p. 338). When she feels that 'someone had deliberately made mischief' (*B* p. 415), she can respond to that also, and when she realizes what Vera is up to, and the danger Timothy is in, 'a tide of anger' rises in her: 'a dry, hot feeling that she had not known for years' (*B* p. 417). She recognizes Vera as evil and dies in the attempt to overcome her.

Does Timothy learn his lesson? We are never quite sure—certainly not finally or totally. Saved from a watery death (by the indirect influence of Mrs. Purbright) he is beginning to feel in 'a happier world', in which Vera's evil is easily overcome and Mrs. Purbright's good lives on triumphant. The 'seesaw' between the two is at rest, with Mrs. Purbright permanently on top—or so he thinks, until he hears the details of her death and her own self-accusation about Vera's. If his dream of the two women forever intertwined is true, he will never afterwards be able to discount evil quite so easily, or be so unaware of his own share in guilt and war. Spattered with red paint by his own former followers, he sees himself, at last, as 'Blood-boltered Timothy' (*B* p. 482). With a 'more realistic attitude to the war . . . a sign that he is taking himself more realistically' (*B* p. 507), he agrees to leave

Upton/Utopia—perhaps for an ultimate involvement with the war effort, in the Censor's Office. His temptations to absolutize and abstract and idealize human nature are still with him: for a moment he sees 'no flaw in a future away from Upton' (*B* p. 508), and he keeps wishing he didn't have to think of Vera and Mrs. Purbright together (*B* p. 509). But Tyro keeps impressing upon him that he is 'just an ordinary sinner' (*B* p. 509) and urges him to practise 'Mental astigmatism' (*B* p. 510). For the first time, as he leaves, he sees 'Upton in curl-papers', and 'Time, which had counted for little in Upton, suddenly became of great importance' (*B* p. 509). Almost the last thing of which Hartley reminds us is that with Timothy as he leaves are Esther and Tyro, 'neither of whom could be joined in thought to the other' (*B* p. 510). It may be that Timothy the theoretician-humanist has become to some extent Timothy the human being; he passes a 'milestone' without noticing, since he is asleep—Hartley's way of telling us that this immense book has merely been the picture of one milestone in one man's life.

[c]

The story of Timothy Casson at Upton is one man's story; it is also one of those Hartley metaphors which show the way the universe works. Specifically, it seems to be the story of humanism and of the war which (Hartley seems to say) put an end to humanism as a viable philosophy of existence.

In the rather mild set of 'Pedants, bigots, cranks, parvenus ...' who surround Timothy we find any number of possible views on existence, from Wimbush's ''Tis only human nature . . .' (*B* p. 102) and Simpson's hangdog 'It makes it so bad for everybody' (*B* p. 310) to Magda's aestheticism and love of luxury and Tyro's moralism, which at times (though he denies it) turns into cynicism. Each of these people objectifies a tendency in Timothy himself and carries it to an extreme; each of their approaches to life attracts him strongly at some point in the book—and so Hartley give us a chance to consider them all in view of the war, of what happens to Timothy, and of the future. None is presented as really satisfactory, although Esther and Tyro survive, at least up to the end of the story, and manage to carry on and to give Timothy some hope of carrying on with them.

Magda appears only through her letters, many of them from a luxurious nursing home in London where she seems to rest up from her exhausting social life. She has adopted Communism and serves to reflect Timothy's own rather ludicrous venture into that philosophy as she combines her wish of 'DEATH TO THE FASCIST DOGS AND TRAITORS' (*B* p. 348) with her devotion to the Daimler hire service (*B* p. 349), her need for the services of a maid, and her self-indulgent life in general. But Magda dies (as, are we to think, Timothy's purely aesthetic view of life finally dies?). It is possible here again, as in so many of Hartley's books, to find a suggestion of Kierkegaard in the background *schema*. There is the aesthetic view of life, with its accent on pleasure and beauty; next step up is the ethical or moral view, as represented by Tyro.[10]

We first meet Tyro the moralist raving, in a letter to Timothy, about human selfishness and British aggression, and the inability of individuals and nations to see that all of them 'have enough malice and meanness among them to be the motive power of a world war' (*B* p. 41); he says specifically to Timothy in Italy in 1939 that the war will be 'brought about by people like you, with no moral sense', the kind of 'well-off English people' who 'hang about in places like this . . . gorging and guzzling . . . killing time and killing thought' (*B* p. 19). Into his mouth Hartley puts the book's most direct criticism of humanism:

> '. . . if ever I quarrel with you, which Heaven forbid, it will be because you are a humanist, as I once was, and believe that man is his own moral criterion, and there is no appeal from what man does to a higher tribunal, a standard of transcendental morality. A little patience, a little forbearance, a little understanding, a little laughter, *gentle* laughter (forgive me, Timothy) and all will be well. . . .' (*B* p. 110).

With the Battle of Britain, Tyro changes his opposition to the war. This is a concrete war, a concrete decision must be made, and 'if you take a sniff at the Nazi cauldron and then at the English alembic surely you can be in no doubt as to which should be preserved?' (*B* p. 251).

> 'What would right be, if it could not be expressed in terms of human behaviour? An abstraction. And what value would that abstraction have, if it could not be apprehended even when confronted by its opposite'? (*B* p. 274).

In Tyro's mind the war is showing itself to be something of a blessing, a challenge and purification for England:

> 'nearly everyone I know is immeasurably the better for it, and by better I do not mean only in the narrow moralistic sense, but more fully alive to social obligations, better adjusted, better integrated, completer men and women. . . .' (*B* p. 252).

Hartley paints Tyro as rather pigheaded and self-deceptive, so that we must learn to pick and choose among his opinions. And surely Timothy is speaking for Hartley when he tells Tyro that 'Your morality is a form of war-mongering too' (*B* p. 20). Tyro does not strike us as having the final answers, nor the clue to peace, though he sometimes comes close, and seems to be coming even closer. Late in the book he shouts his disgust at Timothy for daring still to talk about 'human' values:

> '. . . What are we fighting this way for? Isn't it to establish other, non-human values, the values Christianity teaches? I'm not a Christian, Heaven forbid . . . but surely you realize that Christian values are essential for the preservation of the species?'
> 'Without the Christian faith?'
> 'I should hope so! All that mumbo-jumbo!' (*B* p. 487).

Tyro's rejection of Christian faith seems to go back to the kind of external Christianity which had been his own earlier experience: 'The modern world has legalized bloodshed and practised it on a scale never imagined before, all the while proclaiming from its pulpits and soap-boxes that God is Love' (*B* p. 109).

As in many of his other books, Hartley plays with—all the time undercutting—the idea of Christianity as a viable solution to world problems. One of the best Christians in *The Boat*, pronounced so by the cook Beatrice (*B* p. 293), is the ever-loving and delightful Felix, Timothy's dog of the 'golden nature' (*B*

p. 284), the total freedom from resentment (*B* p. 282), the inexhaustible patience (*B* p. 283) and benevolence (*B* p. 284). But there is at least one human being who could also qualify for the title—Mrs. Purbright, who seems to represent, in the scheme of Hartley's novel, Kierkegaard's third, or 'religious' view of life,[11] a central, unifying position founded upon deep faith, embracing (while surpassing) within its huge vision both the aesthetic and moral views of man.

Mrs. Purbright's Christianity has been discussed above. Hartley keeps us constantly aware also of the aesthetic sense which she shares with Timothy, but which she keeps in its place, as handmaiden to something higher, not as an end in itself. Her appreciation of the world and its beauty comes from and is part of her religious sense, the sense for praise which integrates and motivates her whole being:

> '. . . I wish there was more praise, though. We have so much to be thankful for. Prayer and repentance are very good things, but there would be less need for them if praise came easier to us. . . . God is praised in a beautiful face, for how should we know it was beautiful, unless it reminded us of Him? And when we are happy seeing it, that is in itself an act of praise' (*B* pp. 87–8).

Mrs. Purbright's moral sense, as Timothy also realizes, is quite clear and true. With all her sympathy, she keeps her own sense of values, living them, tempting people with them rather than arguing about them like Tyro. But she knows there is evil in the world and in the end even she is forced to take sides and do battle.

To Mrs. Purbright Hartley gives some of the central statements of this long, intricate book. Talking to Timothy about building our reserves, 'our capital of happiness' afresh, she tells him that 'We can inherit the gifts of Christianity but not hand them on: I mean, the third generation must renew its faith' (*B* p. 131). Humanism, for her—the kind of religion of aestheticism and individualism and self-discipline which Timothy learned from his guardian (*B* p. 129)—was the gift of Christianity, which the Victorian and Edwardian ages could inherit from their predecessors and which might have been sufficient for such as Timothy's guardian in those days when 'there was so much happiness to fall back on—cushions, mattresses of happiness. . . . Life was padded against accident. Now, if one scratches one's fingers, the whole world bleeds' (*B* p. 134). For this generation—Timothy's generation—humanism, the gift of a dead Christianity, is not enough, and 'belated Victorians' like him (*B* p. 131) cannot meet the challenges of the present. She says to Timothy that his guardian's gaze 'condemns what we see; but still, we must look at it, though it is harder for us, who have seen through his eyes' (*B* p. 131). She alone of the local gentry really welcomes the breakdown of the class system, and sees that the 'new blood' brought by the invasion of the townsfolk into their social life can be a 'transfusion', one of those 'rejuvenating processes' (*B* p. 85) which might help bring renewed life to a dead culture. The war itself, for her, might be this kind of blessing—perhaps speeding up the decay of what is old and dead so that something new might be born. Her feelings about the war, as Timothy learns, are 'only an intensified version of her general view of the human lot', her conviction of the redemptive value of suffering (*B* p. 144).

At the end Mrs. Purbright is dead as Magda is dead; Christianity and aestheticism have both gone their way with Timothy's over-romantic humanism and hope of automatic fruition. The chastened Timothy is left with Esther's British tradition and Tyro's moral sense: is there a chance that he will ever understand what Mrs. Purbright was, meant, could mean? Could her spirit, could some form of Christianity be reborn? Will men like Timothy, with their spiritual sense, their longing for integration and for direction towards a great goal find it in praise and love—or will they continue to seek it in boats and factions, in pride and self-assertion and war? Hartley does not leave us over-hopeful, though he seems to suggest that the war itself could be turned from a curse into a blessing. Perhaps, as Esther and Tyro both seem to believe, 'good things . . . grow out of the battlefield as naturally as fruit and crops and flowers do' (*B* p. 195).

The Boat, while still a symbolic novel, marks a shift in Hartley's approach from the primarily romantic—based on myth and striving to express the universal forces in man's life and destiny—

to the primarily satirical or mock-romantic, in which the author, while still on a deeper level dealing with universals, tends to emphasize contemporary social conditions and to make his characters representative of contemporary ideas and philosophies. *Eustace and Hilda* is closer to myth, *The Boat* to satire—although *The Boat*'s satire has a mock-romantic structure and manages to suggest that the idealistic quest is not all wrong but merely, in this case, wrongly directed: that it inheres in the nature of human life, to be discovered by the sensitive person.

The mythical *Eustace and Hilda* is set in the theatre of the past; its world is seen through the imaginative eyes of a child. Hence the book's characters can more easily approach mythical stature and can live in a world of dense and all-pervading symbolism: Eustace's Venice is Venice, no doubt, but it is even more a mysterious world of his supernatural encounter, education, mystical death and rebirth. Hence also the sheer beauty of this book—the re-created, rediscovered world of nature and art which language and symbols and innocent-eye-view bring into being.

We have a different pair of eyes for *The Boat*: the adult eyes of Timothy Casson, while naïve and imaginative, give us a less enchanted world. The romance and myth which he incorporates into his view are slightly ridiculous and give the book its mock-romantic quality; at the same time we are able to see the characters in his world as representative adult types, embodying classical human dispositions in current social and political positions. Mrs. Purbright's view, like Timothy's in so many ways, yet serves as a corrective—it suggests what true imagination and spirituality would make of those people and events he romanticizes.

Timothy's world is one in which design is discernible, in which there are mysterious causalities and inter-relationships—but often we see this in spite of his romantic vision; we see it through the things that happen, their juxtapositions, their parallels with each other, with Nature, with the war. His is a more opaque world than that shining one of *Eustace and Hilda* in which water, land, lighting, colours, clothing speak constantly of meanings beyond the material; his is, in short, an adult's world—one in which we understand, alas, how shortsighted adults can be.

The depth and wisdom of *The Boat* come in large part from its romantic underlayer, which gives the epic of Upton universality and pathos while at the same time serving as a background for satirical contrast. *The Boat* is, I believe, a very fine book: a sensitive, comic probing of human nature as well as a provocative meditation on World War II and our century.

CHAPTER FIVE

AFTERMATH: *THE GO-BETWEEN*

To lose sensibility, to see what one sees,
As if sight had not its own miraculous thrift,
To hear only what one hears, one meaning alone,
As if the paradise of meaning ceased
To be paradise, it is this to be destitute.
This is the sky divested of its fountains.

                                        —Wallace Stevens[1]

[a]

The Go-Between (1953) could be seen as Hartley's 'Young
Goodman Brown', addressed to an England dry and disillusioned
after the *Walpurgisnacht* of world war. Characteristically, however, Hartley's book ends—not, as Hawthorne's story does, with
the death of the innocent-turned-cynic—but at the moment when
he at last comprehends what has happened to him. Hartley wants,
perhaps, to show the postwar world a complex symbolic picture
of the past fifty years. Having put the last piece in place before his
audience, he will step back, his task done, to see if in the flash of
comprehension any spark of new life is communicated.

The Go-Between is also, perhaps, Hartley's *Lady Chatterley's
Lover*, except for a deliberately-added dimension to its examination of love and the nature and implications of the sexual relationship; a frame-story of fifty years in the life-span of a man and
a century renders highly symbolic the centrally-focused affair
between a daughter of the upper classes and an intensely physical,
masculine young farmer.

Harvey Curtis Webster says ('diffidently, particularly when I
remember the high quality of *Eustace and Hilda* and *The Boat*')

97

that 'because it includes almost all of Hartley's varied preoccupations in intense unity *The Go-Between* seems to me his best novel'.[2] It is, indeed, a superbly-crafted unity of complexities, in less than three hundred pages managing at once to affirm and to question the Lawrencian yes to life and love; to tell an absorbing story and suggest the interlocking meanings of a number of lives; to recreate in critical perspective the first fifty years of the twentieth century, its wars, its social and religious revolutions—and the vacuum now left for those who follow after.

Hartley experiments with a new structure for *The Go-Between*, one which can move back and forth between single and 'double' vision and enable us, even more than is usual in his novels, to experience the dialectic between fact and imagination. The book is about seeing, about vision and double vision. Its frame-story is the encounter of a sixty-five-year-old bibliographer—buried for years under 'cliffs' of dingy paper—with his diary, the diary which tells the story of the summer of 1900 and the blighting of his life. In an *Epilogue* we see the final comprehension of, perhaps a slight lifting of that blight, brought about by the reading of the diary. In between, there is the summer itself: mainly the love between Marian Maudsley, of Brandham Hall in Norfolk, and Ted Burgess, the tenant of nearby Black Farm. We see it through the eyes of the too-innocent, too-hopeful young Leo Colston as seen now through the eyes of his soured present self. In fact, the book is the extension of an argument in the Prologue (*GB* pp. 20–1) between the twelve-year-old Leo and the sixty-five-year-old Leo over the content of the diary, the meaning of that summer and love affair, the meaning of life and love in general. Looking through the two pairs of eyes (actually the same pair, fifty years apart) so contrasting in their viewpoint, yet so alike in the extremism and romanticism at the root of their judgements, we are able to see sinners and sinned-against with much more sympathy and understanding than either; able, too, to understand more of the human mixture that has gone into the making of 'this hideous century we live in' (*GB* p. 279). The ageing, dried-up, lonely Leo struggles to bring himself to life again with 'a last flicker of the instinct for self-preservation' by reading his diary, 'facing . . . the scene, the people, and the experience' (*GB* p. 21) which had crushed him. At the end, after reading and thinking it through, after seeing Marian again, after seeing and hearing the aftermath of the tragedy, suddenly he sees spring into view 'the south-west prospect of the Hall, long hidden from my memory' (*GB* p. 281). It is a symbol of the attaining of a true vision which has all along been lacking. At last he can see the thing whole: the house of which he could previously remember only 'the hinder parts . . . higgledy-piggledy and rambling . . . not well lighted' (*GB* p. 33); the love-affair which had seemed so evil and destructive, yet which had also, inevitably, something in it of the good and beautiful; his own romanticism and blindness and that of his century, living on traditions of beauty and self-discipline and forgetting to acknowledge the passion and violence and evil in human nature; love itself, the central secret—not limited to sexual passion (though including it) but reaching out with compassion to embrace all one's fellow-sinners, fellow-sufferers in the human tragicomedy. *The Go-Between* is a book, an experience which can immeasurably increase one's penetration into, one's love for and acceptance of life, one's 'tolerance for ambiguity' in people and events—that primary attribute, according to some social scientists, of true maturity. Leo seems just possibly on the verge of attaining some such maturity, at sixty-five, as we close the book, and Hartley's art is such that we understand the preciousness and rarity of the achievement, even at such an age.

Hartley's frame structure, the single/double pair of eyes through which he has us look, is the means by which he makes his narrative into a romance while yet criticizing those who romanticize. The elder Leo, paging through the diary, recreates each scene for us with the freshness and wonder, the symbolizing imagination of the young Leo—attaching significance to everything just as he did, making a mythical, other-worldly experience, as he did, out of that summer at Brandham Hall. We, like the elder Leo, are aware of the real facts of the case as we watch—can tell that the figures in the central triangle, Marian and Ted and Hugh, are not gods and goddesses of the Zodiac, as young Leo saw them, but very fallible humans playing a dangerous game with a little boy.

Yet this is not the whole truth either. . . . Leo's childlike vision was unreal, it idealized, it left no room for evil and so could be used and crushed by evil, and by the pride and passion within the child himself. But surely there *is* something of a myth here as we look at it; surely Marian and Ted and Hugh *are* archetypal figures; surely there *is* significance in these strange parallels between nature and man and history, these coincidences and repetitions, these strange configurations and colours—surely the heat of that summer, the flourishing of the glossy, deadly Belladonna, the winning and losing of the cricket match, the reverberations from a distant war all have connections with each other and with the triangle at the centre? Surely there is something of transcendent meaning in these people and their story and the century half gone by? And if there is myth and transcendence in their story, it is because there is in all love stories, in all lives, including our own. This romance warns us of the dangers of romanticizing, yet it shows us that the dry, peeled vision Leo has tried to practise since Brandham Hall is also inadequate. There was something of truth in Leo's vision then, and he was never so false, he realizes, as when, on his thirteenth birthday at Brandham Hall, he first tried to curb his imagination:

> I did not realize that this attempt to discard my dual or multiple vision and achieve a single self was the greatest pretence that I had yet embarked on. It was indeed a self-denying ordinance to cut out of my consciousness the half I most enjoyed. To see things as they really were—what an impoverishment! (*GB* p. 251).

How, then, to combine the child's spiritual vision with the grown man's knowledge of evil? It is the same question Blake asked long ago. Hartley gives no very strong and sure answer in the book—he is too concerned with showing us exactly where we are today. But the book as a whole seems to call for a Higher Innocence, for a rebirth of faith and vision in a people whose ideals have been shocked and defeated by the evil and violence and ugliness of our century.

Peter Bien deals at great length with the symbolism of *The Go-Between*,[3] which he sees as a 'tight symbolist' novel. Perhaps it is not, then, necessary to examine the entire symbolic structure in detail, but mainly to point out certain areas of difference or special emphasis. It is also important to stress that the central story of Leo's quest for identity is meant to be the story of twentieth-century man.

The story in the diary at which the elder Leo is looking begins when the young Leo is twelve—just on the threshold of seeing himself as a man, as a separate person. He wonders whether to identify himself with the Archer in his beloved picture of the Zodiac, or with the Water-carrier:

> They were in fact the same man following different callings. He was strong and sturdy and this appealed to me, for one of my ambitions was to become a kind of Hercules. I leaned to the Archer as the more romantic, and because the idea of shooting appealed to me. But my father had been against war, which I supposed was the Archer's profession; and as to the Water-carrier, though I knew him to be a useful member of society I could not help conceiving of him as a farm-labourer or at best a gardener, neither of which I wanted to be. The two men attracted and repelled me at the same time: perhaps I was jealous of them (*GB* p. 10).

If Leo is jealous, it is probably because of the Virgin figured on this circle which surrounds the lettering of the year 1900 on his diary. For Leo she is 'the key to the whole pattern, the climax, the coping-stone, the goddess' (*GB* p. 9), and in imagination he likes to replace the Archer/Water-carrier figures and have the Virgin all to himself on the Zodiac (*GB* p. 11).

Son of an unorthodox, somewhat withdrawn pacifist father and a conventional, inexperienced mother, himself the product of the narrow society of a typical British boys' school, Leo goes off totally unprepared, in the summer of 1900, to his first meeting with the great world and higher society. He is to spend some part of his vacation at Brandham Hall, home of his school friend Marcus Maudsley. Encumbered with heavy, formal clothing, he is unprepared for the summer's unusual heat; intoxicated with the beauty and elegance and ease of life among the country gentry, he is convinced that they are divine, immortal, like the zodiacal figures in his diary, and that he, caught up into their life and given a new green summer suit, is equally powerful and glorious and invulnerable.

Leo, in 1900, sees the twentieth century as the dawn of a new Golden Age (*GB* p. 10)—as Eustace dreamed of one in *Eustace and Hilda* (*EH* p. 504) and Timothy in *The Boat* (*B* p. 395). For him two and two never make four, if he can make them five (*GB* p. 71). His 'favourite religion' is the Zodiac, in which the divinities are noted for their immortality (*GB* p. 157), their immunity from harm and disability, rather than their goodness (*GB* pp. 68–9). Sin has no meaning for him (*GB* p. 69) and, living as he does among the immortals of Brandham Hall, 'I could not find a flaw in the universe and was impatient with Christianity for bringing imperfection to my notice' (*GB* p. 157). He thinks of himself as a magician, able to control Nature and events (*GB* pp. 28, 107, 244): 'luck was in love with me, like everyone else' (*GB* p. 153); 'Truly Providence was on my side' (*GB* p. 157).

The summer of 1900 is, especially, an encounter with the heat which is everywhere, and which Leo comes to see as 'a liberating power with its own laws . . . outside my experience' in which element 'the senses, the mind, the heart, the body, all told a different tale' (*GB* p. 77). The heat had been an enemy for Leo since his experience of the fever of diphtheria (*GB* p. 29), but now, in his Lincoln green suit, in the exalted society of Brandham Hall, he wants to explore it, 'to feel its power and be at one with it' (*GB* p. 77). He longs to discard more and more clothes, 'to travel far, ever farther into it, and achieve a close approximation with it; for I felt that my experience of it would somehow be cumulative, and that if it would only get hotter and hotter there was a heart of heat I should attain to' (*GB* p. 50). He longs somehow to discard even the vague notions of 'decency' he has, longs 'for the release of casting them off with my clothes, and being like a tree or a flower, with nothing between me and Nature' (*GB* p. 50). Through the medium of the summer and its heat he loses his schoolboy ability to distinguish between dreams and reality and 'without knowing it' crosses 'the rainbow bridge from reality to dream' (*GB* pp. 76–7). Here he is somehow master of Nature, of the heat, of the thermometer. He does not take warning from the way the heat is progressively drying up the fields and the water of the river and its pool (*GB* pp. 77–8; p. 112) to reveal 'ghostly, corpse-like boulders, and a "mad disorder" of tangled, ugly weeds and mud-coated rushes' (*GB* pp. 168–9).

The symbol of the heat pervades the entire atmosphere of the book; it is particularly linked with Ted, the Water-carrier, the beautiful young farmer whose 'powerful body . . . spoke to me of something I did not know' (*GB* p. 56). When Leo first visits Ted at his farm, 'All the heat of the afternoon seemed to be concentrated where we stood' (*GB* p. 83). Ted is nakedness, the body, the physical, the utterly masculine; standing in the cornfield, 'the colour of the corn, between red and gold', he is to Leo 'like a sheaf the reaper had forgotten', and Leo fancies 'that it would come back for him' (*GB* p. 101). Talking to Leo about 'spooning', Ted stresses that it is 'Nature' (*GB* p. 116), and says that 'It wouldn't be natural' to be in love with someone without 'spooning' with them. For him, young Leo sees, 'the word "natural" seemed to be conclusive. I had never thought of it as justifying anything. Natural! So spooning was natural! I had never thought of that. I had thought of it as a kind of game that grown-ups played' (*GB* p. 117).

Ted represents Nature and complete oneness with Nature— hedonism: the kind of self-forgetfulness, 'self-glory, depending on nobody's approval but their own' that Leo finds unappetizing in the earthy pictures of Teniers (*GB* p. 205). And Marian, representing ideal beauty for Leo, his Virgin of the Zodiac, his Maid Marian, his fairy-godmother (*GB* p. 222) is also linked with the heat—that powerful force to which Leo responds, which he wants to explore, embrace, control, but whose deadly power he does not begin to comprehend. Perhaps, indeed, Marian is the heat (*GB* p. 245). Constrained by her mother's ambition and her own pride to marry Lord Trimingham, the Archer, she is carrying on a passionate affair with Ted and using Leo as uncomprehending go-between. Leo 'did not understand the force that drew them together, any more than I understood the force that drew the steel to the magnet' (in the thermometer he is always consulting), but he feels its strength, and a suggestion of its beauty and mystery (*GB* p. 118). The 'fierce embrace' of the sun reconciles him somehow to their 'spooning', perhaps by suggesting 'the helplessness of Nature to contend with Nature' (*GB* p. 112). Leo, as Bien points out,[4] is Mercury, the messenger among the planets; he is like the mercury of the thermometer (*GB* p. 96), conveying, conducting heat, registering its effects, 'soaring ever to new heights' in its presence while remaining an alien element. The heat which pervades *The Go-Between* is the heat of Nature— expressing itself in human beings as overriding passion, the passion between Marian and Ted which 'had come to dominate our lives' (*GB* p. 233). Like the heat, it is strong and beautiful; like the heat, it can dry up, wither, kill.

For Leo, this uncomprehended force, exhibiting as it does such power over them all, comes to be an intruder in his world of the Zodiac, a serpent in his imagined (or fallen) Eden. Life, according to his idealized, Pelagian view, should be one unbroken progression of blisses. Without this intrusive love affair, he convinces himself,

> There would have been no ridicule, no making fun of me: every day would have been a highlight. . . . I should have been infinitely valued and esteemed, but at the same time I should have been perfectly free to go my own way. . . . I should have enjoyed it . . . in a mood of continuous, conscious lyricism . . . everything I saw would have ministered to my happiness. . . . (*GB* p. 234).

Convincing himself that he is restoring 'order . . . social order, universal order' (*GB* p. 235), Leo, still uncomprehending, betrays Marian and Ted by falsifying the time for their meeting. They are caught, and tragedy follows.

Leo's destruction of the ambiguous belladonna or nightshade plant—which has come to symbolize both the ambiguous Marian and the ambiguous mystery of sex in its beauty and deadliness— epitomizes the entire experience which he undergoes at Brandham: his innocence, his unknowing but fascinated involvement in sexual intrigue, his terror and the unimagined destruction it wreaks, the living death and burial he brings upon himself:

> . . . I was almost on top of the outhouses before I saw the thick blur of the deadly nightshade. It was like a lady standing in her doorway looking out for someone. I was prepared to dread it, but not prepared for the tumult of emotions it aroused in me. In some way it wanted me, I felt, just as I wanted it; and the fancy took me that it wanted me as an ingredient, and would have me. . . . There was no room for me inside, but if I went inside, into the unhallowed darkness where it lurked, that springing mass of vegetable force, I should learn its secret and it would learn mine. And in I went. It was stifling, yet delicious, the leaves, the shoots, even the twigs, so yielding; and this must be a flower that brushed my eyelids, and this must be a berry that pressed against my lips. . . .
>
> At that I panicked and tried to force my way out but could not find the way out: there seemed to be a wall on every side, and I barked my knuckles. At first I was afraid of hurting the plant, then in my terror I began to tear at it. . . . I heard the roots creaking and cracking, felt their last strength arrayed against me, the vital principle of the plant defending itself in its death-agony. 'Delenda est belladonna!' I chanted, not loudly, but loud enough for anyone listening to hear, and braced myself for a last pull. And then it gave, came away in my hands, throwing up with a soft sigh a little shower of earth which rustled on the leaves like rain; and I was lying on my back in the open, still clutching the stump, staring up at its mop-like coronal of roots, from which grains of earth kept dropping on my face (GB pp. 240–1).

While the symbolism is obviously strongly sexual, Bien's emphasis upon this incident as a 'sexual experience' involving Leo's unrecognized desire for Marian[5] seems not quite Hartley's point. Rather, this seems one of Hartley's characteristic analogues or epitomes or controlling symbols summing up the meaning of the whole book: the encounter of the overly-innocent with the unsuspected—and deadly—force of Nature (and human nature in particular). This is a perfect example of the way in which Hartley can render complexities of inner experience through the detailed description of a symbol or analogy. In the boy's descriptions we catch the strong sexual hints, the suggestion of a harlot standing in a doorway—but the boy does not know what he is describing or why it is so strong, so primeval, so dangerous, so frightening, yet so weak.

In *The Go-Between* it is easy to recognize Hartley's favourite motif—of the very human tendency to believe in the Eden one longs for as already existing, to see human nature as self-perfectible when its wishes, its desires for the beautiful and pleasing are unobstructed. This tendency, Hartley shows us over and over again, in a Lavinia Johnstone, a Eustace, a Timothy, a Leo, can only be destructive. There is evil at the heart of the universe, in Nature, in human nature—it cannot, perhaps, be fully understood, but it must be reckoned with. Leo's plight is an implicit criticism of the education, the Victorian attitudes, that can throw him into life unprepared for its seriousness, can assume that heat, violence, sex, are unmentionables which, if ignored, may disappear ('Getting hot is always a risk. You needn't do anything *violent*, need you?' says Leo's mother [*GB* p. 30], sending him off in his heavy clothes in the hope that the weather will stay cool because she wants it to). But Leo's story is even more a criticism of those who saw and see the twentieth century, culmination of so many years of cultivation and humanism and scientific achievement, as, logically, a Golden Age of human fulfilment—and who cannot comprehend or encompass the devastating wars which have characterized it. It is an indictment of the Marians who cannot or will not connect those wars, the hatreds and terrors of 'this hideous century we live in' (*GB* p. 279) with their own passions, the unconfronted blackness and destructiveness in their own natures, the weakness of the philosophy which preaches complaisance with all that is natural. As in *The Boat* Hartley is offering war as supreme proof that humanism is inadequate to man's needs, that man's animal nature alone is no key to his life and happiness, that there are—must be—transcendental truths and standards and a world of the spirit, a spiritual dimension, which gives meaning to the physical: that without access to that dimension we are lost.

As we have seen and shall see again, Hartley often uses in his novels what might be called a 'go-between' character: a somewhat Hawthornian or Jamesian observer—boy, man, sometimes woman—a kind of middle-class Everyman who represents a more or less innocent, humanistic approach to life, and who suddenly finds himself caught between opposing forces or ideas where choice for either side can only be destructive. The consequences of the choice, whichever side it falls on, are usually so bad as to send the go-between to the opposite side, usually also bad—the end result being to enable us, if not him, to question whether something is not wrong with the world-view that sets up such a choice.[6] Since that world-view is usually not too far-removed from our own, as liberal moderns, Hartley's novels are peculiarly experiential—involve the reader more than the usual novel in self-criticism and search.

And so, here, Leo jumps with both feet into a belief in the 'sufficiency of earthly glory' (*GB* p. 158), the immortality of the beings and concerns among which he lives. When the blow falls, when the glorious Marian and the beautiful Ted, the Virgin and the Water-carrier, in a scene of shocking grotesquerie suddenly become two bodies grovelling together on the earth floor of a squalid outhouse, when their affair ends in death and madness, Leo swings to the opposite extreme. Never again will he venture into the heat of human passion: as far as possible he rejects sex, love, even life and human relationships—he sees evil, deception and death in all that is human, all that partakes of the flux and force of the natural. Never again will he give his imagination free play—he will bury his energies in facts and papers. Like Hawthorne's Young Goodman Brown, 'A stern, a sad, a darkly meditative, a distrustful, if not a desperate man did he become from the night of that fearful dream.'[7]

Like the choice of husbands open to Marian, the choice of identities or ideals of masculinity open to Leo (to man) at the beginning of the twentieth century is inadequate—the Archer or the Water-carrier, Trimingham or Ted. Trimingham is the gentle, chivalrous representative of a dying tradition, bearing the scars of an 'impersonal' war (*GB* p. 162). A complex symbol, he is 'two-sided, like Janus' (*GB* p. 52), like the war, conflict and suffering for which in some ways he stands—entities which can be evil, the result of passion and pride and 'the fear of losing face' (*GB* p. 42), but which can also be good, the nurturer of strength, humility, self-discipline, compassion, the gaiety having the 'background of hospital and battle-field' (*GB* p. 92). Hugh is two-sided like the traditions of the British nobility, like the blind-in-one-eye chivalry which insists that nothing can ever be a lady's fault (*GB* p. 169), like the patriotism which sends soldiers off to kill the Boer, who's 'not a bad feller' (*GB* p. 162) but who happens to be the current prescribed target.

Hugh stands for tradition and the warrior past, but like the English humanism of *The Boat* his tradition is cut off from its roots and dying. Both Marian and the young Leo want desperately to live and grow—and all that is available to them both as an alternative to dead tradition seems to be the ideal of life represented by Ted: the overwhelmingly physical, natural, hedonistic.

In the figure of Ted in *The Go-Between* Hartley explored one of his favourite themes: the duality of the natural, the beautiful yet terrible aspects of Nature—especially, here, the dual nature of sexual love. The heat which is all around young Leo, the passion between Marian and Ted in which he is caught up, are overpowering, dizzying. By letting us experience that heat and that passion through Leo's eyes, Hartley lets us take an oddly fresh look at the mystery and intoxication of sexual attraction. Yet all the time that we are experiencing that intoxication and aware of the sheer physical power and beauty of a Ted and, obliquely, of the force of the passion between him and Marian ('she cried when she couldn't see me', says Ted. 'How do you know?' Leo asks. 'Because she cried when she did see me...' [*GB* p. 115]), we are also being given intimations of its potential deadliness. There is the story of the death of the fifth Viscount Trimingham in a duel over his unfaithful wife (*GB* pp. 158ff.), after which Leo begins to realize that strong feelings between men and women can lead to murder (*GB* p. 178). There is Ted's identification with the sheaf for which the reaper will come back (*GB* p. 101), his constant association with the gun which in the end destroys him (*GB* pp. 101; 171–2; 177; 263): there is the blood he smears on Marian's letter, given him by Leo (*GB* p. 102). There is the belladonna, glossy and beautiful, fascinating, yet poisonous— destroyed all too easily by Leo in his terror, yet showering earth on him as it falls. There is the ugliness, the bestiality, almost, of the scene in the outhouse when Leo and Mrs. Maudsley come upon Marian and Ted:

> 'No, you *shall* come', she said, and seized my hand, and it was then we saw them, together on the ground, the Virgin and the Water-carrier, two bodies moving like one. I think I was more mystified than horrified; it was Mrs. Maudsley's repeated screams that frightened me, and a shadow on the wall that opened and closed like an umbrella (*GB* p. 262).

All Leo sees (all we see through his eyes) is the naked physical act, unsoftened by a human, spiritual component—it is like the 'crude physical sufficiency, at once relentless and unwilling', the 'physical energy . . . dangerous and cruel, just insofar as it was free' that Lavinia Johnstone senses in the strokes of her gondolier's oar (*SP* p. 95). The ugliness, unexpected, uncomprehended, is shattering. Later Leo sees that moment as 'not only worse than death, it was death too' (*GB* p. 269). And death for Ted, madness for Mrs. Maudsley, the withering of Leo, the twisting of the lives of Trimingham, Marian, the new Hugh/Edward Trimingham are its result. Hartley's theme reminds us of at least one of his short stories: '*per far l'amore*' is indeed not 'a kind of game that grown-ups played' (*GB* p. 117): it is a deadly serious encounter with the root forces of life and nature; it is the unleashing of powers stronger than the individual; it is an entry into the black mystery of the universe, human existence and sin and mortality. Entered upon too lightly, it can deal death and destruction.

This is what Leo takes from the supremely ugly moment in the outhouse and its tragic aftermath: life and nature and love become too ugly and painful to touch. Having seen what he has seen, he can now never make a choice between the Hugh/Ted alternatives his century offers him; it is easier not to live. Visiting Marian, fifty years later, he is amazed by her self-deception. How can she see the sordid affair which had ruined so many lives as beautiful, as having given so much to him, to that summer, even to the sad world? How can she miss the connection between her own selfishness and pride and deception, the breakdown of all standards, and victory of outright evil within her own family circle, her own class—and the wars which have plagued her country and the world? Hartley has made sure with his entire book that we do not miss the connection.

And yet . . . Leo, seeing the whole, comprehending Marian's folly and yet seeing her dilemma, her temptation, begins to be able to excuse. There is 'no spell or curse except an unloving heart', she says, and Leo, ageing, almost unacquainted with love after so many frozen years, knows that she speaks the truth. Anyone privileged to look back, as he has been, at a microcosm of the human life and struggle and failure of more than half a century, who has seen the weakness and sin in himself and others and the inexplicable pain and death at the heart of things, knows that human passion, once recognized and reckoned with, is more to be pitied than condemned and that human love, wherever it exists, has always in itself something beautiful and life-giving. The only answer to the 'sadness of human life, its indifference to our wishes' is understanding love, compassion, the kind of caring that sends Leo off to find young Lord Trimingham to try to convince him that living that life, with all its pain, is better than avoiding it. Perhaps there is a third alternative—perhaps what was good and beautiful in both Hugh and Ted can blend and carry on in their descendants. Perhaps this small opening up to love on Leo's part will be the beginning of some kind of life for him. And if Hartley sees Leo as the type of Briton stunned, shattered, discouraged by the impact and horror of war and the destruction of the past, perhaps he is indicating the means—including a healthy merger of the classes—by which a new stirring might come. Nowhere is there much suggestion in this book that institutional Christianity is anything but part of the past—except that the elder Leo, nearing the end of his quest as he returns to the church at Brandham, kneels to pray for himself and for all the souls of the faithful there 'who had passed away in the hope of a joyful resurrection' (*GB* p. 270).

[c]

The Go-Between is unquestionably one of Hartley's most successful romances—if not *the* most successful. It is a small book, tightly unified by its frame structure, its two viewpoints which are really one, its many recurring symbols of colour, heat, natural surroundings, clothing, and the spells, signs of the Zodiac and mythical figures by which a small boy's imagination turns the natural into the supernatural.

Many critics[8] see Hartley as most successful in depicting children and the past, and it is impossible not to agree with them: Hartley is unsurpassed at working through the imagination of a Eustace or a Leo to invest a natural setting or a social gathering—or the world itself—with radiance and significance. *The Go-Between* is, literally, a beautiful book; it manages to recreate the beauty of a child's world before evil inevitably shatters that world. In *The Go-Between* the double-visioned form Hartley created achieves its peak, giving us at one and the same time, within very small compass, an absorbing personal history/love story, an important social/historical description and analysis of the first fifty years of the century, and—running through all this —a fascinating inquiry into the modern workings of good and evil.

The Go-Between is pervaded with sexual feeling, with the sense of the power and heat (literally, since this is one of his chief symbols) of sexual passion. The fact that Leo is uncomprehending and describes all with an innocent eye makes the reader's awareness and understanding all the stronger. What is Hartley saying about sex in letting it be the chief agent of destruction in this novel? Mainly, I think, that it is one of the chief manifestations of that lovely but flawed, deceptive and deadly Nature about which man since Rousseau is apt to be little too naïve and trusting. At the heart of things for fallen man there is a great blackness which he cannot discount; he must learn to face the void with courage and love, but he can never come completely to terms with it. And specifically: if modern man is going to make a *mystique* of sex, going to see it as an agent of salvation, Hartley wants to warn that it could just as easily—given its strength, its potential for deadliness—be an agent of tremendous destruction.

The symbolic method Hartley has evolved seems perfect for the complex world into which he wants to introduce us: a world in which we see men slipping, over and over again, into some version of romanticism, of *hubris*, of the belief that we are immortal, unflawed, can control events, ourselves, our destinies. Each of Hartley's modern romances is a questioning, a probing— usually a tragic refutation—of this attitude, this hope. Yet, refuted, the tendency remains. And the form itself is a witness that we are meant to see more than 'what one sees', are meant to be always striving, imagining, believing—aware though we must be of the shadow of death over all our undertakings. In all these modern romances Hartley deflates the man of imagination, the humanist, the aesthete, the optimist, for their over-simplifications; he shows us the world's blackness. But he is asking that we learn to meet that blackness with imagination and hope, and that we rediscover, before it is too late, the true meaning of man's spiritual aspirations.

CHAPTER SIX

HINTS AND GUESSES, DIRECT AND CROOKED PATHS:

MY FELLOW DEVILS, A PERFECT WOMAN, THE HIRELING, POOR CLARE THE BRICKFIELD/THE BETRAYAL

> . . . But to apprehend
> The point of intersection of the timeless
> With time, is an occupation for the saint—
> No occupation either, but something given
> And taken, in a lifetime's death in love,
> Ardour and selflessness and self-surrender.
> For most of us, there is only the unattended
> Moment, the moment in and out of time,
> The distraction fit, lost in a shaft of sunlight,
> The wild thyme unseen, or the winter lightning . . .
> . . . . These are only hints and guesses,
> Hints followed by guesses . . .
>
> —T. S. Eliot[1]

[a]

BEGINNING with *My Fellow Devils* in 1951,[2] L. P. Hartley wrote a series of tragi-comic novels set, unlike most of his earlier works, in the present: the actual conditions of postwar England. These novels, from *My Fellow Devils* through *A Perfect Woman* (1955),[3] *The Hireling* (1957) and *The Brickfield/The Betrayal* (1964–66) to *Poor Clare* (1968)[4] mark a new stage in his experimentation with modern romance. In each of them Hartley denies himself the child's-eye-view or the slightly-removed 'theatre' of the past which have formerly served his purpose of artistic distancing, and takes on, for his metaphysical exploration, a set of adult characters involved in rather prosaic-seeming problems in a rather ordinary contemporary setting.

Yet Hartley's purpose is, as ever, to probe eternal, universal significances at the same time that he delineates quite recognizable social and psychological temporalities. If he has left behind the rich surfaces of the Edwardian age and the imaginative vision of a Eustace or a Leo, it is only to emphasize that the flatnesses of the present also have their hidden depths, that the great myths and archetypes of human nature operate now as then (even if at times fairly ludicrously), that Evil is still among us and redemption from its power still the main problem behind the other problems. In these novels he experiments with various ways of doing this— of combining the utterly down-to-earth contemporary with the symbolic suggestion of a world of transcendent meaning and power surrounding it—and comes up with variously successful but always interesting blends of novel, romance and mock-romance or satire. For the most part these books combine the painstaking portraiture Hartley sees as essential to the novel (*NR* p. 189) with much suggestion (usually satirical) of the mental or moral climate of the times—in a tight, geometrically-patterned design of relationships and events which points beyond itself to the movement of universal elements in the background of life.

These novels, with their more homely settings, do not have quite the romance 'atmosphere' of the earlier books, but their purpose is still double vision: their characters are, for all their contemporaneity, still psychological archetypes, aspects of one personality or representatives of ideas: modern witches, devils, sibyls and guardian spirits still come and go to perform their respective supernatural duties; words, games, objects, landscapes and works of art still act as 'hieroglyphs' (Hawthorne's word, noted by Melchiori)[5] of deeper meanings. But Hartley has undertaken a difficult task; sifted through an adult consciousness, his symbolism is much less all-pervading, much less a symbolic world, much more a question of isolated moments of vision. And in anti-romantic modern bourgeois surroundings vision and symbolism can often seem forced. In general, also, the more obviously Hartley's symbols seem especially created by him to fit a need, an idea, a specific purpose in a specific novel (and this seems to happen more in his contemporary settings, all more indoor, artificial, citified), the less these symbols are drawn from landscapes or long-standing architectural configurations, the less they suggest a mysterious background world of interrelationships. These more modern symbols can approach the status of signs or signals or Forster's 'banner' symbols; we do not feel they are part of the very nature of things, and therefore we are not so sure they tell us about the nature of things. Some of these novels, too, depend much more than their predecessors on omniscient-author asides or lengthy analyses of characters and their motives; it sometimes seems as if L. P. Hartley grew tired of having people miss the subtleties of his earlier novels and determined to say everything all too explicitly.

In general each of these books deals with a more or less involuntary, more or less successful spiritual search by a modern Everyman. Peter Bien quotes Hartley as saying, in an unpublished lecture, that the vacuum in which the isolated individual finds himself 'should be filled by God, but only in one of my books did I dare to suggest it was'. This one book, says Bien, was *My Fellow Devils*.[6] But in the books with which this chapter deals (and in almost all Hartley has written, I would suggest) one finds life hollowing out just such a vacuum in the soul of the protagonist—a vacuum which indeed seems to call for a God without letting us know whether or not one exists. Here all Hartley's longer works seem to lean upon Kafka, whose *The Castle* Hartley sees as 'a kind of Pilgrim's Progress, the search for God through appearance after appearance which deludes the seeker', and whose *The Trial*, according to Hartley, symbolizes 'the sense of guilt to which any Christian is liable until he is assured of absolution' (*FF* p. 87). In only one of the books with which we are dealing here does the searcher seem really 'to apprehend / The point of intersection of the timeless / With time . . .' but the 'Hints followed by guesses' of the other books, showing the spiritual search as it turns out 'For most of us', often come very close. These are myths of man's search for God (or God's for man) in homely modern settings; given their unromantic exterior surfaces, perhaps 'parables' would be a better name for them.

[b]

My Fellow Devils is one of three Hartley novels of the fifties which try to embody and to interpret, in satiric microcosm, the society (or non-society) which began to come into its own after the second world war. Here, in *A Perfect Woman* and in *The Hireling* the phrase 'postwar world' recurs over and over, with frequent allusions to shortages of gas or food or money, and with even more frequent reminders of the thinning-out of standards. A drab place, not filled, as were the worlds of *Eustace and Hilda*, *The Go-Between* and even *The Boat*, with the trappings and traditions and shapes and colours of a rich, if dying past, Hartley's novelistic postwar world is only a concretization of that of his essays, which claim that 'the individual has been devalued, like the pound' (*NR* p. 11); that 'There is certainly a deficiency of feeling nowadays' (*NR* p. 12); that 'Priggishness is now a deadly sin' and 'excellence is suspect' (*NR* p. 12); that by the 'new humanism' we are 'excused personal responsibility . . . at the cost of being denied Free Will' (*NR* p. 15).

Each of these three novels struggles to detail a particular aspect of the postwar scene: *My Fellow Devils* the 'new humanism', the cult of the criminal, the 'prevailing sin of our day . . . dishonesty' (*NR* p. 74); *A Perfect Woman*, suburban marriage and bourgeois respectability; *The Hireling* the changing class structure. All three deal also with the question of art and the position and problem of the artist.

Each undertaking the close, even exhaustive, study of one post-war character undergoing a crucial postwar experience, the novels nevertheless submit characterization to overall design—they are reminiscent of Hartley's own description of the later Henry James:

... in his later work, his characters only exist in virtue of their relationship to each other, and to their general predicament, which the conclusion of

116

the novel is to solve . . . the tormented quartet in *The Golden Bowl* are almost like unknown factors in a quadratic equation or lines in a parallelogram of forces, so interdependent are they (*NR* p. 180).

These Hartley books could, in fact, be thought of as three slightly fantastic parables—*The Magistrate and the Movie Star . . . The Suburbanite and the Bohemian . . . The Chauffeur and the Lady*—little constructs borrowing from the manner of Kafka: often rather simple and homely, utilizing enough contemporary detail to be recognizable, but given enough mythical or archetypal content to suggest an indefinite number of universal relationships and meanings.

My Fellow Devils is the parable of the Magistrate and the Movie Star, with Margaret Pennefather as the neo-humanist do-gooder who marries and tries to reform a ne-er-do-well film actor. When Colum McInnes turns out to be all too like the charming thieves he plays on screen, Margaret, a social worker and justice of the peace (from Fair Haven, in Dittingham), finds her own strictly regulated private life brought into conflict with her publicly professed compassion for crime and criminals—and herself an accessory to her husband's dishonesty.

Father McBane, a Catholic priest, appears, to exemplify for her a new, disturbing, much more exacting definition of compassion—one which refused to compromise truth and personal integrity. Through his agency Margaret leaves Colum to settle down at Fair Haven with their child. But 'It was not true that she was returning to her old life; she was entering upon a new one, about which she knew nothing' (*MFD* p. 413). Her choice involves becoming a Catholic, accepting a transcendental standard of truth and morality—the only way in which she seems to be able to reconcile love and justice:

'I want the liberty to love, without having to ask myself whether what I love is a good thing. I want my love to be centred in something—someone —that I know is true, something that I can trust. Where shall I find it, except in the Church?' (*MFD* p. 406).

The basic geometric figure of *My Fellow Devils* gives us Margaret and three men, in shifting relationships. These three, representing three possible attitudes to life, are also three aspects of Margaret's character and three stages in her growth. There is Nick, the discarded fiancé, whose rigidity and legalism seem to reflect the originally rather rigid Margaret—who lives according to law and custom without recognizing any transcendent basis for doing so, and whose inadequate morality dissolves (just as does Nick's regard for the law) under the influence of Colum's charm. There is Colum, who is, as Father McBane tells Margaret, 'the worser self of anyone who is with him, for he has no self of his own' (*MFD* p. 249). Certainly the worser self, the shadow side, of Margaret, he brings out the dishonesty latent in her ambiguous moral standard; as a 'bad Catholic' (*MFD* pp. 84, 94), he seems to be Hartley's embodiment of 'faith without morals'—the chief modern heresy:

> Nearly all our present troubles are owing to it; it is the state of mind that produced the Nazi regime and the Communist regime and it is the most dangerous state of mind a human being can get into (*NR* p. 15).

Father McBane, of course, stands for the absolute integrity which is Margaret's best self, and which her encounters with Colum (in paradoxical, *felix culpa* fashion) help, by contrast, to develop. The 'sense of loss' she encounters in the gangster-image of Colum McInnes (*MFD* p. 40) sends her seeking first Father McBane, then her own integrity, eventually a faith in God and a standard of morality 'lost' to her generation. Father McBane tells her unequivocally that her search itself has been an answer to prayer. 'Life doesn't let us alone, and God doesn't either . . .', he says. 'And do not think the seeking is all on your part. You are being sought for, too' (*MFD* p. 249). The Margaret-Colum marriage lasts exactly nine months (*MFD* p. 360): out of it something new has been born for Margaret and, we suspect, also for Colum. The Renaissance child's head which Colum steals, and then deliberately breaks, helps to link the story to the theme of Fall and Redemption, death and rebirth.

Margaret Pennefather's dilemma and solution are, perhaps, more apt to outrage us than amuse or delight us—so thoroughly do we as modern liberals detest the proposal of absolutes in any form, so convinced are we with Nick (at his moment of weakening) that 'we must all bow to life, of which high principles are only one part' (*MFD* p. 372). Since 1951 even theology, even the Catholic Church itself has shown signs of adopting a new, more relativist ethics. One cannot say that Hartley exaggerates in seeing all the guests at the book's climactic banquet toasting the Devil—if this is toasting the Devil. Most of us *would* see Margaret McInnes as a prig, and find prigs unattractive; most of us would be shocked at Father McBane's uncompromising abhorrence of 'sin' (*MFD* p. 245). Precisely. This *is* the temper of the time, the temper which Hartley is so broadly satirizing and so sharply probing.

In *My Fellow Devils* he is trying to force us to face the fact that there is another pole, that there is a problem which we cannot quite dismiss. If there are no transcendentals, no absolutes, if morality is an outgrowth of time and experience, if truth is not terribly important, if honesty and integrity must bow to 'love', and if we have no clear standard even for what love should be, could we not all, sooner or later, find ourselves in some such position as Margaret McInnes's symbolizes? In the last analysis she cannot know when to believe what her husband says; she cannot really even find him, cannot know who or what he is, under the too-easily-alternated masks which serve him for life's shifting situations. Dishonesty, which Hartley, as shown above, sees as the chief sin of the day, does, he wants us to understand, undermine the contractual basis of society and of all human relationships.

Hartley carries the problem, which evidently fascinates him, to its extreme on either side: he is not trying to be 'realistic' when he sets Margaret between a gangster-film-actor husband and the Catholic Church. He is playing, laughing a little at them and at us and himself, but nevertheless pointing out that there is a question. The question, like that posed by Molière's Misanthrope, seems insoluble: one must choose between absolute honesty and life in society (in which absolute honesty is impossible). Margaret's settling squarely for the Absolute is one solution to such a dilemma, Hartley suggests—but he also makes it clear that it doesn't quite take care of everything. She can only make the choice she does by abstracting Colum into a symbol of evil ('She must not let herself think of Colum as a person. As long as she thought of him as an evil influence her way was clear' [*MFD* p. 403]), and we are left with the feeling that she may have to reconsider this in the future—especially since Colum has, it seems, become a better person (*MFD* p. 410). Hartley wants to show us that there has been a wholehearted and uncompromising acceptance on Margaret's part of a new standard for life, a new basis for and understanding of love, a complete spiritual change underlying what looks like the same material structure. But he does seem to suggest that when Margaret is strong enough or settled enough in her new convictions she will have to put them to the test. The end of this story leaves us with one half of a marriage which seems to call for the other half: it seems that Hartley is saying, finally, that the Absolute and human life are two poles, like male and female (with which he often identifies them, in this and other novels), and that our supremely difficult, perhaps impossible, task is to try to choose both.

The incidental symbolism of *My Fellow Devils* depends heavily upon works of art which, apart from the revelatory roles which they play in the story, seem to suggest a Hartley warning about art itself. Besides the Renaissance head which reveals Colum's destructiveness to Margaret there is the 'art' of the film (and we sense Hartley would only speak of it as such here within quotation marks), allied with that of the Press. Films and press together seem to be doing the major portion of the work of creating the modern cult of the Devil which Hartley is satirizing, and alongside the Margaret-Colum story we are treated to the plots of a number of egregiously sentimental Colum McInnes films—*The Secret Thief, The Devil is so Distinguished*—which help tip us off to the inner meaning of events, and which show us how much modern life is imitating art (or 'art'). The theme of the mask, also, runs through the book, allied to Colum's lack of integrity, of self, and culminating in the sinister masked party from which Margaret flees and from which Colum also finally breaks away.

Colum is, in his own words, 'only . . . a film-actor with no meaning of my own' (*MFD* p. 83). And his concept of art is that 'the artist gives himself entirely to something that, for the ordinary purposes of life—just isn't there, and has to be created out of nothing . . .' (*MFD* p. 116). Margaret sees that 'that's the reality to him, and the rest is a kind of make-believe, to be got through somehow—as Art is to me, I expect. I regard Art very highly, of course, but not as one of the most important things in life . . .' (*MFD* p. 117). By stressing this, along with the illusory, the miraculous in Colum's approach to film, Hartley seems to be questioning modern aesthetic theory in making art so independent of reality and of morality, as well as condemning the *use* of modern arts such as the film, which flatter and sentimentalize and feel no obligation to maintain truth or a moral stance.

And how well does *My Fellow Devils* itself answer the problem —what kind of relationship does it achieve between aesthetic creation and moral concern? Peter Bien sees the striving towards this union as the basic impulse behind all Hartley's work;[7] in *My Fellow Devils* he deplores the dispensing with 'symbolic under-layers', and feels that it, 'though admirable as a tract, fails as a work of art'.[8] And a *TLS* reviewer called Margaret McInnes 'one of the dullest heroines in modern fiction', complains of the unconvincing nature of the plot, and concludes that 'if *My Fellow Devils* fails to carry conviction upon the plane of realism (as it does), then it must fail also as a parable'.[9]

Establishing standards for criticism is difficult, because Hartley is here again experimenting with a new version of an old genre— a kind of combination of a romance, in the Hawthornian sense, with a novel of character and a satire of contemporary life. He tries to show us the Devil walking around in evening clothes as a popular film star who is also a thief, and who marries a good, rather priggish lady judge. Some imbalance between the realistic and symbolic elements does seem to be the problem—Hartley's own feelings about modern times seem to prevent him from giving the Devil his due, giving the dilemma enough real depth and complexity. The book tends to rely too much on analysis and exposition; it becomes too long, too heavy, too didactic, and its form, its design—which ought to carry the meaning—become lumpy and obscured.

And as suggested before, Hartley's symbols in this contemporary novel often seem forced. Earlier he sought for his symbol in natural surroundings, in the architecture and art which naturally express an entire culture, in the quirks of personality and dress which can express a class or occupational type, especially in a particular historical period. In the more modern books, where he does not have quite the same rich cultural and social fabric from which to draw, he tends to create symbols to fit ideas rather than to choose pre-existing objects which are suggestive, many-sided. The Renaissance child's head is an example—it seems a little too pat, too artificial, too tailor-made to symbolize innocence, Margaret's expected child, and all the other complexities demanded of it.

In searching for symbols of absolute truth and of the 'distinguished devil', the casual immorality of modern times, it seems again too pat of Hartley to make his mighty opposites the Catholic Church and a tough-guy film actor. He tries to make Margaret's a strictly personal and concrete choice, meant to point to God and an absolute order more than to the Church as institution. But unfortunate overtones are inescapable in symbols drawn so directly from the present moment: when Hartley makes his heroine choose between the Catholic Church and a gangster-movie actor he is, whether he wants to or not, setting up a choice between what most moderns would see as the intransigence of traditional institutional religion and what most moderns would not agree to see as the cheapness and amorality of modern culture. He is loading the dice; he is oversimplifying enormous complexities; he is presenting us with a false dilemma—and even if he does it with tongue slightly in cheek, we resent it. *My Fellow Devils* marks an interesting initial try in Hartley's search into modes of contemporary romance, but not a completely satisfactory one.

A Perfect Woman is more successful. In a 1957 article in *Die Neueren Sprachen*, August Closs sees it as Hartley's finest work of art after *The Go-Between*:[10] a judgement with which I do not completely agree, though the Jamesian 'quadratic equation' of this novel is far more clear-cut—at the same time more believable and more non-realistic, more symbolic—than the figure of *My Fellow Devils*.

A Perfect Woman is the story of Isabel, the over-idealistic housewife who tries to play Muse to an erratic artist—her fall from suburban stagnation, her rise to a new life; secondarily it is the story of Alec, artist and catalyst. And where *My Fellow Devils* was the story of a separation, of the way of the saints, *A Perfect Woman* is the story of a marriage, or reconciliation, of the longer, slower way to salvation that serves 'For most of us'.

The quadrangle in *A Perfect Woman* is a metaphor for the economy of selfhood and salvation in four different lives, for the relationship of art to life and life to art, and for the operation of some kind of paradoxical destiny or Providence or meaning in existence itself. Harold the conventional businessman and Isabel the suppressed idealist have found reasonable contentment in their conventional suburban marriage and their two children. Then Harold meets Alec Goodrich, the novelist, helps him on a business basis, and introduces him into the family circle. Isabel, who has sometimes 'had to stifle a longing to be more to someone than she (or perhaps anybody) could ever be' (*APW* p. 15) casts herself in the role of the Muse who, through her love, will enable Alec to write, finally, a book about a good woman—but not before Harold, also through Alec's agency, has become involved with a loving, yielding Austrian barmaid called Irma, who makes him feel strong and masculine and protective again.

Alec lives in a wild, half-pagan setting in Wales and has long been in the power of his witchlike mistress Elspeth Elworthy (seemingly the *liaison dangereuse* with his subconscious which he claims is essential for an artist). It is Elspeth, jealous at being replaced, who goes to an infernal sort of fair at Blastwick, finds a ready instrument in huge and jealous Otto Killian, and gets him to fulfil the promise of his name by murdering Alec and Irma.

The finished equation leaves us Harold and Isabel, at Marshport:

. . . there was another thing, much more important. The episode had brought her very close to Harold: theirs was now a real relationship of heart and mind. They had no secrets from each other. She did not always want to confide in him or he in her, but when they wanted to, they could. Each was conscious of the other as a person in his or her own right, a person who for a short time had meant to someone else as much as any human being can do—a sovereign with one adoring subject—no, that wasn't true, for Harold had meant more to Irma than she, apparently, had ever meant to Alec. Still it was nearly the same thing. Each brought to their relationship, and pooled, this gift of personal sovereignty which neither had possessed before, or recognized in the other (*APW* pp. 327–8).

As for Alec, he has died in giving birth to his 'best book, the book that Isabel had always wanted him to write' (*APW* p. 299); there is in the book, the posthumous reviews say, a 'Sense of having come to terms with life' (*APW* p. 331). Anyone familiar with the Hartley myth would know that no one, and particularly no artist, could live on in that abnormal condition. The perfection, the perfect reconciliation that all Hartley heroes seek, is found only at the moment of (or the moment after?) death: what is possible in life is a kind of delicate, precarious balance of opposites such as Isabel and Harold finally achieve in their marriage. And that balance is an uneasy one: *A Perfect Woman* ends with Isabel concealing some rather disgraceful thoughts from Harold—a certain exultation over the role she has played in Alec's book. She and Harold and the children—it is 'a pious quartet' now—set off for church, 'with stiffened Sunday faces', but they are aware now that Elspeth is still roaming about, like the devil, seeking whom she may devour. They both remember to shut the door—a precaution their more unsuspecting, over-innocent earlier selves always forgot (*APW* p. 333).

The Jungian or monomythic (or Christian) shape of the metaphor is quite plain in *A Perfect Woman*. Everyone who counts goes through a necessary fall and rebirth (a meeting with the *anima*, the *animus*, the shadow, and an integration of the Self). For each of these widely-differing personalities it is exactly the right moment, and the operative law is that the needs of one serve as the agent of salvation for the other. This intricate quadratic equation is one of Hartley's hints about the nature of existence, the way things happen, universally—its ultimately mysterious inter-relationships correspond to that unplumbable sea which surrounds Marshport, the sea on which ships plunge and labour so that 'One did not connect them with their future in some far-off port; only with their immediate present, their hand-to-hand encounter with the grey, monotonous sea' (*APW* p. 159).

Hartley shows us two sides, two myths of Woman or the feminine in the book—the yielding, loving Irma, the witchlike *femme fatale* Elspeth; the domesticated Isabel has to recognize both potentialities, angelic and demonic, in herself. And we see in Alec the problem of the artist, beset by his daemon and introducing the daemonic into the lives of others; through the favourite Hartley symbol of money—of blackmail, investment and bequest —we also see in Alec the artist as outsider, taker, exploiter, non-lover, who learns, ultimately, to give (he leaves the profits from his book to Isabel's children).

As always, there are figures, scenes within the story which echo its overall form: the ludo game, played by two German men and two English girls ('the peaceful meeting of once enemy nations' [*APW* p. 303]) which languishes in the presence of Elspeth, the book's witch; the ladder game played by Janice and Jeremy, Isabel's children, with its continual warning refrain of ' "Janice, go back!" ' (*APW* p. 232); the plots of Alec's novels—notably *After the Storm*, with its crisis and tragi-comic resolution (*APW* p. 12) and *The Italian Maid*, with its discovery by a 'roving sensualist' that 'in woman, or in some women, could be found a quality of intelligent self-sacrifice which nourishes life, as opposed to the sheer will of the male, which devastates it' (*APW* p. 308). Pre-eminently there is the changing landscape and seascape of suburban Marshport. The sea impinging on the town yields a storm and then a calm in Isabel's life, and after it she sees Marshport itself anew. It is 'snug . . . with the great church tower standing sentinel':

Yes, and more than snug—it was romantic, picturesque, unique, with its enfolded contrasts of civilian and soldier, hill and plain, slow waveless canal and, outside, the hungry, howling sea. How could she have ever thought it tame and townish when so much history clung to it, when round the corner, only just out of sight, was the castle from which the four knights rode away? (*APW* p. 316).

A Perfect Woman's landscape and sea and storm is a rich one, mysteriously and suggestively used (as Closs has pointed out),[11] giving visible form to life's conflicting elements and at last attempting to show us, like Isabel, that life at its best consists of 'enfolded contrasts' (*APW* p. 316). Not all the symbols of this book are so successful: to highlight the presence of good and evil among these rather dull participants in typical suburban family life, Hartley has had to exaggerate and simplify, to contrive some rather artificial types and situations and signals which, without the softening influence of a setting in the past, do reveal a little more of the paint and paste-board Hawthorne feared could show through in a Romance when 'an atmosphere of strange enchantment' was lacking.[12] As a *TLS* reviewer has noted,[13] even Hartley's children here are rather artificial, uncharming creations, their games and questions too obviously rigged to parallel the grownups' problems.

Despite these faults, *A Perfect Woman* has much to recommend it as a reflection upon the meaning of modern middle-class existence. As an experiment, the book achieves a better balance between design and realistic portraiture than *My Fellow Devils*— but it is perhaps in *The Hireling* that Hartley brings this genre and this balance to a sort of perfection. For one thing, *The Hireling* is shorter, a kind of miniature, with far less exposition and explanation, and its size and scope seems more appropriate to the kind of macrocosm-in-the-microcosm aim Hartley seems to have. One also suspects Hartley of being more at home with a male protagonist: as a *TLS* reviewer says, his 'characterization of the proud, lonely, half-articulate Leadbitter is almost wholly convincing'.[14]

The Hireling is only secondarily a quadratic equation: the basic figure here is an exchange, perhaps a symbolic marriage, between the archetypally male Steven Leadbitter, ex-soldier, realist, driver (in every sense of the word), and the archetypal woman (or one archetype of woman), the gentle, unawakened, idealistic Lady Franklin. Other-worldly, aspiring, unbounded by time, she has something in her of the cathedrals she visits, and, in her blue and white (*H* p. 237), of the Virgin of those cathedrals about whose cult she discourses to her hired-car driver (*H* pp. 103–4). He—the postwar man, basically a cynic—embodies the world of matter-of-fact experience, the world bounded by time.

To bring herself more in touch with reality, Lady Franklin tries to interest herself in the daily life and troubles of her driver; to respond to her interest, Leadbitter invents a non-existent wife and family and tells her involved little tales about their crises and joys. She gives him money—symbol of immense transformations beginning to take place in them both. His misguided attempt to respond by making love to her does, though gently rejected, signal his loss of 'the self that he was used to, the hard impersonal life that war and Army life had polished into a shell' (*H* p. 131) and also her awakening to a new awareness of the possibilities of life and love. In the end Leadbitter, the erstwhile cynic and non-involved man, saves her from a disastrous marriage but crashes in his car, killing her fiance—a sell-out artist—and himself. The St. Christopher medal he has sent her is left to reveal to Lady Franklin that he loved her, and to jolt her from the withdrawal and non-life into which she is about to relapse. He 'had awakened her once', she sees, 'though into other arms than his, and had he not awakened her again?' (*H* p. 248).

The cathedral image is crucial in this novel. It represents Hartley's idea of love and human relationships and Providence: in Winchester Cathedral Lady Franklin shows Leadbitter how:

'These arches and pillars aren't made to a pattern like those others in the nave—those are Perpendicular, as I expect you know, and too cold and uniform for my taste. But these don't repeat themselves, or not exactly. There's a kind of living relationship between them, if you see what I mean, as there is between human beings, not just structurally, but spiritually as well, the likeness and the unlikeness, which somehow draws us to each other—the contrast you sometimes see between ill-matched couples which helps to make them one' (*H* p. 98).

The cathedral image serves also to point up contrasting views of the relationship between art and life—a subject which continually fascinates Hartley. 'Most art is the work of individuals, and often of individuals at odds with their lot', Lady Franklin tells Steven: '. . . the fruit of loneliness and separation. The cathedrals were a collective effort, a family affair—the result of an epidemic, not a personal, non-infectious illness' (*H* p. 105). Hartley seems to be probing here into the isolation of modern artists whom, in Alec Goodrich and even Colum McInnes, he painted as empty, exploitative men with little capacity for love.

More simply and essentially than almost any of Hartley's works, *The Hireling* is a novel of the marriage of opposites: masculine and feminine, time and eternity, reality and imagination, earthiness and aspiration, life and art—even upper and lower classes. It is also one of his own best marriages of realism and symbolism and, therefore, of content and form—a book about unity and complexity which achieves a remarkable unity and complexity within its own 248 pages. Steven Leadbitter and Lady Franklin help to make each other whole; he is enabled to aspire and to sacrifice and to relinquish life; she is enabled to live it. At the end Steven's nature of clash and conflict has found a kind of rest; he sees a mission accomplished, an account almost closed, when he dispatches his medal to her (*H* pp. 206–7) and, by inference, accepts his own sacrificial death. But, lest we have doubted it, Hartley emphasizes that it is the nature of *life* to be unresolved, to be un-abstract, to be unpeaceful.

'What is there for me in Life,' Lady Franklin cries at one point, 'but to flounder forever in these cruel uncertainties, not even knowing what I want to believe? Far better not to think and not to feel . . .' (*H* p. 243). This is no solution, and neither we nor she are allowed to think so. Forced ' "out of my shelter into a world where every fact is painful to me" ' (*H* p. 246), she is given strength and reassurance for the conflict by the knowledge of Leadbitter's love. And he has done the one thing important in life, something he learned from her: loved, and told his love. ' "Is there anything in life that matters—really matters—except that somebody you love should know you love them?" ' (*H* p. 26).

[c]

Hartley's *Poor Clare* (1968) was greeted by Angus Wilson in a London *Observer* review as 'an unexpected and splendid display of his powers', a 'beautifully-plotted and well-told story' which 'should be read'.[15] It is a small (156 pages) book which belongs with the novels we have been considering because like them it touches a present-day social setting with 'absolute overtones' (Mr. Wilson's phrase).[16] The setting is no longer the fifties, no longer merely postwar or traditional: this climate of rather accepted amorality is, despite its rarefied atmosphere (Wilson identifies the setting as 'the very centre of Mr. Hartley's Bloomsbury universe')[17] recognizable as the feeling of our own late sixties. Mr. Wilson makes an unkind remark about Mr. Hartley's time sense becoming increasingly inexact after 1920, but in *Poor Clare* he seems somehow to have caught something of the moment in which we live—perhaps all the more so because (still in Wilson's phrases) he has pencilled in 'only the outline of a neutral and comfortable milieu', given 'the whole short novel a discreet Christian religious framework', and left much of the book's final judgements in reserve.[18] And that the setting is an artistic milieu and the chief characters professional artists, that the narrator is an artist who tells the story in the first person (the only one of Hartley's longer works, besides *The Go-Between*, to be told this way), that so much of the framework is explicitly Christian and set in the town of Assisi where Christianity has taken on visible form, that the novel is so brief and delicate, helps to create more nearly the sense of a shimmering symbolic world which we miss in the other adult novels.

At the centre of the novel is another quadratic equation. There is Gilbert, the artist (musician) to whom reality speaks in terms of discords and conflict and Edward, the lesser artist (painter) who imposes his inner vision—of harmony, within a limited scope— on reality; there is Myra, Gilbert's inspirer, and Barbara, Gilbert's interpreter. The story seems to be about giving and receiving, about the economy of human (and, one would suspect, Divine) relationships and the growth to Selfhood. One would also suspect, especially from the title, that Hartley wishes to emphasize the importance of poverty in this paradoxical economy and growth: poverty of all kinds—the 'vacuum'.

At the outset Gilbert seems to be one of those maladjusted and lonely artists whose ability to create comes from his quarrel with the world. He (something like Alec) is a taker—for his art's sake —and the other three are content, to some extent, to serve his life and art with theirs. But a mysterious bequest from Gilbert's austere but benevolent Aunt Clare has suddenly intervened to change this long-standing arrangement, and set Gilbert to giving her gifts away, in his turn.

No one is too clear about what is happening to Gilbert, probably least of all the (probably unreliable) narrator, Edward. But it seems that Gilbert is somehow being pressured by the spirit and love of Aunt Clare to seek *life* rather than art ('one's art is of one's life a thing apart, dear Edward', he writes [*PC* p. 10]): to choose 'Perfection of the life', in Yeats's terms, over that of 'the work'.[19] His hesitation over giving Myra a gift seems to stem from his growing understanding that having hinders being, that, in the spirit of *Saint* Clare, 'to do people good, you must exact the utmost sacrifices from them' (*PC* p. 36). And well he might think that, since his gift to Edward sets off a greedy reaction in which Edward takes Myra away from Gilbert by misrepresentation and settles down to use her for his own gratification and for the success of his own attempts at art.

Thus Edward aids in the partly voluntary, partly involuntary denudation of Gilbert, who had really loved Myra and wanted to give her not simply a gift but his love, himself. The total vacuum which it is life's work to create has once more been accomplished, in Gilbert, and the novel ends with his mysterious death. But we understand that the chain reaction will go on: a new cycle is commencing. Gilbert's gift to Edward has jolted him out of his niche, the tiny room he had contented himself with painting, and the restricted harmony he was able to see there. In the sunshine and shadow of Italy he has found far greater challenges and become a better artist; he has risked love for Myra and known a measure of fulfilment and happiness, the possession of life's 'gifts'. 'It was the first time in my life', he says, 'that I felt the totality of this or any relationship' (*PC* p. 107). Those gifts of life have made him more of a Self; now perhaps the denudation process can begin in him. His betrayal of Gilbert has been exposed to himself and to others, and his love affair with Myra has broken up. The book ends with his spending a day at Assisi, at the Church of St. Clare, 'meditating on her death and Gilbert's, and trying to reconcile myself to mine' (*PC* p. 156).

What would lead us to a Christian or para-Christian interpretation of the story, apart from our knowledge of other of Hartley's works, is the emphasis on specifically Christian symbols. Aunt Clare, the rich woman who gave everything away (Ditch-worth is her other name) before her death and lived on, 'wraithlike', in her home with its 'under-water' feeling (*PC* p. 53), is many times identified with Clare, the saint who epitomized poverty. Key symbols of the book are the churches and towers and streets of Assisi: the Church of St. Francis, for example, with its bright, sunlit, *glad* Upper Church and its shadowed Lower Church, where one finds the portrait of St. Clare in its 'withdrawn' austerity and that of the 'rough vigorous little figure' of St. Francis (*PC* pp. 70–1). Or the crypt of St. Clare: led there by 'an intentionally crooked path' (*PC* p. 111), Edward feels 'nearer to the presence of death, nearer to the fact of death, than I had ever done' (*PC* p. 115).

It is this closeness to death which explains St. Francis and St. Clare and the 'direct route' which, in ages past, they so 'certainly knew'—this *sense* of death and shadow which seems to underlie the sunshine and flowers, the 'general joyousness', the 'lasting alliance with and confidence in life' which still marks Assisi (*PC* p. 111). And it is this understanding of the dark side of life which insures that 'there is, and perhaps always has been, a Merrie Italy', whether or not Merrie England ever existed (*PC* p. 83). Gilbert Finstock—symbol of a dying line, a dying England—sees quite clearly that 'The architecture of humanism has broken down—it's quite flat. All we have left are the pieces' (*PC* p. 39). Gilbert is led, by mysterious ways—by gifts and then by deprivations—to rediscover, if not an old faith, then the old realities which underlay that faith: that in what looks forbidding, exacting, severe and death-like can in reality be found the greatest love and benevolence (*PC* pp. 36–7; 73), and perhaps the greatest joy. One should dread the Greeks—or anyone—bearing gifts, as the epigraph warns: what happens at their coming is 'a myth as old as humanity' (*PC* p. 23). Life's gifts are instruments for invasion, subversion, which lead us to Selfhood, but then teach us to give away Self, or rather to extend Self by giving (*PC* p. 11). It all, as Gilbert writes at one point, 'seems to make a synthesis of something, but Heaven knows what!' (*PC* p. 11).

In *Poor Clare* we can discern Hartley's vision of our century as it now stands—a time in human history in which he saw, in the Matthew Arnold phrase he liked, increasingly, to quote, 'nothing to rejoice or comfort us'. *Poor Clare*'s is a bleak picture—of men without roots or real social milieux, caught in petty, random, self-serving relationships which they are only too easily capable of betraying. Men of no past and no particular thought about the future, they have few contacts with the life of the spirit. Real love, though rare, is one such contact; another seems to be the art and architecture of a still partly-living Christian culture. Hartley's 1968 men seem sad and lonely and unwilling searchers, all too ready to betray and deny in a world where nothing seems to transcend the present moment, the transient experience. Yet Hartley shows even these uncaring searchers finding, or beginning to find, in spite of themselves. This is still the terrible world of the shrimp and anemone, though devoid of much of its colour and life; great and terrible forces still strip and crush man and ask, in the end, his life—but Hartley still suggests that there is meaning, that the meaning transcends death, and that man goes on finding that meaning.

On the whole, *Poor Clare* is a disappointing book, the more so because, in giving us a thin, contrived, near-allegorical version, almost a parody, of his characteristic symbolic form, Hartley almost makes us question the beauty and richness and delicacy of his earlier achievements. Most of Hartley's more recent books have been disappointing: *The Love-Adept* (1969),[20] *My Sister's Keeper* (1970),[21] *The Harness Room* (1971),[22] *The Collections* (1972),[23] *The Will and the Way* (1973),[24] and *Mrs. Carteret Receives And Other Stories* (1971).[25] Hartley himself would probably concur in this judgement; in a 1970 interview he described his latest books as a different *kind* of work from that he had previously done: 'lighter', with no particular 'message', and written mainly because for him writing was almost to be equated with living.[26] And in a letter dated 25th November 1972 he wrote, ' "The Collections" is a light-weight novel, and I don't think would affect your opinion of my work either for good or bad.'[27] Less and less symbolic (though on occasion allegorical), more and more confined to a rarefied social milieu, these books seem valuable mainly as insights into Hartley's personal world and preoccupations. Freudian critics in particular will find much material for speculation in the more daring topics, including homosexuality, which Hartley touched on in his last years. But in this study I have felt justified in regarding these books as unrelated to what I see as the main thrust of Hartley's literary art.

[d]

The 'betrayal' of Hartley's most ambitious work of the sixties, the two-part *The Brickfield* / *The Betrayal*, is a multiple one. There is author Richard Mardick's half-imagined betrayal, in his teens, of the young girl Lucy who loved him and died, perhaps through his fault, in the Brickfield where they used to meet. There is the betrayal by Richard's secretary, Denys Aspin, of that guilty secret which has marred Richard's life and which Richard has revealed to him, in strictest confidence, in a state of increasing age and ill health. Denys cheats the all-too-trusting Richard, he blackmails him, he breaks up his miraculously-found love relationship with Lucilla Distington, and finally he has the egregious taste to throw himself, mortally and painfully ill, upon the responsibility of the also-ailing Richard.

But there is a further betrayal, underlying all the others, which seems to be the real key to this story. Hartley's epigraph is from Sir Thomas Browne: '. . . it is in the power of every hand to destroy us, and we are beholding unto every one we meet, he doth not kill us' (*BET* p. [vi]). Hartley's concern—linked to his familiar motifs of money, obligations, investments, blackmail, gifts—seems to be with the death man owes God: that basic betrayal, original sin, which has left man in a state of debt, with that proneness to evil which is for Hartley at the heart of human nature and human life.

Richard Mardick, like many Hartley heroes, has allowed guilt over his early escapade to ruin his life and separate him from people. This sense of guilt is actually due, however, to his unwillingness to face up to the common burden of sin and evil in human nature; he is weighed down with a *false* sense of debt which makes him insist on being always the giver, the pleaser, always the one who pays and overpays for what he receives, always the fearful parrier of offers of unconditional love from anyone else. When the two-part novel begins he is a sixty-seven-year-old author who lives in a 'snug, cosy flat' (*BET* p. 49), who in his novels has 'invented rather than observed' nuances of human behaviour (*BET* p. 81), and who tries amid the buffets of the uncongenial Welfare State world, to 'keep out some of the winds of change' (*BET* p. 79). His revelation of the past to Denys sets off a series of fantastic calamities and betrayals which shake his false snugness and force him back into life. Tested to the ultimate point by Denys the Betrayer, who suddenly drops himself upon Richard's doorstep, mangled beyond recognition, dying, needing care which is both expensive and exceedingly personal and distasteful, Richard finds himself, through many circumstances, brought into the strange position of pleading to be allowed the privilege of performing an ignominious service for his worst enemy. And it is at that moment that he dies. . . .

Hartley never tells us whether the vacuum so carefully created in Richard's life is filled. He shows us only what he has shown us in other novels: that each man's life does seem to add up to a vacuum, that life seems to conspire to create one. Significant in Richard's transformation is someone whom we might have expected to turn up: a loving, unconventionally Christian older woman, his Aunt Carrie. Aunt Carrie has always stood for *love* to Richard, since his childhood days, and has something of the supernatural about her (she married a 'James Eldridge' from 'the West Country' whom she met 'in a wood' [*BR* pp. 138–41]). It is she who argues with the rebellious Richard that Denys, whom he sees as 'the albatross . . . the evil principle that had tracked him down the years, and had at last caught up with him' (*BET* pp. 292–3) is not the cause of his own villainy—that suffering, persecution even, are marks of God's favour—an invitation, perhaps, to help even out the balance:

> . . . Because such experiences are not under our control, they are what God means for us—they are His arrows and we are His target, they are messengers from Him, and whatever hits the bullseye, and gives the greatest pain, is the surest proof that we are chosen by Him . . . for whom the Lord loveth he chasteneth. . . . (*BET* p. 309).

We are left to agree or disagree with Aunt Carrie as to the ultimate meaning of this man's, and every man's life.

Chief symbols in this work are the abandoned Brickfield, scene of Richard's teen-age Fall, and the thriving Brickworks, basis of his financial security. The Brickfield is explicitly identified with the Garden of Eden and sometimes called 'the Spoilt Acres' (*BR* p. 140); the clay of the Brickfield is a symbol of failure to Richard as the clay of the Brickworks is a symbol of success. It is only as a result of his many sufferings that he begins to see these sharply antithetical symbols coming together. 'Perhaps everything tended to coalesce as one grew older . . .' (*BET* p. 223). When Richard, returning to his childhood surroundings, finds that the ugly *M* buttress has been removed from Rookland Abbey to reveal a glorious traceries window beneath (*BET* p. 266), and that the barren Brickfield has been turned into 'twelve acres of the best land we have' (*BET* p. 271), he asks himself 'Did it mean that evil had vanished from the world?' It seems, rather, to mean what his dawning identification of Brickfield and Brickworks means—that humanity, weakness, suffering, mortality, perhaps even evil itself can be blessings, if we face them. That which strips, defrauds us, kills us, may be bringing life. The Brickfield, emblem of Richard's Fall, has been sown 'with rich golden grain that was ripening under his eyes, as he was ripening too, he felt, for a spiritual harvest he had never hoped to yield' (*BET* p. 274).

Under its metaphysical overtones Hartley's book is also a satire on very contemporary England: the Welfare State in which the mediocrity of the postwar years came to full bloom. One reviewer of *The Betrayal* deplores

> those middle chapters where he over-develops some light relief seasoned with hits at welfare state ethics, half-witted psychology in the law courts and the anti-hero cult. Here, as in his best earlier work—the *Eustace and Hilda* trilogy and *The Go-Between*—his major creative preoccupation is itself an indictment of such aberrations.[28]

There is validity to this objection, but at least one such satirical section, detailing the depredations of Richard's fiendish 'daily women' and man-servants, reads something like a Waugh–Dickens collaboration. There is the redoubtable Mrs. Stonegappe, always at tooth-and-nail with Nurse (Sister) Tranter—who, in turn, wouldn't dream of staying a moment longer if Richard were *dying* at closing time, 'because that would be to let down the side' (*BET* p. 145). There are Kinklecross, Ladbroke Grove and John Chinnery. Kinklecross is 'an old public schoolboy' (*BET* p. 127) who steals Richard's car and smashes it into someone else's; Ladbroke Grove is an ex-actor who arrives with fifteen suits (one for each occasion of his day) in two white suitcases, and who, by giving wild midnight parties in Mardick's living room, brings down the ire of Richard's fellow-tenants; John Chinnery is an 'outsize' man with a moustache who has been a big-game hunter and who, instead of suits, brings skins. The agents of the flat complain when it appears that he is selling the skins on the premises; the police arrive to arrest him for receiving stolen goods. And a policeman also arrives to chide Richard for his over-kindness to his employees in the matter of paying for insurance stamps. ' "... By your thoughtless, though excusable generosity, you undermine their sense of civic responsibility." "I didn't know they had any," ' says Richard (*BET* p. 155).

Through all this Richard does much thinking (and letter-writing), especially about the modern belief that 'the conceptions of right and wrong are based on human behaviour' rather than on 'abstractions invented by a divine law-giver, unrelated to human needs and impulses' (*BET* p. 159). Richard's observations and questions sound all too much like Hartley's own in, for example, essays in *The Novelist's Responsibility*. But then we realize that Hartley is also satirizing, questioning *Richard* and his mistrust of the modern—as usual making his book not a tract for setting forth his own received opinions, but for testing those opinions, for raising what are real questions in his own mind. And it is significant that Hartley has Richard, in his almost-completely-reformed state, go back to his idealized home of the past, 'divided in his mind between desiring change and dreading it' (*BET* p. 266), and find that much *has* been changed, and decide that it is good. He is glad that there are telephones and that the outdoor privies have gone while the flower gardens remain:

> What had been changed was for the better, and what was unchanged was for the better, too. . . .
> . . . In every room there was something new and something old—something changed and something unchanged—in either case, making for reassurance (*BET* p. 274).

While it is likely that this change and stability refer to the person of Richard himself, and to his comprehension of the human condition, it is also, I think, rather clear that Hartley does not want modern man to live in the past or to refuse change. He is a writer who has seemingly exploited every stage of his own life for its artistic fruits; here he explores the implications of age and impending death and seems, like Eliot, to feel that 'Old men ought to be explorers'. As always Hartley is urging that men must go on growing, changing, all their lives—must undergo many small deaths and transformations before the final death which, hopefully, might mean a final rebirth. There is pain in childhood, in youth, in middle age, in old age—this is Hartley's verdict on life. But then we must learn to look twice at pain and ask what it means.

This pair of novels is especially reminiscent of *Eustace and Hilda* and *The Go-Between*. Here Hartley (true to his own urging that men go on changing, experimenting all their lives) seems to make still another try at combining realism and symbolism in an examination of contemporary life. In *The Brickfield | The Betrayal* he combines what he has learned from creating his 'adult novels' of the fifties with the 'atmosphere of strange enchantment' in the world of childhood and the past. He uses the frame-story pattern of *The Go-Between*, but this time expands the frame—the present-day section—to more truly contain the childhood idyll that fits within the frame. And he has the present-day ageing author go back to that childhood world and live in it again after both he and the world have changed for the better.

This new Hartley experiment on a basic theme suffers from its likeness to the others, its adherence to the formula—as well as from a tendency to over-explain, over-consider, over-talk, and some over-doneness and under-funniness in the satirical portions. These 'modern' sections, with their deliberately cerebral and moralistic character, are less than satisfying aesthetically, and detract from the believability of the novel as a whole. And some of the book's symbols, like the 'M' on Rookland Abbey, for example, seem much too contrived-to-order for Hartley's specific purpose, serving as 'sign' rather than genuine symbol.

The Brickfield / The Betrayal does not come near greatness, as some of Hartley's earlier novels did, but it is an unusual and at times beautiful meditation on age which rounds out Hartley's explorations of the spiritual searchings of man in the various modern circumstances and at the various stages of life. If these adult contemporary novels are less magical in their beauty, less convincing in their symbolism than the Hartley world which we have seen through a child's eyes, it is partly because he is here trying to depict life as he feels it must appear to those upon whom 'the shades of the prison-house' (*BR* p. 94) of adult life have closed forever.

CHAPTER SEVEN

TOWARD THE GOLDEN AGE:
FACIAL JUSTICE

> . . . the dreamt land
> Toward which all hungers leap, all pleasures pass.
> —Richard Wilbur[1]

[a]

L. P. HARTLEY'S earlier romances tended to portray (and warn against) the excessively romantic humanist vision which waited too happily for the Golden Age of the twentieth century to crown the striving of the nineteenth. Hartley's wartime and immediately postwar novels grew more grim, more satiric; they showed how thoroughly that hopeful humanist vision could be crushed by the overwhelming revelation of human sin and guilt brought by the century's battlefields. In 1960 Hartley seemed to feel compelled to experiment with a new emphasis in his symbolic fiction: one with which he could satirize the dullness and barrenness of a world which now mistrusted and banished the life of the spirit, the imagination—while at the same time he could suggest the eternal viability and beauty of that spiritual dimension and the possibility of a true goal for man's infinite longings.

Hartley's typically, even outrageously, unique solution was to create his own kind of fictional *1984* state—in which everyone had to be as alike, as equal, as lowly and earthly and unaspiring and uninspiring as possible—and to have one of its repressed inhabitants counter by falling in love with an Angel. The genre thus produced is not easy to place. Anthony Burgess, in a popular book on the contemporary novel, terms it 'dystopian',[2] and sees

139

Facial Justice as partly a moral fable; a *Times Literary Supplement* reviewer seems to come nearer the mark when he classifies it as 'a kind of religious science-fiction, part fantasy about the future and part satirical fable about the standardization and neutralization of men and women'. He says, further and very well, that the book is

> . . . a love-story about humanity, comic in spirit, not tragic, religious, not political; the regime it portrays is more pathetic than horrific, while the narration has the odd, contrived remoteness of a dream rather than the inevitability of a nightmare.[3]

Facial Justice is, essentially, a religious work—more an apocalypse or myth perhaps than a romance, if one accepts Frye's judgement that the romantic is 'the tendency to suggest implicit mythical patterns in a world more closely associated with human experience'.[4] *Facial Justice* is seen as though with some kind of X-ray vision or in some state of dream whereby one can seemingly watch bodies acting independently of spirits and spirits (of which there are very few) of bodies. Mankind is in a future stage which Hartley seems to see as having developed very logically from its present one, and is very near to the apocalyptic finale which will conclude the novel and the known earth at the same time. The form seems a logical one for Hartley's experimentation. Concerned as he has been in all his works to show the operation of a spiritual world in the background of the social worlds he gives in such detail, seemingly moved above all by the good/evil battle in human existence, and feeling, perhaps, like Hawthorne, that 'the very fabric of the earth is as unstable as it is presented in the Book of Revelation' (*NR* p. 129),[5] it would seem only natural that Hartley would come at last to writing as directly as he could of the spiritual struggle (or love affair) which for him was ultimate reality. The form he has found is flawed because he tries to do and to combine so many things, but *Facial Justice* is a fascinating experiment by a man determined to say things never quite said before. The book is dedicated, 'with homage, acknowledgments and apologies to the memory of Nathaniel Hawthorne' (*FJ* p. [5]).

Beginning with the proposition which most of his own previous books might be said to have expounded—that man has an inherent tendency to evil, violence, murder, war—Hartley posits a state which is trying to play down, to condition away that tendency. Then he shows us in detail how this well-meaning effort, like the experiment in democracy which preceded it, ends in utter destruction.

Once again Hartley seems to leave us with a sense of the impossibility of absolutes, prescriptions, final solutions in man's dilemma: a sense of man's condemnation to constant striving and repeated failure—the terrible yet beautiful fate which seems to be Hartley's concept of human existence. It is, again, the story of Sisyphus. But in the background of *Facial Justice*, more even then in the other Hartley novels, we sense a possible God, a possible Plan behind it all, a possible real Golden Age towards which man's always frustrated desires and efforts point—finally, the possibility that all man's abortive attempts, his falls and resurrections (in each person, in each age) are so many re-enactments of Redemption, leading, in a slow, painful spiral, to the desired fulfilment.

Redemption. Then again, possibly only redemption. We are never sure whether the spiral upwards is really there; we are never sure whether its source is human or divine: whether Hartley implies the existence of a transcendent, all-powerful Force outside of time, drawing us to Itself, or means that man's spirit must be/is his own divinity—or both. Hartley gives us a modern myth: a strange yet appealing love story, which can be read as embodying the traditional view of man's traffickings with God, as a Christian philosophy of history—or as a completely parallel psychological view in which man comes more and more to terms with his own spirit, his own nature. Hartley may be saying that these are one and the same; he may be saying nothing of the kind. Like all myth or parable, this newly-created one refuses to yield to one meaning or one line.

Hartley starts from what he evidently sees as the levelling tendencies of the England in which he writes, tendencies which he has discussed in several lectures and articles on the novelist's art—

especially in 'The Novelist and his Material'. Dealing at length there with collectivism and its effect upon human individuality, and noting the danger that the individual submerged in the community may develop automatic reactions and a protective colouring which will render him indistinguishable from the rest, Hartley nevertheless concludes his essay with an expression of hope in the enduring quality in man's personality:

> But I cannot help believing that this will not happen, and that an awareness of other people's personalities and their right to be themselves, and of one's dependence, for the fulfilment of one's own personality, on them as individuals—not just fellow-sufferers or fellow-criminals with identical faces—will survive, and with it the novel, which thrives on that belief (*NR* p. 190).

His own novel beings 'In the not very distant future, after the Third World War. . . .' We are in a New State. Immediately after the War, which 'had all but eliminated the human race' (*FJ* p. 22), the twenty million survivors lived for a time in caves below ground, their lives conditioned to an absolute, machine-like, artificial routine. Led out of the Underworld by a mysterious child, after several unsuccessful revolts and a Slaughter of the Innocents, a remnant of the English people set up a new life in a land where organic life has all but disappeared, where the climate is perpetual March, where the golden Voice of an unseen Dictator organizes them into a regime of calculated equality, conformity, non-violence. Here all is relaxed, slow-paced; the air is warm and conditioned, the buildings pink with rounded edges. There is little compulsion, except towards obligatory recreation, the taking of one's daily bromide, the eschewing of pronounced preferences, hurry, worry, anxiety or guilt. All is geared towards eliminating envy, promoting equality—women are urged to have their faces altered to an ideal (though not excessively exciting) standard to achieve this end. Especially frowned upon are imagination and all upward-looking, all 'vertical aspiration', all seeking of heights of any kind. 'Only through the imagination', says one of the Dictator's emissaries (*FJ* p. 90) 'can one kill a man.'

The entire experiment seems to be based on the principle that 'Nature is nasty' (*FJ* p. 15), that pronounced personal identity makes more trouble than it is worth. The Dictator, as it turns out (*FJ* pp. 150ff., 199ff.), wants (through surprises and risks built into the programme) to develop free will in his 'Patients and Delinquents', as he calls them, with the hope that they will mature into more than that (*FJ* p. 31). The ultimate goal he has for his people is a Golden Age in which each individual would find complete personal fulfilment:

> So each should have his paradise, her paradise, to be enjoyed by him or her alone, and inaccessible to the others. And yet not inimical to the others—oh no! Side by side, touching but not colliding, each cell enshrining a perfect individuality, that owed nothing to and took nothing from the rest. A hive of private paradises, fashioned not by working together, or playing together, or talking together, or thinking together, not created by any communal activity—perish the thought! But coming insensibly, miraculously into being by the simplest of all expedients: the exercise of free will, all your free wills, all operating on their own, without reference to others, guided by that inner light, that infallible sense of right direction that, as is well known, we each of us possess (*FJ* pp. 153–4).

Facial Justice is, in particular, the story of Jael 97 and her education in personhood—within/in spite of/because of (?) the New State. Tending towards conformity, prevailed upon by her conformist brother to have her too uncommon prettiness scaled down to ideal Beta specifications, she is persuaded at the last moment, by her friend Judith, to keep her own face. The effort of the decision makes her, for the first time, begin to discern a purpose in her life (*FJ* p. 84)—mainly a compulsion to be her own self.

Jael takes a frowned-upon motor expedition to the ruins of Ely Cathedral, looks up at the tower's soaring height and leads others to look up. The experience, for her and for them, leads first to a sense of sin and guilt, then to an ecstasy, a going out of self, a merging in dance and song, 'until the current passing through their linked hands seemed to sweep away the barriers of individuality and leave a single personality, as homogeneous and indivisible as a wedding ring' (*FJ* p. 56). The result of this risky experience of height, ecstasy and desire is a motor accident, meaning death for some, meaning the grafting of a new, standard face on the unconscious and unwilling Jael—but not before her aspiration and risk has given her a further, fleeting experience of ecstasy (not 'earthbound', this time, but 'timeless' [*FJ* p. 60])—in the arms of a godlike 'Inspector' for the regime, named after and resembling the Archangel Michael.

The mysterious, mystical 'embrace among the stars' to which her risk-defying aspiration brings her is one which 'her mind and her flesh would remember for ever' (*FJ* p. 94). She sees Michael again, but only fleetingly, and (perhaps) is brushed fleetingly by another kiss. 'It was a ravishing moment, a moment not in time or place, the longed-for moment, the moment of moments; and yet she could not, afterwards, tell how it came to her' (*FJ* p. 106). Michael, though supposedly an arm of the regime, had seemed to encourage her to be different, a 'rebel' (*FJ* p. 105); he gives her a plant, a real plant, a live blue cineraria unlike the neat plastic ones accepted by all the others in her hospital ward. The memory of her meeting with him stays with her as a kind of talisman support-ing 'the tottering fabric of her emotional life' (*FJ* p. 85), and the flower, fading as it is, becomes a symbol of her dreamlike ex-perience of love. Often close to dying, it is with Jael through all that subsequently happens to her—is, perhaps, Jael: her indivi-duality, her soul.

Finding that her face has been tampered with, Jael tries to lead a revolution against the state; she succeeds in hardening, rather than developing, her own personality, and in bringing anarchy and destruction to the people. Concurrent with her struggle to be herself and her revolutionary activities is her wooing by the Doctor (Wainewright) who has altered her face and fallen in love with it. He is extremely physical, with a 'roughhewn face, to remind her of reality and her mission' (*FJ* p. 167). His job, seemingly, is to get her to accept things as they are, herself as she is, reality as given.

In her rival lovers Jael is faced with Hartley's usual polarity of ideal/actual, physical/spiritual, earth/heaven—but this choice seems to be even more concrete than usual in Hartley's novels: Jael is choosing whether to have a soul, a personality, or not. Asking those who are trying to keep her earthbound 'But don't we all rely on things outside ourselves, and people, for what makes life worth living, indeed for life itself?' (*FJ* p. 90), Jael nevertheless involves herself enough with the regime and the Doctor to lead a rebellion against it. She becomes obsessed (as did Timothy in *The Boat*) with the idea of being herself—a desire intensified by the standardizing operation on her face and the outward pressures against her. But in trying to attain and hold on to the past, pre-accident self she had known, she becomes rigid, quite different (*FJ* pp. 119-21)—then destructive, detached from her brother, her friends (*FJ* pp. 207-8). Michael is absent during this entire phase of Jael's life, though the cineraria is still with her.

Nearly at the end of *Facial Justice* we find Jael alone at home, waiting for death. The Dictator gone, the State replaced by anarchy and repression, she has volunteered to be one of the propitiatory victims demanded by the now-powerful Underworld. Outside an unusual rain beats down, turning the parched land into a swamp. The rain seems to exemplify the Nature which has come to life again within the realm, but so savagely that it brings nothing but destruction.

All Jael has left, 'the only thing she cared for in the world . . . far more than for herself' (*FJ* p. 209), is the cineraria, only half-alive. Her volunteering for death has in it something of altruism, of a desire to give herself for others, to be free of self and the 'collective self' which sometimes visits her (*FJ* pp. 207, 213)—a gesture like this, she realizes, is the only way at this stage to reassert 'the uniqueness of her personality', to use the 'faculty of private judgement and the power of choice' which she alone, of all the people, has retained (*FJ* p. 207).

The final chapter of *Facial Justice* is the most puzzling of all, the most disconcerting to any attempt to emerge with a single meaning for this novel. Identifiable by a Hawthornian birthmark (a heart-shaped one which seems at the same time to indicate love and 'mortal weakness' [*FJ* p. 186]), the Dictator turns out to be a little old lady—formerly beautiful, now wet through by Nature's onslaughts and very near death. Fire is raging outside: 'the world that Jael knew was being destroyed' (*FJ* p. 220), but the people are calling again for their Dictator, for a Voice to guide them. As the former Dictator dies and is consumed, she leaves this task to Jael and Michael together, with the hope that the 'play' they devise for the people will be a better one, will profit from her mistakes, will have a 'happier ending' (*FJ* p. 219). In a place 'unknown to her, as were the faces that surrounded her', Jael is 'clothed in authority, a ritual began of which she seemed to be the centre; Michael bent his knee'. The Voice speaks to the people. 'But Jael did not speak with her own voice, she spoke with Michael's' (*FJ* p. 220).

[b]

Like Kafka's parables, like all his own romances, Hartley's story yields possible meanings on the socio-political, the psychological, the religious-metaphysical levels. Most immediately and obviously, it is a satirical comment on current social attitudes—like Jael herself, Hartley attacks the prevailing mental climate (as described in his comments on postwar England, above) by carrying its precepts of 'fairness' to their ridiculous extremes. The Dictator of his New State is a kind of God, omnipresent and omniscient, whose nature and wishes are only guessed at from his promulgated laws. 'The Dictator forbid' (*FJ* p. 165) and 'For the Dictator's sake don't do that' (*FJ* p. 168) are common expressions. But this is a false and mortal god—the god of public opinion, perhaps, or of the current accepted standard of morality as created by the people themselves ('. . . people say . . . that he doesn't initiate, he only follows . . .' [*FJ* p. 75]), 'he' himself says that he behaves like a tyrant because that is how the people expect him to behave, and 'it is our principle to give our people what they want' [*FJ* p. 80]). Equality, fairness, 'justice' is what the Voice seems to be decreeing, in response to the will of the people —an absence of all aspiration to anything the 'highest common factor' of the people cannot understand or accomplish. The human mean governs all. The Doctor is, perhaps, science, common sense, even psychology—earthly, sensual sight as opposed to vision: helping the patient to forget disturbing transcendentals and adjust to things as they are.

Jael is an Everyman who proves that the imagination, the surge towards an ideal (however dangerous this can be to the status quo) can never be quite destroyed in man. Michael seems to stand for that ideal, for perfection, for the transcendental—something completely beyond the ordinary powers of man, tangible only to the spirit, the imagination: a 'presence' in darkness which calls forth a death to self, fulfilment in a mystical union. Since Michael spoke for the Dictator and now, even more fully, rules with and speaks for Jael, since he is timeless and looks down somewhat on the plant which is 'only an annual' (*FJ* p. 103), the suggestion would seem to be that he, Michael, was the 'pretty gentleman' behind the original revolt from the Underworld (*FJ* p. 26): the perennial spirit which gives rise to and inhabits (in greater or less degree) man's perennial attempts to cast off the unsatisfactory, to seek and establish the good upon earth. Michael is Blake's Divine Imagination, perhaps, or Emerson's World Soul, or simply God —that Divine life and energy, that Kingdom and fullness of life, which is uniquely and continually coming to birth within each man. (Something in this portrayal of the Spirit, if such it is, would make us connect Hartley even more directly with some aspects of romanticism, even American transcendentalism: a possibility strengthened by his liking for the organic metaphor, the pathetic fallacy, and types of symbolism which suggest a unity between men and nature, a common spirit inhabiting and uniting all forms of life.)

Hartley's social satire in *Facial Justice* is at times delightful (especially when understated), at times contrived and—depending on one's own allegiances—often rather annoyingly reactionary. Jael's idea for destroying the state is precisely Hartley's own method—to exaggerate the ideal of 'fairness' and show by a *reductio ad absurdum* to what destruction such levelling leads. Tongue in cheek, she writes a mock treatise on the unfairness of excellence in art, in which she attacks 'the priggishness and fancied superiority of the Failed Alpha class, in whom the cult for "serious" music has always been strongest' (*FJ* p. 170). (Since the Alpha class, or accepted elite, is composed of those who rule, because of their superior brains, brawn or beauty, no doubt the

147

Failed Alphas, of whom Jael is one, represent for Hartley the middle class which he sees, in his previously-quoted lecture, as being 'squeezed out of existence' in England, along with the altruism—the going out of oneself for an ideal, for art—which 'the middle classes believed in . . . and sometimes practised' in the past. This middle class he, with Goethe, sees as having been the key to the 'finest culture' [*NR* p. 190].)

Along the same lines, Jael urges the people to do everything badly in order to lessen envy, and they pull down the standard of every occupation, every undertaking to previously unheard-of slovenliness—so that the state's own order of business suffers. Urged to equalize housing, the people raze quite adequate homes in so-called 'slums' (*FJ* pp. 197–8) and force the occupants to move in with others (here Hartley aims directly at certain aspects of social welfare); urged to find and punish the overprivileged man among them who has a heart-shaped birthmark (Jael has learned that this is the way to distinguish the still-hidden Dictator), they fall to challenging, uncovering, fighting and killing each other.

What Hartley's parable and satire say on the level of social organization is that one cannot arrange life according to a merely physical, behaviouristic, statistical standard and expect it to satisfy man's needs. Imagination and ideals and striving for perfection may be dangerous—but man without these qualities is even more dangerous, and the herd instinct can lead to war and destruction even more surely than the superman cult. The kind of free will and autonomy the Dictator hopes for will never be developed by merely responding to public opinion, will never arise from 'that inner light, that infallible sense of right direction that, as is well known, we each of us possess' ([*FJ* p.154]: one must always be on one's guard when a Hartley character says 'as is well known', or 'of course'). The satire itself is uneven, as in most of his novels of the fifties and sixties, and tends to stress many of the same concerns found there and in his essays. This does not seem Hartley's greatest forte or most welcome contribution—one must respect the 'sincere, brave and unfashionable' quality to which the *TLS* reviewer calls attention.[6] But one cannot help agreeing to some extent with Angus Wilson's review on

Poor Clare which deplores the fact that in earlier works (not *Poor Clare*),

> Mr. Hartley's social standpoint, however one views it (and let me say at once that I cordially detest it), threatens to swallow up his deep moral concern and his power to translate that concern into art, to reduce everything to petulance, grousing and nagging.[7]

Hartley's book seems to call for a resurgence of the British tradition of self-governance, self-restraint, individual responsibility. But he sees this self as not to be attained by obsessive self-assertion (as Jael, like Timothy Casson, discovers), but by finding something beyond self—an ideal, a perfection, towards which self can go out, give, strive.

As the story of Jael's personal integration, *Facial Justice* can be seen as a picture of the realm of the self, Jael's self, and who or what is to rule over that realm. Seen this way, each character is an aspect of Jael herself. The book tells us several times that the revolt 'seemed to be going on inside the room, inside their own heads' (*FJ* p. 149), that 'the same noise and the same colour [as the fire and revolution outside] were in her mind' (*FJ* p. 216). Her hatred for the Dictator is, Dr. Wainewright points out, linked to self-hate (*FJ* p. 162). Jael begins as a conformist, the kingdom of her life under the control of public opinion, accepted morality—without being conscious that this is the case (*FJ* pp. 84–5). She tends to equate her self, her identity, with her appearance (*FJ* p. 78); rebelling, questioning enough to hold on to her own face, she is drawn to look higher, to see something (in Ely Cathedral tower) of the aspiration, the art, the different approach, of men of other times. This experience and the sense of unity with humanity which it brings gives birth in her to a desire for an ideal, a love of her own—and an inkling of the fulfilment, the expansion there can be in losing self to, uniting oneself with the Other-than-self.

The human Ego is the question (see *FJ* p. 74): suppressing it, or dulling it by submission to public opinion, is not the answer, nor, on the other hand, is letting it run rampant, asserting and insisting on it to the destruction of all else. Hartley's solution to this problem of the duality of the Ego, its good/evil ambivalence (linked to the 'face-saving' which elsewhere in Hartley is asserted as the cause of war but here is linked to personhood [*FJ* p. 148]) seems to be along lines which could be called traditionally Christian or just good psychology. The following, from anthropologist/theologian Pierre Teilhard de Chardin, seems to say what Hartley intimates in Jael's crooked path to selfhood:

> Egoism, whether personal or racial, is quite rightly excited by the idea of the element ascending through faithfulness to life, to the extremes of the incommunicable and the exclusive that it holds within it. It *feels* right. Its only mistake, but a fatal one, is *to confuse individuality with personality*. In trying to separate itself as much as possible from others, the element individualises itself; but in doing so it becomes retrograde and seeks to drag the world backwards towards plurality and into matter. In fact it diminishes itself and loses itself. To be fully oneself it is in the opposite direction, in the direction of convergence with all the rest, that we must advance—towards the 'other'. The goal of ourselves, the acme of our originality, is not our individuality but our person; and according to the evolutionary structure of the world, we can only find our person by uniting together.[8]

It is, then, in feeling responsible for others that Jael's selfhood will come most fully—and it is only this kind of selfhood and freedom, won through meeting and overcoming the worst in oneself, which could lead to anything like the Dictator's dream of a Golden Age. That Golden Age itself sounds like a slightly perverse version of Teilhard de Chardin—of a modern Christian view of 'heaven', of the goal to which human evolution should rightly lead, an 'Omega point' where human consciousnesses, retaining their uniqueness, would meet at the centre of Space-Time. Evolution, according to Teilhard de Chardin (and it is, of course, a 'romantic' view, reminiscent of the transcendentalists) is ultimately a process of love, of the 'uniting of living beings in such a way as to complete and fulfill them', joining them 'by what is deepest in themselves'.[9]

The flaw in the Dictator's plan (and it is a flaw many attribute also to Teilhard) is that he forgets original sin, the blackness in man's nature—or thinks that it can be conditioned out of being by blandness, by the smothering of all natural instincts that might possibly lead to wrongdoing. There can be no free will without the freedom to do wrong, as Simonetta Perkins discovered (*SP* p. 53). There can be no crown without the cross, as Leo Colston (and indeed all Hartley's innocent heroes) finally know (*GB* p. 147). Man will only attain this kind of fulfilment and happiness by learning, at his own expense, to go beyond himself in the interests of a whole which is greater than he.

Jael the individual, Everyman, is also, of course, Jael the writer, the artist—the creative person whose own imagination is awakened and who takes it as her task to stir up the atrophied imaginations of her captive countrymen. Many of Hartley's articles are concerned with the question of the artist in an age notable for its 'devaluation of the individual' (*NR* p. 11), and in one he wonders 'Well, what is the novelist of today to do, faced by this swing-over in public opinion? Is he to accept it, or is he, as the eighteenth-century novelists did, to take up a governessy attitude?' (*NR* p. 14). Hartley deplores those novelists who accept this 'fashion in thought' (*NR* p. 16), who refuse to allow their characters any guilt or responsibility, or else wipe out all guilt by the intervention of faith and grace. The novelist, he thinks, 'must believe that *something matters*' (*NR* p. 16). In the story of Jael he shows us the creative person and the kind of lonely and dangerous struggle for self which is his. The artist can, often through ridicule, change public opinion as Jael did—but it seems that he should not be ensnared into seeing only destruction, hate and self-assertion as freedom.

Facial Justice speaks perhaps most deeply on a religious/ metaphysical level. Hartley suggests here much about the relationship between God and man and humanity's ultimate destiny which serves to clarify his possible meanings in other works. Jael gives us some reason to think we may be dealing with a philosophy of history when she muses, 'Some writers said that history had come to an end with the Second World War; how little they knew! She herself could not remember that time; but this was like another incarnation and needed a new language' (*FJ* p. 101). And within the covers of *Facial Justice* we can trace an entire Bible history, a complete cycle from Genesis through to an Apocalypse. There has been the Fall of the Third World War, after which man lives in the Underworld (i.e. in a state of sin and alienation). The 'pretty gentleman' (Michael? God's emissary? God's grace?) speaks through a child to urge the people to seek a better life, and the Slaughter of the Innocents helps them to understand the evil of their present state, the need to raise themselves a step nearer freedom. In the 'Exodus' (*FJ* p. 36) which follows, a million people follow a child up into daylight.

Above on the earth, they are ruled by a mysterious Voice whose laws and New State are said to reflect their own wishes and capacities. The State with its constant changes and surprises and mysteries is designed, the Dictator later tells them, to educate them to choosing good freely. Hartley does seem here to be giving us a picture of fallen man in his earthly state. Redemption is within his power, but he must choose it for himself. Meanwhile he is ruled by government, Church, moral code, public opinion—any or all of which are, perhaps, agents of God's educating and healing Providence, but all of which can only represent man's current stage of moral development, and all of which demand to be superseded by man's own initiative, creativity, moral growth. Only the individual who overcomes the pressure of groupthink, the fear of a 'higher authority', only the person who discovers that institutions and codes are mortal, grow old and die, only the one who finds that freedom is not anarchy or self-seeking but goint out of oneself to give, only the one who values and seeks and unites himself with the spirit, over the letter, moves himself and humanity on to the next stage. The goal would seem to be a state in which man's spirit reigns more and more fully within each individual and in relations among men, and in which the letter, the rules, the guidelines wither away.

Hartley's picture of the consuming of the old earth in flames and the birth of a new, more spiritual kingdom, could be a final apocalypse, the beginning of the new heaven and new earth at the end of all—or merely *an* apocalypse, one of many successive endings and reincarnations of the spirit which make up human history. Is Hartley saying that the process, on a human level, is rather black and hopeless? That man's ego, left to itself, turns more easily to 'some form of activity that would fill the hospitals and the coffins' than to opening, 'each one of you with a special, private key' the door to the Golden Age (*FJ* p. 153)? Yes. Most often the human imagination seems to be used to kill (*FJ* p. 90). But Hartley lets us see, too, by very contrast, the achievement of the human imagination which can fall in love with God, the good, an ideal, and cling to it through all the blackness of earthly life and disappointment with oneself and one's efforts; which can be led, through God, through one's ideal, to burst one's limitations and, transcending self, to bring about a new order of life. Hartley's parable is a paradigm of the purgative, illuminative, unitive stages in individual spiritual development, a journey through Hell, Purgatory and Heaven in modern dress, a history of mankind's progress through successive incarnations of God to the point where man today understands that he himself is in control and can, if he chooses, make his own destiny. Yet always, even here, Hartley keeps us aware of man's propensity to evil on the one hand, and, on the other, of a golden, inescapable Something beyond him which is always available to him, drawing him, *for* him.

It is this aspect of religious fantasy with which Hartley is, it seems to me, most successful in *Facial Justice*. The delicacy and depth which are always with him in creating imaginative mythical worlds touch the shadowy love story of Jael and Michael—in any case a creative symbol—and give it something of the spiritual force of the myth of Cupid and Psyche. And by contrast, the rougher overtures of Dr. Wainewright have an appealing human quality which does not leave the choice all one-sided.

Apart from the love story, Hartley is at his best in this novel where he is most suggestive and mysterious, in the sections which reveal the history of the apocalyptic and of the State and the beginning of the new era, whatever it may be. These passages seem genuinely symbolic—can be translated on many levels into human and religious experience.

With his depiction of the State and with the combining of the various elements, Hartley is less successful—mainly, as is obvious, because his undertaking is so ambitious and the strands to be combined so very disparate. With regard to the State, Hartley searches for concrete symbols to express what are perhaps some of his deepest philosophical convictions or detestations—but unfortunately the symbols are too often like mere allegorical signs: over-simple, contrived, reducing the problem too easily to the ridiculous or unworthy. The central symbol itself, of the standardizing of faces, might be objected to on these grounds, and so might the recurrent symptoms of the debasement of words —the slogans like 'Nature is nasty', for example—whereby Hartley tries to incorporate into *Facial Justice* something of a theory of language.

Peter Bien criticizes *Facial Justice* for so mixing 'the techniques proper to parable and allegory with those proper to the conventional novel, that each destroys the effectiveness of the other';[10] the *TLS* reviewer mentioned above feels Hartley 'has not entirely succeeded in fusing into a single whole the various elements of satirical fable and religious fantasy of which his book is composed'.[11] While I prefer the terminology of *TLS*, I do agree with Bien that Hartley's authorial intrusions and inconsistency of tone keep *Facial Justice* from aesthetic wholeness. Nevertheless, this book is an exciting attempt in a rare genre, trying to suggest the constant change, revolution, striving, death and rebirth at the heart of man's existence and common history. Man must let the body, the institution, the present, the abstraction, go, *Facial Justice* suggests, to seek the spirit, the life, the future. The pains, the deaths, the flaming apocalypses of the world—the World Wars, even, which we bring upon ourselves—are like the flames which lick at every page of Blake's apocalyptic *Marriage of Heaven and Hell*: they destroy legalism, conventionality, timidity, tyranny, abstraction, materialism, empty religiosity; they purify man, over and over, further and further, and free him more and more for poetic vision, prophetic inspiration, the gift of self, the exercise of his own genius or gift from God. Hartley's novel remains with us as an image of inevitable change suggesting at one and the same time historical, political, economic, religious, moral and aesthetic extensions of itself. This time Hartley has not left his apocalyptic world in the background, but has made it the subject of his story.

CHAPTER EIGHT

CONCLUSION

MANY critics have praised L. P. Hartley's achievement while stressing the 'limited' sphere in which it takes place.[1] Hartley protagonists, as has been shown, tend to be men and women of one mould, their experiences basically similar; Hartley settings (with the exception of *Facial Justice*) are eminently predictable. But one must perhaps find another term than 'limited' to describe an artist who tries to create a new genre—lightly comic but deadly serious—in order to raise, amid the pettinesses of everyday social life, the ultimate questions of existence. Hartley may sometimes fail, his failures may even approach the ludicrous or the maddening, because he attempts so much; his trying to locate eternal, implacable Evil in a West End flat or a suburban garden may approach the absurd, may end, as Angus Wilson believes it does,[2] in confusing manners with morals. But those who would confine his interests to exploring certain types of neurotic personality, certain classes in British society or periods in British history, even certain moral conflicts between the individual and the collectivity, certainly misread. The Hartley subject is Everyman: the meaning of his love, life, death in the modern world; and Hartley's novels, far from fitting into an established pattern, have been worthwhile investigations into forms whereby such a subject may be exploited. Walter Allen sees Hartley—I believe correctly—as one who carried on the necessary search for ways of integrating the technical discoveries of the great innovators like Joyce and Lawrence into 'an adequate conception of structure'.[3] Where is the novel to go, post-Joyce, post-Woolf? Hartley gives a very different answer from those today who have returned to the

Victorians, stressed empiricism, social realism and an almost deliberate disregard for form. In him a unique conjunction of existentialist, Christian and mythical thought demanded unique embodiment; his answer has been a genre new to contemporary English fiction—an adaptation of the nineteenth-century Hawthornian romance which gives symbolic dimension to the carefully-described realities of everyday contemporary life. And in that genre he has given us—in *Eustace and Hilda*, *The Go-Between* and *The Boat*—some works of modern fiction worth treasuring.

The romance genre, that blend of mythical patterns and everyday experience which is basic to most of Hartley's experiments, is at one with the meaning it seeks to convey. From the total body of Hartley's work emerges a shadowy, shifting world-picture in which images of absurdity, contradiction, negation and death seem to mingle or alternate with those of self-discovery, radiance and renewal. Now these prevail, now those, and it is a risk to try to fix a Hartley 'system'. If there is consistency, it is a consistency in which Jungian and Kierkegaardian concerns seem to meet—both of which visions would insist first of all that salvation and truth are of no system, but of the individual.

And so the individual search for salvation, for meaning, is the core of, the key to, the Hartley cosmos. The search takes place amid the seemingly opaque properties and petty events of contemporary urban and suburban life—except that always an imaginative eye within the story (usually the protagonist's own) gives us a vision of these landscapes and homes and clothes and pleasures as the stuff of dreams and Golden Ages, of gods and demons, heavens and hells. When the dreams fail, as they always do, when absurdity and irrationality are seen to prevail, when all that the individual has been building and planning comes to grief as it invariably does—we know we have watched something suggestive of life, ending, as life does, in death. We are left to decide whether what we watched was tragedy or fulfilment—because somewhere along the way the vision by which we have seen has suggested that the other world was there after all, that the destruction of illusions may be lifegiving, that the facing of nothingness and death may be the beginning of the birth of self, that heaven and the Golden Age are lost by illusion and self-seeking but may reveal themselves to self-transcending love and faith. Hartley's stories build upon (often play upon) the age-old archetypal patterns discerned by Jung in dream, romance, fairy-tale, religious rite—the monomyth of heroic quest, ordeal, death and rebirth which can also stand for Jung's process of psychic individuation as well as for Kierkegaard's reading of man's progress from aesthetic to ethical to religious consciousness. The heroic quest of the romance, as Joseph Campbell illustrates in detail,[4] is a figure of man's psychological growth, his learning to live from the centre of his own being. It is also an image of the redemption of the world, the introduction of divine life and power into the weakness and mortality of the human condition.

[a]

It is not, perhaps, immediately easy to see this heroic pattern in Hartley's stories of rather ineffectual 'little men' lost in the confusion of the postwar world. But the way in which Hartley recreates, restructures the myth is highly significant. He is emphasizing the need of a mythic consciousness for our time, and the hero he give us is the anti-hero of our time. In general Hartley's protagonists stand before us quite recognizably as lone, modern, post-Protestant Everyman—tied still, perhaps, to some remnants of a Christian moral code (like Lavinia, Eustace, the Margaret of *A Perfect Woman*), but never dreaming of taking Christianity seriously as a key to the enigmas of modern life. And enigmatic that life is—the loneness of Hartley's heroes (with a preponderance of live-alone, work-alone bachelor writers and artists among them) seems meant to emphasize the absence of communal life, work, standards, goals, rituals, meaning. One has the sense of a world in which most men are cast alone into the flux of time and phenomena to flounder about with no clue towards comprehension, no useful traditions or rituals from the past to lend design to the welter of experiences. World War II looms as a kind of boundary line in each of Hartley's novels; after it, all is different (Richard Mardick thinks of it as the Great

Divide of 1939 [*BET* p. 4]). The connection with the past is severed; each man is born frighteningly alone in an alien world. Joseph Campbell states thus the problem which Hartley, too, seems to be setting himself:

> There can be no question: the psychological dangers through which earlier generations were guided by the symbols and spiritual exercises of their mythological and religious inheritance, we today (insofar as we are unbelievers, or, if believers, insofar as our inherited beliefs fail to represent the real problems of contemporary life) must face alone, or, at best, with only tentative, impromptu, and not often very effective guidance. This is our problem as modern, 'enlightened' individuals, for whom all gods and devils have been rationalized out of existence. Nevertheless, in the multitude of myths and legends that have been preserved to us, we may yet see delineated something of our still human course. To hear and profit, however, one may have to submit somehow to purgation and surrender. And that is part of our problem: just how to do that.[5]

Each of Hartley's novels is structured in the mythical, suggestive form of a circle—a circle which could be seen as closed and dead-ended or which could be a loop in a spiral. In each the hero or heroine, after going through an adventure, a change (often a purgation and surrender), comes back to the point of departure. In some cases it is easy to believe that he or she now stands there on a slightly higher level than at the beginning; in some, though there is hope, we are left agonizingly unsure. Hartley's artistry usually refuses to allow too easy conversions, and one sometimes senses that his pessimism about the modern world finds it impossible to believe in them. But usually his books end with some measure of insight on the part of the protagonist, some degree of stripping of illusions and masks, leaving at least the opening for new and authentic life.

The pattern can be seen in miniature (as pointed out above)[6] in the short story 'The Crossways'. Here we have a heroine and hero, the husband and wife Michael and Lucinda, who are like the split halves of a single personality. Lucinda seems to represent the soul or spirit, Michael the flesh—or perhaps they are nearer to the consciousness and the unconscious. Lucinda longs for the Land of Heart's Desire and goes off into the dark forest to seek it. At the end of her quest she meets a now penitent and open Michael and realizes that her Land of Heart's Desire can only be achieved in union with him, back in their own home.

This little parable seems a clear parallel to the monomyth, as described above. By going through the dark forest and hurting her foot, Lucinda comes to terms with her own body, her unconscious, the dark side of her nature—previously cut off from her spiritual side and rendered brutish. She finds that male/female unity or wholeness which is her Self; she discovers that eternity, the Land of Heart's Desire, is to be found and lived in time, in the circumstances of one's real life. The story itself is a beautiful little *mandala*, fulfilling some of the functions of that symbol as described by disciples of Jung in the book *Man and His Symbols*. 'The contemplation of a mandala', says M.-L. von Franz[7] 'is meant to bring an inner peace, a feeling that life has again found its meaning and order.' And Aniela Jaffé describes a particular variety of Eastern mandala which throws light on Hartley's pattern:

> Aside from the circle, a very common yantra motif is formed by two interpenetrating triangles, one point-upward, the other point-downward. Traditionally, this shape symbolizes the union of Shiva and Shakti, the male and female divinities, a subject that also appears in sculpture in countless variations. In terms of psychological symbolism, it expresses the union of opposites—the union of the personal, temporal world of the ego with the non-personal, timeless world of the non-ego. Ultimately, this union is the fulfilment and goal of all religions: It is the union of the soul with God. The two interpenetrating triangles have a symbolic meaning similar to that of the more common circular mandala. They represent the wholeness of the psyche or Self, of which consciousness is just as much a part as the unconscious.[8]

All Hartley's novels, with their circular-spiral form, the almost geometrical symmetry of the relationships and movements within, the repetition of symbols and leit-motifs, and the stress on male/female interchange and mutual completion, seem to share in this nature and function of mandala-symbol. *Simonetta Perkins* carries a Bostonian Puritan to Venice (Italy, seen as primitive, sensual, uninhibited, or as religious and ritualistic, is often used by

Hartley as a kind of exact opposite shadow-land or reverse mirror-image into which to plunge English or American Puritans), and lets her experience there the deep split in her seemingly secure psyche when her Simonetta-Perkins-half steps forward and develops an embarrassing and degrading physical passion for a gondolier.

Emilio might be seen as Lavinia Johnstone's *animus*, Simonetta Perkins as her shadow. While the contemplated physical union with the gondolier never does take place, there is a certain spiritual recognition and assimilation, and the Lavinia who is, in her mother's company, metaphorically back in Boston at the end of the book, is a somewhat more complete, self-knowing and self-propelled young woman, who has come through at least one small stage in the spiral of her individuation.

Eustace, like so many of Hartley's heroes, is aimless and directed from without when he starts forth on his quest from Anchorstone. He is a half-person, living in dreams of a Golden Age or the kind of timeless unity he sees embodied in the mandala-window of Frontisham Church—estranged from the Puritan ethic, the almost mechanical morality and determination to control Nature represented by his sister Hilda. It takes a fall into the 'abyss'—the recognition of the fate his false persuasions and hopes have brought upon her—to make Eustace comprehend the force, the potential evil in that Nature, and to bring him back to Anchorstone determined to be, himself, more conscious and realistic towards its manifestations. It is difficult to say with certainty, but it would seem that Hartley wants us to know that Eustace's death, terrible as it is, does represent a kind of fulfilment. He has followed his destiny, he has responded to his moment of truth on the cliff-edge—has loved and given himself, as only a Self can do. The dream of universal salvation he has just before dying seems to corroborate both this fact, and his own awareness of it. The terrible shrimp/anemone symbol is, among other things, a symbol of wholeness, the union of opposites—the unions Eustace has been longing for, accomplished willingly and lovingly by his gift of self to 'something more precious than itself' (see *EH* p. 513). The symbol itself is reminiscent of one described by Jung as appearing in an ancient allegory[9] in which life is brought back to a barren wasteland by the ritual union of a brother and sister, his death (in one text, through disappearing into her body) and rebirth. 'The brother-sister pair', says Jung, 'is an allegory of the idea of opposites in general.' In this case the brother represents 'the masculine, spiritual principle of light and Logos, which . . . sinks into the embrace of physical nature. The death is therefore, the completed descent of the spirit into matter.'[10] Similar also is the Indian legend cited by Joseph Henderson in which a pair of twins represent the first fully human generation on earth:

> Though the Twins are said to be the sons of the sun, they are essentially human and together constitute a single person. Originally united in the mother's womb, they were forced apart at birth. Yet they belong together, and it is necessary—though exceedingly difficult—to reunite them. In these two children we see the two sides of man's nature. One of them, Flesh, is acquiescent, mild, and without initiative; the other Stump, is dynamic and rebellious.[11]

The twins, together or separately, are invincible—but they abuse their power and commit crime for which they deserve death. But 'Though the Twins erred, and though the punishment should have been death, they themselves became so frightened by their irresponsible power that they consented to live in a state of permanent rest: The conflicting sides of human nature were again in equilibrium.'[12]

Hartley never shows us the Eustace and Hilda, shrimp and anemone principles in equilibrium; they are in perpetual, agonized battle, for man's life is perpetual battle. The kind of unity and perfection Eustace longs for has an infinite quality; it can only be achieved, Hartley seems to suggest, by breaking through the limitations of life and self—by the gift of Self to something one truly sees as greater and more beautiful than oneself, worthy of love and self-immolation. Eustace's story shows us an entire life-cycle, a destiny completed and sealed with death. The following, from Campbell, suggests, however, the kind of implication of victory and hope that clings to the end of the Eustace/Hilda story:

> The hero, whether god or goddess, man or woman, the figure in a myth or the dreamer of a dream, discovers and assimilates his opposite (his

own unsuspected self) either by swallowing it or by being swallowed. One by one the resistances are broken. He must put aside his pride, his virtue, beauty, and life, and bow or submit to the absolutely intolerable. Then he finds that he and his opposite are not of differing species, but one flesh.[13]

The Boat, on the other hand, is one of the novels that shows us only a loop in the spiral, a stage in the life-process. The loop—a middle-aged interlude in the life of writer Timothy Casson—deals with his obsession with a boat (which coincides also with his obsession for a blonde *femme fatale* and for the revolutionary cause in which she embroils him). M.-L. von Franz notes that a man may project his 'anima', the personification of all the feminine psychological tendencies in his psyche, on to a ship or car.[14] For Timothy the boat does bring to a focus all the unsuspected, undiscovered tendencies in himself and reveal to him their (his own) potential for evil and destruction in the calamities and deaths they cause. The Timothy who leaves Upton at the end of *The Boat* has met and absorbed a great deal of knowledge about the dark side of his character; he is no longer under quite so many illusions about his innocence of war guilt, or about the possibilities of a Golden Age for humankind being brought about by free access to boats.

(One of the best examples, incidentally, of Hartley's utilization of the romance tradition for his own purposes, is his practice of educating his heroes by successive [sometimes rather comic] apparitions of Woman—taking all the traditional forms the *anima* or 'woman within' can take for a man, from the witch-figure to the Mary-like or Wisdom-like idealization: in each case challenging him to recognize and come to terms with unconscious elements within his own psyche. In other terms, Campbell speaks of the ultimate adventure of the hero as a mystical marriage with the Queen Goddess of the World, at the nadir of the earth or the central point of the cosmos. The Queen Goddess stands for the cosmos, the material universe—here the traditional myth attributes to matter the feminine attributes of the mother, good and bad, and uses the image 'for the purpose of the purging, balancing, and initiation of the mind into the nature of the visible world'. Campbell goes on to show that 'The meeting with the goddess [who is incarnate in every woman] is the final test of the talent of the hero to win the boon of love [charity: *amor fati*] which is life itself enjoyed as the encasement of eternity'....

> Woman, in the picture language of mythology, represents the totality of what can be known. The hero is the one who comes to know. As he progresses in the slow initiation which is life, the form of the goddess undergoes for him a series of transfigurations: she can never be greater than himself, though she can always promise more than he is yet capable of comprehending. She lures, she guides, she bids him burst his fetters. And if he can match her import, the two, the knower and the known, will be released from every limitation. . . .[15]

My Fellow Devils reveals a stage, a spiral, in the life of Margaret Pennefather. She starts out a rather conventional suburban spinster whose life is transformed by her meeting with and marriage to Colum McInnes, a charming but twisted movie star who plays (and lives) gangster roles. Life with Colum, who is a liar and a thief, is beginning, Margaret sees, to warp her and make her a sharer in his deceit. But the experience has at least awakened her to spiritual and moral realities, as well as to her own weakness. The spiral's end finds Margaret back at her own suburban home and tasks, but different—she has left Colum and become a convert to Catholicism, as a tangible evidence of her desire to dedicate herself positively to good and truth, and to renounce compromise with evil. For Margaret, as for all Hartley's other protagonists, the confrontation with her opposite, the recognition of the dark side of her self, was needed, and has enriched her own growth. What Hartley seems to be stressing here is, however, that recognizing one's shadow side does not mean giving in to its darker propensities. Margaret's estrangement from Colum and cleaving to the Church alone may be just a necessary stage: one feels she may be strong enough later in life to take on (and help make a man of) her erring husband. But first she is called upon to make a clear and unhesitating choice.

In *The Go-Between*, Leo Colston's spiral brings him back, at the end, to the Norfolk country house where, as a child, he had met and refused to face evil and betrayal. There at last, in old age, he is able to confront all that happened: able to recognize, to forgive, and even to see the elements of love in the human weakness and folly that blighted so many lives; able, too, to see the part his own exaggerated and over-innocent expectations had played. As a child the zodiac-mandala had seemed to him a true picture of the people among whom he lived, and the history of his times; disillusionment had let him remember only scattered details, and the 'hinder parts of the house . . . higgledy-piggledy and rambling' (*GB* p. 33). The vision of the front view of Brandham Hall which comes to him at the very end, after having been hidden for so long, is the symbol of the new wholeness (and the new, down-to-earth reality) his quest into the past, the dark, has won for him. Whether that understanding can bring him back to any measure of life is an open question, but he does undertake an act of unselfish giving as the book ends.

Isabel and Harold in *A Perfect Woman* must meet and grapple with their own hidden or repressed sides before being able to resume their married life on a more mature and conscious, more mutually aware level. Isabel has pushed her intellectual and literary sides into the background and repressed her desire to be some artist's inspiration; Harold has become a business machine, all but eliminating feeling and tenderness. Their escapades with Alec and Irma, upon whom they project their needs, their missing halves, are anything but harmless—two deaths are the result. But greater self-awareness also comes, greater capacity to understand the other—the ability, finally, to live out well this particular marriage which is their destiny.

The Hireling is a spiral both for Steve Leadbitter and for Lady Franklin. He, the completely isolated postwar cynic, trained in the school of war to a machine-like, purely pragmatic existence, learns from her to value the feminine side of life, the intangibles signified by her cathedrals and her own person. She learns from him to come down to earth. They meet in a dream-world (the non-existent family life of Leadbitter) spun from his imagination through her inspiration—but they do meet. When Leadbitter dies, at the end of the book, he has completed his mission. He has loved and has told his love; he has twice awakened Lady Franklin to life. Each has become more whole through encounter with the opposite.

The Jael–Michael love affair of *Facial Justice* seems a clear symbol of the longing of the human soul for something completely beyond its ken and powers. Jael attains selfhood in attaining the capacity to give up that self for others—this is her union with Michael and the beginning of their joint reign over (seemingly) a new heaven and a new earth: a new loop in the spiral. Whether this mandala refers to psychic wholeness, to the union of the soul with God on earth or in heaven, or to the apocalyptic end of the world, one really should not say—probably, like other myths, it means all these things.

Hartley's duo *The Brickfield* and *The Betrayal*, set in Welfare State England, show the circle or spiral of an ordinary life ending in old age and death. Richard Mardick ends where he began, in the home and village of his youth. But he ends as a man who has been forced by circumstances to face and assimilate the tragedy, the forgotten blackness of his youth, and, ultimately, to face and care for his betrayer. He has not been allowed to eliminate or to cast off and despise evil, whether in himself or others; perhaps he has been enabled to transcend, to forgive it. Again, we do not know with any certainty.

Hartley's myth seems to imply that this is or ought to be the meaning of life—this awakening of each person to consciousness and personal responsibility, this meeting with sin and suffering and disappointment, this stripping away of masks and externally imposed standards and false or unworthy ideals, this coming to a certain wholeness by interchange with others who embody one's missing qualities—finally, this attainment of the ability, at the moment of destiny, to go out of oneself totally in love, in the gift of self to an adequate ideal. Eustace's meditation on the fireworks, quoted in Chapter III, seems the best summary of this sombre, exacting vision of life and death:

> Viewless, perceptible only by the energy, the winged whizz of its flight, desire started up through the formless darkness of being; its goal reached, it burst into flower—a flower of light that transfigured everything around it; having declared and made itself manifest, it dropped back

released and fulfilled, and then at a moment that one could never foresee, it died, easily, gently, as unregretted as a match that a man blows out when it has shown him something more precious than itself (*EH* p. 513).

Lady Franklin suggests somewhat the same thing in her initial talk with the cynical and unresponsive Leadbitter in *The Hireling*. She is upset that in her life with her late husband, 'the meaning hadn't revealed itself', because of 'the curtain coming down so suddenly, leaving it all unfinished and meaningless' (*H* pp. 24–5). 'Is there anything in life that matters—really matters', she says to Leadbitter ('whom nobody loved and who assuredly loved nobody'), 'except that somebody you love should know you love them?' (*H* p. 26). This is the lesson Leadbitter learns from her, so that he is able to repeat it, as an explanation of what he has done for her, just before his own death. 'She said to me once, "If you have anything to tell anyone, tell them, or it may spoil your life, as it has mine." I thought it funny at the time . . . but now I don't, I want to tell her . . .' (*H* p. 227). His death seems to come almost naturally after his metamorphosis, a metamorphosis indicated by his act of love for Lady Franklin. Getting into the car for what will turn out to be his final journey 'he had the feeling of having accomplished a mission, he was happy in her happiness of which he now almost believed himself the architect; and if no other mission lay before him, no other outlet for his emotions, no one for him to identify himself with, well, it was just too bad' (*H* p. 206).

Hartley's protagonists are lone modern men—but his myth seems to insist that there is that in the nature of things which looks after men even in these denuded days: which throws into each man's path precisely the people and events and trials and experiences he needs to awaken him, bring him to wholeness and equip him for his moment of destiny. In a more fairy-tale-like book such as *Eustace and Hilda* these people and events have a more fabulous or supernatural quality, like the Fortuna-like Lady Nelly (*EH* p. 633), or the Venus-like Hilda (*EH* pp. 642–3). But even in more down-to-earth books like *A Perfect Woman* there is Elspeth, perfectly recognizable as a modern witch from the moment she materializes out of the fog and wild garden of Alec's house until, at 'Blastwick', in the midst of a kind of *Walpurgisnacht* ('Here there were sideshows mounted on lorries. . . . One truck was styled The Devil's Cookhouse. Men with blackened faces and blackened bodies, wearing white cooks' hats but dressed as devils where they were not naked, with pitchforks stoked a smoking tar-boiler . . .' [*APW* p. 304]), she arranged for Otto to revenge her upon Alec and Irma. And of course there are Timothy's good and bad angels, Mrs. Purbright and Vera Cross, in *The Boat*; the triangle of lovers who double as gods of the zodiac in *The Go-Between*; the Colum who plays Devil in *My Fellow Devils*; the Steve Leadbitter who plays St. Christopher in *The Hireling* (*H* p. 248). Good or bad, these agents of destiny play a positive role in the hero's (or heroine's) growth: Hartley seems to be agreeing with St. Paul that in the mixed affairs of this world, somehow 'all things work together unto good . . .': for spiritual good if not for earthly happiness. Here is Margaret musing about her relationship with Colum, at the very end of *My Fellow Devils*:

> After many minutes had passed this way, Margaret sat down to write a letter to the father. The father, her child's father, was the Devil, and the Devil was the father of lies. There should be no communication between them and the letter must be merely formal. 'Dear Devil, Good old Devil,' —the phrases that accompanied Colum's toast came back to her. But Margaret could not call him that. 'My dear Colum, I am so very grateful to you. . . .' But how could one be grateful to the Devil, even formally? One had nothing to be grateful to the Devil for. Yet she was grateful, or she had been: in the flood of emotions that Colum's note let loose, gratitude had certainly been present. But not gratitude to Colum; gratitude to St. Anthony, perhaps, who had restored what had been so nearly lost. . . . (*MFD* pp. 408–9).

One is not sure whether or not to be grateful to the Devil, to one's betrayers and persecutors, in a world in which their action is a needed condition of one's growth and fulfilment. Timothy of *The Boat* guesses dimly that some guiding force is at work in his life:

> Was it the more comforting, he wondered, to regard the mistiming of Captain Sturrock's letter as a blind hit of chance, or as one of a series of seeming mischances, ordered and inevitable as the rungs of a ladder, which

the logic of his nature required for its development? In either case he was the loser; but if character was destiny, and if he attracted to himself fiascos as a magnet attracts iron filings, the outlook was dismal (*B* p. 211).

Father McBane, in *My Fellow Devils*, unequivocally interprets that guiding force for Margaret as God's Providence (*MFD* p. 249). Aunt Carrie, too, at the end of *The Betrayal*, places Richard's almost incredible trials squarely within the context of a Christian philosophy of experience:

> . . . .But you, who have evidently come up against so much dishonesty, and ingratitude, all done *against* you, how can you feel, as I do, that it's a kind of fulfilment? But try to think it is. . . . It isn't our happiness that counts with God, or is a sign that we are accepted by Him, if I may put it so—it's our unhappiness, for whom the Lord loveth he chasteneth and scourgeth every son whom he receiveth. (*BET* pp. 308–9.)

It is the same message as that of the Scripture quotation with which, in his final dream, Eustace passes his examination:

> But the souls of the righteous are in the hand of God, and there shall no torment touch them. In the sight of the unwise they seemed to die: and their departure is taken for misery, and their going from us to be utter destruction: but they are in peace. . . . (*EH* p. 734).

One can see the life-quest, the spiral growth which each of Hartley's heroes goes—or almost goes—through as engineered by this Providence through innumerable agents, who are the ordinary companions of everyday life but who are, knowingly or unknowingly, entrusted with the keys to each other's growth and happiness. Leadbitter fulfils his life-purpose by bringing Lady Franklin several steps forward; she helps to awaken him to the love which completes him. One presumes that she, and people like Lavinia of *Simonetta Perkins*, Margaret of *My Fellow Devils*, Harold and Isabel of *A Perfect Woman*, Timothy of *The Boat*, still have more stages to go through before they accomplish their destinies: their small deaths and rebirths are rehearsals and preparations for the final test. People like Eustace, Leadbitter and Richard Mardick, on the other hand, who die at the close of their stories, have, perhaps, despite the outward appearance of failure and waste ('their departure is taken for misery, and their going from us to be utter destruction'), completed their lonely tasks of self-realization. For Kierkegaard, true faith can only operate in the face of absurdity and uncertainty.

Campbell, in his study of world myth, stresses throughout that myth transcends tragedy. In building his modern novels on the designs and figures of myth, surely Hartley is aiming at something of the same effect?

> The basic principle of all mythology is this of the beginning in the end. Creation myths are pervaded with a sense of the doom that is continually recalling all created shapes to the imperishable out of which they first emerged. The forms go forth powerfully, but inevitably reach their apogee, break, and return. Mythology, in this sense, is tragic in its view. But in the sense that it places our true being not in the forms that shatter but in the imperishable out of which they again immediately bubble forth, mythology is eminently untragical. Indeed, wherever the mythological mood prevails, tragedy is impossible. A quality rather of dream prevails. True being, meanwhile, is not in the shapes but in the dreamer.[16]

[b]

Hartley's myth—depicting life as the setting for the mysterious trial and growth of innumerable individuals, guided by some superhuman power—is, like all myths, also a philosophy of history. *Facial Justice*, that myth of a hypothetical next stage in humanity's long life, is the most explicit of Hartley's books in suggesting this philosophy.

According to Hartley's myth, the history of humanity seems also to be a spiral with each stage representing a new 'incarnation' —also, seemingly, a new Fall, a new redemption growing out of that Fall and involving sacrifice and death, and the beginning of a new cycle (all this is basically in keeping with the cosmic aspect of the monomyth).[17] Jael alerts us to the fact that Hartley does want us to think in these terms when she talks about new 'incarnations' needing a new language (*FJ* p. 101).[18]

Throughout his novels Hartley seems to stress change, becoming, process as the basic reality of the world of time—and to insist upon the necessity that each man (and each nation, humanity itself) respond to, co-operate with that process, or run the risk of atrophy. Jael distorts and rigidifies her own personality by trying to preserve it as it was in the past, according to an externally-conceived standard. 'How can I tell how I feel till I know how I look?' she asks at one point, indicating that her image of herself comes from without rather than within (*FJ* p. 63). And her solution for the change in her external appearance is to try to hold on to her old self by repeating actions and attitudes of the past:

> She tried to reproduce the pattern and routine of her Failed Alpha days; to do things at the same time as she used to do them, think the same thoughts and say the same things. 'I won't let myself be different,' she kept telling herself: 'I won't!' To repeat herself became almost a religion with her; the smallest deviation from her remembered routine, she tried to curb; she walked to and from work on the same side of the pavement, she even tried to make her footmarks tally. These efforts to recover her lost self were a great strain, for all the time, partly unknown to her, she was developing a new personality quite unlike her old one. Sometimes in her attempts to force herself into the old grooves she felt herself going physically rigid (*FJ* p. 120).

Jael does not know the danger of which Margaret, in *My Fellow Devils*, is at least aware:

> . . . I must bring my journal to an end. . . . I don't think it's healthy to put down all one's thoughts on paper. One ends by making a sort of image of oneself, which one feels one must live up to. It retards and makes one static. A mistress told me that at school and I'm sure it's true. . . . I remember the same mistress telling me she had made a rule for herself and copied it out on paper: 'I must not take my spiritual pulse',—and I never have, until now. . . . (*MFD* p. 130).

But it is mainly the comic sibyls, the ubiquitous older-woman guides in Hartley's novels who seem to have grasped the sense of life as an organic, meaningful, ordered growth in which each person's individuality and destiny seem to unfold from within like a plant, like the seasons. For individuals and for human history there must be continual change if there is to be life and growth: it must supersede the past, but it must grow organically out of the past. On the personal scale, Mrs. Purbright always speaks to Timothy in terms of organic growth (*B* p. 216); Lady Nelly hints to Eustace that his absent sister Hilda must be changing like all living things:

'I remember how well that blue dress suited her. But she might like something different now.'

'Something older?' suggested Eustace.

'Well, not exactly older. She's not much older, is she? She's still very young. But flowers change as the season passes.

'. . . I don't think of her as a dahlia now. That's over, her dahlia phase. I think of her as a night-scented stock—no, that's too bunchy. An iris, perhaps. I'm no good at analogies. But something fragrant.'

'That would be a great change,' exclaimed Eustace, to whom Hilda had always seemed as scentless as dew.

'No, no, not a great change, but I dare say a welcome one.'

'But scent is for someone else's benefit,' objected Eustace.

'Well, there's no harm in that.'

. . .

. . . An instinctive conservative, Eustace thought all change was for the worse.

'I don't think Hilda would change easily,' he said at last.

'No change is very easy.'

'I hope it didn't hurt her.'

'Perhaps it did, but we long for it' (*EH* pp. 589–90).

And Richard's Aunt Carrie, in *The Betrayal*, sees the changes that life's sufferings have made in her as having been totally beneficial, and that which she was 'meant for' (*BET* p. 308).

'I often think' Aunt Carrie said, 'that the self I had then wasn't my real self—it was an image, a golden image that your dear mother and my sister Florrie, and indeed all my family except Ada, who had sharper eyes, set up— . . .

. . .

'And when I got to Australia, where they didn't know anything about all this . . . well, I stopped being one, and slipped back into being something else—something perhaps that God had always meant me to be. I hope I stuck to some ideals, but they were mine, or what the circumstances out there imposed on me, not the ideals of what Austin used to call the Holy Family, do you remember? I became another person, that's why I said I'd changed' (*BET* p. 303).

Change and suffering, Hartley seems to say in these figures, are the stuff of individual growth; they are necessary also for humanity, history, human life as a whole. Complete equilibrium is impossible in this world where opposing forces must be continually struggling, and alternating 'solutions' taking hold.

Life is a dialectic, a series of necessarily imperfect and doomed-to-be-superseded stages, of necessarily incomplete liberations, in which human beings tend to seize upon each successive stage as finality and can only with difficulty be pried loose for the next step, the next lesson. Mrs. Purbright has this sense of the need for repeated deaths and rebirths in history, as she does for individual human life. She welcomes the 'new blood' of the intruding lower classes as a rejuvenating process not unlike the hypodermic needle which, while it pricks, restores health to listless patients (*B* p. 85). She sees that humanism might well have been enough in the past, but that now we must build afresh, and for her the new stage must be an explicitly Christian one, refreshed from the sources. 'We can inherit the gifts of Christianity,' she says, 'but not hand them on: I mean, the third generation must renew its faith' (*B* pp. 131–4). In *Facial Justice* we see a complete historical cycle running its course, failing, dying and being superseded by the next—as was the cycle before it, our own. As the dying Dictator turns her task over to Jael and Michael, she hopes that they will learn from her mistakes. 'You must think out a new play for them,' she says, '—a better one than mine' (*FJ* p. 218). Gods and religions, philosophies and systems of morality die too, this book seems to say; we must let them go, to be ready for the new 'incarnation'. But we must not totally discard the past and what it can teach us. Organic growth builds on the past. The mandala which symbolizes wholeness links something old with something new—is itself, in fact, really a spiral:

> The mandala serves a conservative purpose—namely, to restore a previously existing order. But it also serves the creative purpose of giving expression and form to something that does not yet exist, something new and unique. The second aspect is perhaps even more important than the first, but does not contradict it. For, in most cases, what restores the old order simultaneously involves some element of new creation. In the new order the older pattern returns on a higher level. The process is that of the ascending spiral, which grows upward while simultaneously returning again and again to the same point.[19]

Scourges like wars come from individual human weakness and evil (note that Timothy learns to recognize his own complicity in the guilt of World War II, and that in a dream Margaret of *My Fellow Devils* sees herself, with her acquiescence in Colum's deceit, helping him to prod victims into a gas-oven with a pitch fork [*MFD* pp. 239–40]). But these repetitions of the Fall, like the ugly riots in *Facial Justice* which bring the New State to an end, can have their place in history just as individual falls and trials have their place in individual vocations. Mrs. Purbright and Tyro both see the war, Timothy discovers, as a potential blessing for humanity (*B* pp. 144, 252). But there are many possible reactions to human evil, individual or collective. ('The Fall, the Fall, how often it has been repeated ...' says Tyro [*B* p. 41].) One can ignore it, as so many of Hartley's heroes do initially. Or, brought face to face with it, one can become a cynic. ('. . . I will not, I *will* not, Timothy, adopt a cynical attitude,' Tyro writes, 'perhaps the truest of simplifications, but the most boring and the most despairing' [*B* p. 41].) Jasper Bentwich is a cynic; Leo Colston, as he re-opens his diary is a cynic; Steve Leadbitter, released from the War and the army, is a cynic. On the other hand, one can try to excuse and almost exalt crime, as Margaret the magistrate tends to do at the beginning of *My Fellow Devils*, as Welfare State psychology seems to in *The Betrayal*. One can try to condition it out of existence as the Dictator does in *Facial Justice*. But none of these solutions seems to work—evil and sin, suffering and frustration remain constants in human life which can not be rationalized or edited out of the picture: men must discover or re-discover a philosophy adequate to dealing with them, able to answer those mutterings of Dostoevsky's Underground Man which must have sounded often in Hartley's ear:

> ... Oh, tell me, who was it first announced, who was it first proclaimed, that man only does nasty things because he does not know his own interests; and that if he were enlightened, if his eyes were opened to his real normal interests, man would at once cease to do nasty things, would at once become good and noble. . . .
>
> Oh, the babe! Oh, the pure, innocent child! . . .[20]

Total man, allowed his free will, his imagination, as the *Facial Justice* experiment knows well, is capable of enormities. But without them he is not man, and the enormities come anyway, perhaps in a more animalistic form. The only solution, Hartley seems to force us to see—the only road left open to twentieth-century man, if he really digests the ghastly message of World War II—is to admit the inadequacies of rationalistic and humanistic panaceas for human ills, and to discover or rediscover a philosophy (the myth, the religion, the renewed Christianity?) which treats of man in his wholeness and which recognizes the organic principle, the continual death and rebirth that must characterize human existence. Jael-and-Michael just may succeed where the purely humanistic Dictator ('I had to do it alone' *FJ* p. 218) had to fail.

But Jael-and-Michael and the body/soul, time and eternity kind of union they represent may only be possible, finally, *in* eternity. The goal of human history, Hartley's myth implies, is the Golden Age that most of his characters long for: a state of complete and cosmic unity and harmony in total diversity—in which each one's fully developed individuality and personality would fit into a perfectly attuned whole. The Dictator sees it as a hive of private paradises (*FJ* p. 153).[21] Eustace envisions his when he describes his novel in an imaginary colloquy with Jasper Bentwich:

'Is that all? Do you leave them there, Pericles and Aspasia, co-educating in Little Athens?' 'Oh, they would have children, of course, who wouldn't have to go through what they had—I mean, in the way of making mistakes, and taking the wrong path, and having temperaments at odds with what they really wanted. They would find everything ready for them, so to speak, and start being happy straight away.' 'In fact, you would be describing the dawn of the Golden Age?' 'Well, I hadn't thought of it like that, but I should try to get the feeling of light into the book, gradually spreading, you know, until finally it enveloped everything, so that every-thing shone of itself, in the way it sometimes does here.' 'But as you describe the book, there would be no darkness, only this appalling daylight growing stronger till everyone had to wear blue spectacles or go blind?' 'Oh, it wouldn't go quite like that—you see, there would be some shadows at the beginning—obstacles to the marriage, and so on, and then the parents being killed, and perhaps some other setbacks as well—I haven't quite decided. No, I should try to give the effect of the light growing out of darkness' (*EH* p. 504).

Timothy Casson's obviously fatuous dream involves setting

everyone truly free to go boating on the river (*B* p. 395), while young Leo Colston's dream (of the year 1900) has attached itself very specifically to the twentieth century:

> . . . my imagination was then, though it is no longer, passionately hierarchical; it envisaged things in an ascending scale, circle on circle, tier on tier, and the annual, mechanical revolution of the months did not disturb this notion. I knew that the year must return to winter and begin again; but to my apprehensions the zodiacal company were subject to no such limitations: they soared in an ascending spiral towards infinity.
>
> And the expansion and ascension, as of some divine gas, which I believed to be the ruling principle of my own life, I attributed to the coming century. The year 1900 had an almost mystical appeal for me; I could hardly wait for it: 'Nineteen hundred, nineteen hundred,' I would chant to myself in rapture; and as the old century drew to its close, I began to wonder whether I should live to see its successor. I had an excuse for this: I had been ill and was acquainted with death; but much more it was the fear of missing something infinitely precious—the dawn of a Golden Age. For that was what I believed the coming century would be: the realization, on the part of the whole world, of the hopes that I was entertaining for myself (*GB* pp. 9–10).

But if there is one thing we learn from the bittersweet experience of Hartley's novels, it is that the Golden Age is not to be attained by ordinary human effort or in the ordinary process of evolution: neither by the most wide-eyed of dreams nor the most enlightened social welfare schemes; the contradictions of the large, concrete, unpredictable angel-beast called man keep getting in the way. Whether Hartley means that these contradictions can only be resolved and equilibrated in the repose of death and the life of eternity or whether he is intimating that a Jael-Michael regime would be possible on earth if we would recognize again the claims of the human spirit and the laws of love, sacrifice, death and rebirth, it is difficult to say. One is only sure that he rejects humanistic optimism as well as misanthropic cynicism, clinging to the past as well as cutting oneself off from it—and that neither Eustace's complete capitulation to circumstance and external influence nor Hilda's rigid Puritanism, her attempt at complete control of events, seems to be an adequate response to life's complexities. Somehow one must find a metaphysic that combines a sense of inner identity and continuity with the ability to respond sensitively to fact and event, and that recognizes that something greater than one's small self is, after all, involved both in the infinitesimal moments of one's life and in the cataclysms of one's world. In the face of all the evidence and of the many sly and not so sly hints, it does not seem outlandish to suppose that Hartley, like Mrs. Purbright (like Kierkegaard), thinks a renewal —a radical and true rebirth—of the essence of Christianity within the individual might be an answer to humanity's post-war destitution. In any case, one feels that he does see that monomyth which exalts love and self-sacrifice as expressing the deepest wisdom about life and the only way out of its tragedy and absurdity.

Novelists, Hartley has written, often make their works an extension of themselves, or at any rate 'are haunted by a particular idea or situation which embodies what they feel about life. . . . This idea or situation goes on in them like a murmur . . . a magnetic north for . . . private musings . . .' (*NR* p. 5). This is obviously the case in those novels of Hartley's own with which we have been dealing, and the most casual reader of his work would soon acknowledge a certain basic repetitiousness. But his theme of life's tragedy and transformation is a great and central one, and in his books he has explored it systematically as it appears in all the human conditions from childhood to old age and as it has characterized itself in each decade of our century. In the interests of this exploration he has introduced a new and playful form of an old and powerful genre to the literature of our age and has experimented with its symbolic possibilities in various combinations and adaptations and with the aid of the technical and psychological resources of twentieth-century novelistic sophistication. If we judge him as a metaphysical rather than as a social or psychological novelist, as a creator of romance and mock-romance, symbol and design rather than case-study, as experimenter rather than traditionalist, we find many faults in Hartley. But they are the faults of a fine writer whose contribution has not yet been fully recognized.

NOTES

PREFACE

1. L. P. Hartley, 'The Future of Fiction', *New Writing and Daylight*, ed. John Lehmann (1946), p. 1. Subsequent references will be designated *FF* and identified by page number within the text.
2. Giorgio Melchiori, 'The English Novelist and the American Tradition', *SR*, LXVIII (1960), 502–15.
3. Melchiori, 509.
4. Melchiori, 512–13.
5. Melchiori, 513.
6. Lord David Cecil, 'Introduction' to L. P. Hartley, *Eustace and Hilda*, collected ed. (New York: The British Book Centre, 1958), pp. 7–13. Subsequent references to any of the novels which make up *Eustace and Hilda* will be to this edition, will be designated *EH*, and will be identified by page number within the text.
7. J.-P. Vernier, '*La Trilogie romanesque de* L. P. Hartley', *Études anglaises*, XIII (1960), 26–31.
8. Vernier, 27.
9. Vernier, 28ff.
10. Peter Bien, *L. P. Hartley* (London: Chatto and Windus, 1963).
11. E. K. Brown, *Rhythm in the Novel* (Toronto: University of Toronto Press, 1950).
12. E. M. Forster, *Aspects of the Novel* (New York: Harcourt, Brace and Company, 1927), pp. 164–9.
13. Brown, p.59.
14. Brown, p. 115.
15. Northrop Frye, *Anatomy of Criticism* (Princeton, New Jersey: Princeton University Press, 1957).

CHAPTER I

1. Frye, p. 305.
2. Frye, p. 136.
3. Frye, p. 139.

4. Frye, pp. 304–5.
5. Frye, p. 306.
6. Frye, p. 187.
7. Frye, pp. 186–206.
8. Frye, p. 193.
9. See Frye, p. 233.
10. See Frye, pp. 223ff.
11. See especially L. P. Hartley, 'Nathaniel Hawthorne', *The Novelist's Responsibility* (London: Hamish Hamilton, 1967), pp. 55–141. In all subsequent references this volume will be designated *NR* and its constituent essays will be identified by page number within the text.
12. Frye, pp. 137–8.
13. Nathaniel Hawthorne, 'Preface', *The House of the Seven Gables* (Columbus, Ohio: Ohio State University Press, 1965), p. 1.
14. Hawthorne, pp. 1, 3.
15. F. O. Matthiessen, *American Renaissance* (London, Toronto, New York: Oxford University Press, 1941), pp. 262–71.
16. Nathaniel Hawthorne, 'Preface', *The Blithedale Romance* (Garden City, New York: Doubleday, 1962), pp. 22–3.
17. Nathaniel Hawthorne, 'The Threefold Destiny', *The Works of Hawthorne* (New York: Walter J. Black, Inc., [1932]), pp. 519–25.
18. Hawthorne, 'The Threefold Destiny', p. 519.
19. Hawthorne, 'The Threefold Destiny', p. 525.
20. Hawthorne, 'The Threefold Destiny', p. 523.
21. Hawthorne, 'The Threefold Destiny', p. 525.
22. John C. Stubbs, 'Hawthorne's *The Scarlet Letter*: The Theory of the Romance and the Use of the New England Situation', *PMLA* LXXXIII (Oct. 1968), 1439–47.
23. Stubbs, 1439–40.
24. Stubbs, 1440.
25. Stubbs, 1441–7.
26. Matthiessen, pp. 253–8; 344ff.
27. See, for example, Carl G. Jung, 'Approaching the Unconscious', *Man and His Symbols*, ed. Carl G. Jung and M.-L. von Franz (Garden City, New York: Doubleday, 1964), pp. 18–103.
28. Emily Brontë, 'A Day Dream', *The Complete Poems of Emily Jane Bronte*, ed. C. W. Hatfield (New York: Columbia University Press, 1941), pp. 199–200.
29. L. P. Hartley, *The Betrayal* (London: Hamish Hamilton, 1966). Subsequent references will be designated *BET* and identified by page number within the text.
30. Sir Thomas Browne, *Religio Medici*, Part I, Sec. 12, *The Works of Sir Thomas Browne*, I, ed. Geoffrey Keynes (London: Faber and Faber, 1964), p. 21.

31. 'Sir Thomas Browne', *Seventeenth Century Verse and Prose*, I, ed. Helen C. White, Ruth C. Wallerstein and Ricardo Quintana (New York: Macmillan, 1951), p. 314.

32. William Blake, *A Vision of the Last Judgement*, in *Complete Writings of William Blake*, ed. Sir Geoffrey Keynes (London: Oxford University Press, 1966), p. 611.

33. L. P. Hartley, *Simonetta Perkins*, 2nd ed. (London: James Barrie, 1952), p. 44. Subsequent references to this novel will be designated *SP* and identified by page number within the text.

34. Forster, p. 167.

35. L. P. Hartley, *The Brickfield* (London: Hamish Hamilton, 1964). Subsequent references to this novel will be designated *BR* and identified by page number within the text.

36. L. P. Hartley, *The Hireling* (London: Hamish Hamilton, 1957). Subsequent references to this novel will be designated *H* and identified by page number within the text.

37. L. P. Hartley, *Facial Justice* (Harmondsworth: Penguin Books, 1966). Subsequent references to this novel will be designated *FJ* and identified by page number within the text.

CHAPTER II

1. Richard Wilbur, 'Advice to a Prophet', *The Poems of Richard Wilbur* (New York: Harcourt, Brace and World, Inc., [1963]), pp. 6–7.

2. Frye, p. 305.

3. L. P. Hartley, *Night Fears and Other Stories* (London and New York: G. P. Putnam's sons, 1924). Subsequent references will be designated *NF* and identified by page number within the text.

4. *TLS*, 3 July 1924, 218.

5. L. P. Hartley, *Two for the River* (London: Hamish Hamilton, [1961]). Subsequent references will be designated *TR* and identified by page number within the text.

6. *TLS*, 23 June 1961, 385.

7. L. P. Hartley, *The Travelling Grave* (Sauk City, Wis.: Arkham House, 1948). Subsequent references will be designated *TG* and identified by page number within the text.

8. *TLS*, 16 March 1951, 161.

9. *The Collected Short Stories of L. P. Hartley* (London: Hamish Hamilton, 1968). Subsequent references will be designated *CS* and identified by page number within the text.

10. Q. D. Leavis, 'Hawthorne as Poet', *Hawthorne*, ed. A. N. Kaul (Englewood Cliffs, N. J.: Prentice-Hall, 1966), p. 45. Reprinted from *SR*, LIX (Spring 1951 and Summer 1951).

11. See above, Preface, comments by Vernier.

12. Matthiessen, pp. 276ff.
13. Yvor Winters, 'Maule's Curse, or Hawthorne and the Problem of Allegory', in *Hawthorne*, ed. Kaul (see above, note 10), pp. 21ff. Reprinted from Winters, *In Defense of Reason* (New York: The Swallow Press and W. Morrow and Co., 1947).
14. Richard Harter Fogle, *Hawthorne's Fiction: The Light and the Dark* (Norman, Okla.: University of Oklahoma Press, 1964), pp. 11ff., 23.
15. L. P. Hartley, *The Killing Bottle* (London and New York: Putnam, 1932). Subsequent references will be designated *KB* and identified by page number within the text.
16. Hawthorne, 'Preface', *The Blithedale Romance*, p. 21.
17. L. P. Hartley, *The White Wand and Other Stories* (London: Hamish Hamilton [1954]). Subsequent references will be designated *WW* and identified by page number within the text.
18. See above, Chapter I.
19. Harvey Curtis Webster, 'The Novels of L. P. Hartley', *Critique*, IV (Spring–Summer, 1961), 45.
20. *TLS*, 12 November 1925, 754.
21. See quotation from *TLS* review, above, Chapter II.
22. Ralph Freedman, *The Lyrical Novel* (Princeton, New Jersey: Princeton University Press, 1963), p. 2.

CHAPTER III

1. Wallace Stevens, 'The Well Dressed Man with a Beard', *Poems by Wallace Stevens*, ed. Samuel French Morse (New York: Vintage Press, 1959), p. 104.
2. The word 'shimmering' as description of a certain kind of symbolism is one I have seen used in commentary on (I believe) Hawthorne, but I cannot locate the exact reference. It seems a very satisfactory way of describing the effect Hartley achieves.
3. Walter Allen, *Tradition and Dream* (London: Phoenix House, 1964), p. 254.
4. Bien, p. 94.
5. See above, Chapter I.
6. Allen, p. 255.
7. Walt Whitman, 'Of the Terrible Doubt of Appearances', *Leaves of Grass*, ed. Emory Holloway (New York: Doubleday, 1926), p. 100.
8. Whitman, p. 101.
9. Frye, p. 119.
10. Bien, pp. 56–7.
11. Letter from L. P. Hartley, quoted in Bien, p. 58.
12. Freedman, p. 25.
13. Bien, pp. 70–4.

14. Hawthorne, 'Preface', *The House of the Seven Gables*, p. 1.
15. Søren Kierkegaard, *Kierkegaard's Concluding Unscientific Postscript*, trans. David F. Swenson, completed Walter Lowrie (Princeton, New Jersey: Princeton University Press, 1941). See especially summary on pp. 507ff.
16. Albert Camus, *The Myth of Sisyphus*, trans. Justin O'Brien (New York: Knopf, 1955), p. 91.
17. Wright Morris, 'The Territory Ahead', *The Living Novel*, ed. Granville Hicks (New York: Collier Books, 1962), p. 147.
18. Stevens, 'Connoisseur of Chaos', *Poems*, p. 97.
19. Stevens, 'Connoisseur of Chaos', p. 97.
20. Stevens, 'Esthetique du Mal', *Poems*, p. 120.

CHAPTER IV

1. W. B. Yeats, 'Parnell's Funeral', *The Collected Poems of W. B. Yeats* (New York: Macmillan and Co., 1956), p. 276.
2. Frye, pp. 223–39; 308–12.
3. L. P. Hartley, *The Boat* (London: Transworld Publishers, 1966). Subsequent references will be designated *B* and will be identified by page number within the text.
4. Bien, pp. 106ff.
5. Frye, p. 223.
6. Frye, pp. 309–10.
7. Frye, p. 311.
8. Frye, pp. 223–39.
9. Bien, pp. 126–51.
10. See Kierkegaard, pp. 283ff.
11. Kierkegaard, pp. 493ff.

CHAPTER V

1. Stevens, 'Esthetique du Mal', pp. 120–1.
2. Webster, 50.
3. Bien, pp. 169–81.
4. Bien, p. 174.
5. Bien, pp. 178–80.
6. See Matthiessen, pp. 253–8; 344ff.; also see Roy R. Male, *Hawthorne's Tragic Vision* (Austin, Texas: University of Texas Press, 1957).
7. Nathaniel Hawthorne, *The Celestial Railroad and Other Stories* (New York: New American Library, 1963), p. 100.
8. For example, see Angus Wilson, 'The pursuit of evil', *The Observer Review*, 27 Oct. 1968, 29; Anon, rev., *TLS*, 28 May 1964, 449.

1. T. S. Eliot, 'The Dry Salvages', *Four Quartets* (New York: Harcourt, Brace and Company, 1943), p. 27.
2. L. P. Hartley, *My Fellow Devils* (New York: British Book Centre, 1959). All subsequent references will be designated *MFD* and identified by page number within the text.
3. L. P. Hartley, *A Perfect Woman* (London: Hamish Hamilton, 1955). All subsequent references will be designated *APW* and identified by page number within the text.
4. L. P. Hartley, *Poor Clare* (London: Hamish Hamilton, 1968). All subsequent references will be designated *PC* and identified by page number within the text.
5. Melchiori, 507.
6. See Bien, p. 132, and n. 21 to Bien's Chapter IV.
7. See Bien, pp. 9 ff.
8. Bien, p. 191.
9. 'Modern Parable', *TLS*, 14 Dec. 1951, 801.
10. August Closs, 'Leslie Poles Hartley', *Die Neueren Sprachen*, VI (1957), 41.
11. Closs, 41.
12. Hawthorne, 'Preface', *The Blithedale Romance*, pp. 21–2.
13. 'The End of the Affair', *TLS*, 14 Oct. 1955, 601.
14. 'Sentimental Journeys', *TLS*, 12 July 1957, 425.
15. Wilson, *Observer Review*, 29 (see Chapter V, n. 8).
16. Wilson, 29.
17. Wilson, 29.
18. Wilson, 29.
19. Yeats, 'The Choice', *Collected Poems*, p. 242.
20. L. P. Hartley, *The Love-Adept* (London: Hamish Hamilton, 1969).
21. L. P. Hartley, *My Sister's Keeper* (London: Hamish Hamilton, 1970).
22. L. P. Hartley, *The Harness Room* (London: Hamish Hamilton, 1971).
23. L. P. Hartley, *The Collections* (London: Hamish Hamilton, 1972).
24. L. P. Hartley, *The Will and the Way* (London: Hamish Hamilton, 1973).
25. L. P. Hartley, *Mrs. Carteret Receives and Other Stories* (London: Hamish Hamilton, 1971).
26. Anne Mulkeen, personal interview with L. P. Hartley, August 1970.
27. Letter from L. P. Hartley to Anne Mulkeen, 25 November 1972.
28. 'A Sense of the Past', *TLS*, 15 Sept. 1966, 853.

CHAPTER VII

1. Wilbur, 'A Baroque Wall-Fountain in the Villa Sciarra', *Poems*, p. 105.
2. Anthony Burgess, *The Novel Now* (New York: Norton, 1967), pp. 41, 44.

3. 'Pretty Gentleman and Betafied Lady', *TLS*, 20 May 1960, 317.
4. Frye, pp. 139–40.
5. Also see above, Chapter I.
6. *TLS*, 20 May 1960, 317.
7. Wilson, 29.
8. Pierre Teilhard de Chardin, *The Phenomenon of Man*, trans. Bernard Wall (New York: Harper, 1961), p. 263.
9. For the views summarized here see Teilhard de Chardin, pp. 257–67.
10. Bien, p. 225.
11. *TLS*, 20 May 1960, 317.

CHAPTER VIII

1. See, for example, James Hall, *The Tragic Comedians* (Bloomington, Ind.: Indiana University Press, 1963), p. 111; P. H. Newby, *The Novel 1945–1950* (London, New York and Toronto: Longmans, Green and Co. for the British Council, 1951), p. 35.
2. Wilson, 29.
3. Walter Allen, *The English Novel* (New York: Dutton, 1954), pp. 412–13.
4. Joseph Campbell, *The Hero with a Thousand Faces* (New York: Meridian Books, 1956).
5. Campbell, pp. 104–5.
6. See above, Chapter II.
7. M.-L. von Franz, 'The process of individuation', *Man and His Symbols* ed. Jung, p. 213.
8. Aniela Jaffé, 'Symbolism in the visual arts', *Man and His Symbols*, p. 240.
9. Carl G. Jung, *The Integration of the Personality*, trans. Stanley Dell (New York and Toronto: Farrar and Rinehart, Inc., 1939), pp. 221ff.
10. Jung, *Integration of Personality*, p. 242.
11. Joseph L. Henderson, 'Ancient myths and modern man', *Man and His Symbols*, p. 113.
12. Henderson, p. 114.
13. Campbell, p. 108.
14. von Franz, p. 183.
15. Campbell, pp. 108–18.
16. Campbell, pp. 269–70.
17. Campbell, pp. 255ff.
18. See also above, Chapter VII.
19. von Franz, p. 225.
20. Fyodor Dostoevsky, *Notes from Underground and The Grand Inquisitor*, trans. Ralph E. Matlaw (New York: Dutton, 1960), pp. 18–19.
21. See above, Chapter VII.

WORKS CONSULTED

(British and American editions are given where pertinent)

I. BY L. P. HARTLEY

Night Fears and Other Stories. London and New York, G. P. Putnam's Sons, 1924.

Simonetta Perkins. London and New York, G. P. Putnam's Sons, 1925; 2nd ed. London, James Barrie, 1952; London, Hamish Hamilton, 1957.

The Killing Bottle. London and New York, Putnam, 1932.

Eustace and Hilda, a trilogy; collected ed. London and New York, Putnam, 1958; New York, British Book Centre, 1958. (First published separately as *The Shrimp and the Anemone,* London and New York, Putnam and Co. Ltd., 1944; *The Sixth Heaven,* London, Putnam and Co., 1946; *Eustace and Hilda,* London, Putnam and Co., 1947. *The Shrimp and the Anemone* was published as *The West Window,* Garden City, New York, Doubleday Doran and Co. Inc., 1945.)

'The Future of Fiction', *New Writing and Daylight,* ed. John Lehmann (1946), pp. 86–91.

The Travelling Grave. Sauk City, Wis., Arkham House, 1948; London, James Barrie, 1951; London, Hamish Hamilton, 1957.

The Boat. London, Putnam and Co., 1949; Garden City, New York, Doubleday, 1950; London, Hamish Hamilton, 1961; Corgi ed., London, Transworld Publishers, 1966.

My Fellow Devils. London, James Barrie, 1951; London, Hamish Hamilton, 1957; New York, British Book Centre, 1959.

The Go-Between. London, Hamish Hamilton, 1953; New York, Knopf, 1954; Harmondsworth, Penguin Books, 1958; New York, British Book Centre, 1959; New York, Stein and Day, 1967.

The White Wand, and Other Stories. London, Hamish Hamilton, 1954.

A Perfect Woman. London, Hamish Hamilton, 1955; New York, Knopf, 1956.

The Hireling. London, Hamish Hamilton, 1957; New York, Rinehart, 1958.

Facial Justice. London, Hamish Hamilton, 1960; Toronto, Collins, 1960; Garden City, New York, Doubleday, 1961; Harmondsworth, Penguin Books, 1966.

184

Two for the River. London, Hamish Hamilton, 1961; Toronto, Collins, 1961.

The Brickfield. London, Hamish Hamilton, 1964; Toronto, Collins, 1964.

The Betrayal. London, Hamish Hamilton, 1966; Toronto, Collins, 1966.

The Novelist's Responsibility: Lectures and Essays. London, Hamish Hamilton, 1967; Toronto, Collins, 1967.

The Collected Short Stories of L. P. Hartley. London, Hamish Hamilton, 1968.

Poor Clare. London, Hamish Hamilton, 1968.

The Love-Adept. London, Hamish Hamilton, 1969.

My Sister's Keeper. London, Hamish Hamilton, 1970.

The Harness Room. London, Hamish Hamilton, 1971.

Mrs. Carteret Receives and Other Stories. London, Hamish Hamilton, 1971.

The Collections. London, Hamish Hamilton, 1972.

The Will and the Way. London, Hamish Hamilton, 1973.

The Complete Short Stories of L. P. Hartley. London, Hamish Hamilton, 1973.

II. SECONDARY SOURCES

Allen, Walter, *The English Novel.* New York, Dutton, 1954; London, Phoenix House, 1954.

—. *Tradition and Dream.* London, Phoenix House, 1964. Published as *The Modern Novel,* New York, Dutton, 1964.

Anon. rev., *TLS,* 23 June 1961, 385.

Anon. rev., *TLS,* 3 July 1924, 418.

Anon. rev., *TLS,* 16 Mar. 1951, 161.

Anon. rev., *TLS,* 28 May 1964, 449.

Anon. rev., *TLS,* 12 Nov. 1925, 754.

Barrett, William. *Irrational Man.* Garden City, New York, Doubleday, 1962.

Bien, Peter. *L. P. Hartley.* London, Chatto and Windus, 1963; University Park: The Pennsylvania State University Press, 1963.

Blake, William. *The Complete Writings of William Blake,* ed. Sir Geoffrey Keynes. London and New York, Oxford University Press, 1966.

Bloomfield, Paul. *L. P. Hartley.* (Also Bernard Bergonzi, *Anthony Powell.*) *Writers and Their Work* No. 144, pp. 5–23. London: Longmans Green and Co., for the British Council and the National Book League.

Brontë, Emily. *The Complete Poems of Emily Jane Bronte,* ed. C. W. Hatfield. New York, Columbia University Press, 1941.

Brown, E. K. *Rhythm in the Novel.* Toronto, University of Toronto Press, 1950.

Brown, James. *Kierkegaard, Heidegger, Buber and Barth.* New York, Collier Books, 1962.

Browne, Sir Thomas. *The Works of Sir Thomas Browne,* ed. Geoffrey
185

Keynes, 4 vols. London, Faber and Faber, 1964; Chicago, University of Chicago Press, 1964.

Burgess, Anthony. *The Novel Now*. New York, Norton, 1967; London, Faber and Faber, 1967.

Campbell, Joseph. *The Hero with a Thousand Faces*. New York, Meridian Books, 1956.

Camus, Albert. *The Myth of Sisyphus*, trans. Justin O'Brien. New York, Knopf, 1955; London, Hamish Hamilton, 1955.

Cecil, Lord David. 'Introduction', L. P. Hartley, *Eustace and Hilda*, pp. 7–13. London, Putnam, 1958; New York, British Book Centre, 1958.

Closs, August. 'Leslie Poles Hartley', *Die Neueren Sprachen*, VI (1957), 39–42.

Dostoevsky, Fyodor. *Notes from Underground and The Grand Inquisitor*, trans. Ralph E. Matlaw. New York, Dutton, 1960.

Eliot, T. S. *Four Quartets*. New York, Harcourt, Brace and Company, 1943; London, Faber and Faber, 1944.

Ellmann, Richard and Charles Feidelson, Jr., eds., *The Modern Tradition*. New York, Oxford University Press, 1965.

'The End of the Affair', Anon. rev., *TLS*, 14 Oct. 1955, 601.

Fiedler, Leslie. 'Class War in British Literature', *On Contemporary Literature*, ed. Richard Kostelanetz, pp. 64–81. New York, Avon Books, 1964.

Fogle, Richard Harter. *Hawthorne's Fiction: The Light and the Dark*. Norman, Okla., University of Oklahoma Press, 1964.

Forster, E. M. *Aspects of the Novel*. New York, Harcourt Brace and Company, 1927.

'Fragments of Experience', Anon. rev., *TLS*, 17 Sept. 1954, 587.

Fraser, G. S. *The Modern Writer and His World*. Baltimore, Md., Penguin Books, 1964; London, Deutsch, 1964.

Freedman, Ralph. *The Lyrical Novel*. Princeton, New Jersey, Princeton University Press, 1963; London, Oxrord University Press, 1963.

Frye, Northrop. *Anatomy of Criticism*. Princeton, New Jersey, Princeton University Press, 1957; London, Oxford University Press, 1957.

Grindea, Miron. '*Un maitre du roman anglais*', *Adam International Review*, XXIX, Nos. 294–295–296 (1961), 2–4.

Hall, James. *The Tragic Comedians*. Bloomington, Ind., Indiana University Press, 1963.

Hawthorne, Nathaniel. *The Blithedale Romance*. Garden City, New York, Doubleday [1961].

—. *The Celestial Railroad and Other Stories*. New York, New American Library, 1963.

—. *The Works of Nathaniel Hawthorne*. New York, Walter J. Black, Inc. [1932]. *The Centenary Edition of The Works of Nathaniel Hawthorne*, Columbus, Ohio State University Press, 1962—; *The Selected Works of Nathaniel Hawthorne*, London, Chatto and Windus, 1971.

Henderson, Joseph L. 'Ancient myths and modern man', *Man and His Symbols*, ed. Carl G. Jung and M.-L. von Franz, pp. 104–57. Garden City, N.Y., Doubleday, 1964; London, Aldus Books, 1964.

Hubben, William. *Dostoevsky, Kierkegaard, Nietzsche, and Kafka*. New York, Collier Books, 1962.

Jaffé, Aniela. 'Symbolism in the visual arts', *Man and His Symbols*, ed. Jung and von Franz, pp. 230–71. Garden City, New York, Doubleday, 1964; London, Aldus Books, 1964.

Jung, Carl G. *The Integration of the Personality*, trans. Stanley Dell. New York and Toronto, Farrar and Rinehart, Inc., 1939; London, Routledge and Kegan Paul, 1940.

—. 'Approaching the Unconscious', *Man and His Symbols*, ed. Jung and von Franz, pp. 18–103. Garden City, New York, Doubleday, 1964; London, Aldus Books, 1964.

— and M.-L. von Franz, eds., *Man and His Symbols*. Garden City, New York, Doubleday, 1964; London, Aldus Books, 1964.

—. *Psychology and Religion*. New Haven, Yale University Press, 1938; London, Oxford University Press, 1938.

Kauffman, Walter, ed. *Existentialism from Dostoevsky to Sartre*. New York, Meridian Books, 1956.

Kierkegaard, Søren. *Kierkegaard's Concluding Unscientific Postscript*, trans. David F. Swenson, completed Walter Lowrie. Princeton, Princeton University Press, 1941; London, Oxford University Press, 1942.

Leavis, Q. D. 'Hawthorne as Poet', *Hawthorne*, ed. A. N. Kaul, pp. 25–63, repr. from *SR*, LIX. Englewood Cliffs, New Jersey, Prentice-Hall, 1966.

Levin, Harry. *The Gates of Horn*. New York, Oxford University Press, 1966.

—. *The Power of Blackness*. New York, Knopf, 1958; London, Faber and Faber, 1958.

L. P. Hartley edition, *Adam International Review*, XXIX Nos. 294–295–296.

Male, Roy R. *Hawthorne's Tragic Vision*. Austin, Texas, University of Texas Press, 1957.

Mann, Thomas. 'The Making of *The Magic Mountain*', *The Magic Mountain*, trans. H. T. Lowe-Porter, pp. 719–29. Reprinted from the *Atlantic*, Jan. 1953. New York, Knopf, 1961.

Matthiessen, F. O. *American Renaissance*. London, Toronto, New York, Oxford University Press, 1941.

Melchiori, Giorgio. 'The English Novelist and the American Tradition', *SR*, XVIII (1960), 502–15.

'Modern Parable', Anon. rev., *TLS*, 14 Dec. 1951, 801.

Morris, Wright. 'The Territory Ahead', *The Living Novel*, ed. Granville Hicks, pp. 123–57. New York, Collier Books, 1962.

Newby, P. H. *The Novel 1945–1950*. London, New York and Toronto, Longmans, Green and Co., for the British Council, 1951.

'The New Novelists', *London Magazine*, V (Nov. 1958), 13–31. A symposium

187

with articles by Anthony Quinton, Lettice Cooper, Frank Kermode and Maurice Cranston.

O'Connor, William Van. *The New University Wits, and the End of Modernism.* Carbondale, Ill., Southern Illinois University Press, 1963.

Phelps, Gilbert, 'The Novel Today', *The Modern Age,* ed. Boris Ford. 2nd ed., Baltimore, Md., Penguin Books, 1961; Harmondsworth, Penguin Books, 1963.

'Pretty Gentleman and Betafied Lady', Anon. rev., *TLS,* 20 May 1960, 317.

Rabinovitz, Rubin. *The Reaction Against Experiment in the English Novel, 1950–1960.* New York, Columbia University Press, 1967.

'A Sense of the Past', Anon. rev., *TLS,* 15 Sept. 1966, 853.

'Sentimental Journeys', Anon. rev., *TLS,* 12 July 1957, 425.

Stevens, Wallace. *Poems by Wallace Stevens,* ed. Samuel French Morse. New York, Vintage Books, 1959.

Stubbs, John C. 'Hawthorne's *The Scarlet Letter:* The Theory of the Romance and the Use of the New England Situation', *PMLA,* LXXXIII (Oct., 1968), 1439–47.

Teilhard de Chardin, Pierre. *The Phenomenon of Man,* trans. Bernard Wall. New York, Harper [1959]; London, Collins [1959].

Vernier, J.-P. *'La Trilogie romanesque de L. P. Hartley', Études anglaises,* XIII (1960), 26–31.

von Franz, M.-L. 'The process of individuation', *Man and His Symbols,* ed. Jung and von Franz, pp. 158–229. Garden City, New York, Doubleday, 1964; London, Aldus Books, 1964.

Webster, Harvey Curtis. 'The Novels of L. P. Hartley', *Critique,* IV (1961), 39–51.

White, Helen C., Ruth Wallerstein and Ricardo Quintana, eds., *Seventeenth Century Verse and Prose.* New York, Macmillan, 1951.

Whitman, Walt. *Leaves of Grass,* ed. Emory Holloway. New York, Doubleday, 1926.

Wilbur, Richard. *The Poems of Richard Wilbur.* New York, Harcourt Brace and World [1963]; *Poems 1945–1956,* London, Faber and Faber [1957].

Wilson, Angus. 'The pursuit of evil', rev., *The Observer Review,* 27 Oct. 1968, 29.

Winters, Yvor. 'Maule's Curse, or Hawthorne and the Problem of Allegory', in *Hawthorne,* ed. Kaul, pp. 11–24. Englewood Cliffs, New Jersey, Prentice-Hall, 1966. Reprinted from Winters, *In Defense of Reason,* New York, The Swallow Press and W. Morrow and Co., 1947.

Yeats, William Butler. *The Collected Poems of W. B. Yeats.* New York, Macmillan and Co., 1956; London, The Macmillan Co., 1952.

INDEX TO MAJOR REFERENCES